Public Health
in
America

This is a volume in the Arno Press series

PUBLIC HEALTH
IN
AMERICA

Advisory Editor

Barbara Gutmann Rosenkrantz

Editorial Board

**Leona Baumgartner
James H. Cassedy
Arthur Jack Viseltear**

See last pages of this volume
for a complete list of titles.

A REPORT

ON

STATE PUBLIC HEALTH WORK

BASED ON

A SURVEY OF STATE BOARDS
OF HEALTH

CHARLES V. CHAPIN

ARNO PRESS

A New York Times Company

New York / 1977

Editorial Supervision: JOSEPH CELLINI

———∞———

Reprint Edition 1977 by Arno Press Inc.

Reprinted from a copy in
  The University of Illinois Library

PUBLIC HEALTH IN AMERICA
ISBN for complete set: 0-405-09804-9
See last pages of this volume for titles.

Manufactured in the United States of America

———∞———

Library of Congress Cataloging in Publication Data

Chapin, Charles Value, 1856-1941.
    A report on state public health work.

    (Public health in America)
    Reprint of the 1916 ed. published by the American
Medical Association, Chicago.
    1. Health boards--United States--States.
2. Public health--United States--States. 3. Health
surveys--United States--States. I. Title. II. Series.
RA446.C47 1977   353.9'3'77   76-25657
ISBN 0-405-09807-3

A REPORT

ON

STATE PUBLIC HEALTH WORK

BASED ON

A SURVEY OF STATE BOARDS OF HEALTH

BY

CHARLES V. CHAPIN, M.D.

Commissioner of Health

PROVIDENCE, RHODE ISLAND

Made under the direction of the Council on Health and Public Instruction

of the

American Medical Association

AMERICAN MEDICAL ASSOCIATION
FIVE HUNDRED AND THIRTY-FIVE NORTH DEARBORN STREET
CHICAGO

FOREWORD

The Council on Health and Public Instruction presents herewith the report of Dr. Charles V. Chapin, special representative of the Council on public health organization in the United States. In the fall of 1913 Dr. Chapin was selected by the Council as special representative and directed to make a comprehensive study of the activities, equipment and accomplishments of the various State Boards of Health. This work, carried on at intervals with his duties as Commissioner of Health of Providence, R. I., occupied the entire twelve months of 1914 and the early part of 1915. The compilation of his report, its consideration by the Council and its completion and verification required another six months. While the survey on which this report was based was made in 1914, the report was brought completely up to date before publication.

The object of the Council in having such a survey made and such a report prepared and the relation of this work to the general plans of the Council can best be made clear by the outline of those plans and purposes which appeared in the report of the Council to the House of Delegates at the Atlantic City Session in 1914.

"The plans of the Council have now developed to a point where a comprehensive program can be outlined, which will embrace all of the present and future activities of the Council and will show clearly their relation to each other, their relative importance and the order in which they can be taken up. In outlining such a program, the Council assumes that its primary object is to place before the profession and the public of the United States the objects, purposes and work of the organized medical profession, as represented by the American Medical Association and its constituent and component branches, and to place the Association and its efforts before the public in such a way as to secure public support and endorsement for our efforts for the improvement of public health conditions in the United States.

"Careful study of the present situation leads to the conclusion that a rational program must include three general lines of action. These are:

"1. A thorough investigation of present public health conditions in the United States, with a view to securing more accurate information on all phases of the public health problem than is now available.

"2. Education of the public by every possible means in order that the people may understand the enormous advances in scientific medical knowledge during the last generation and the possibility of utilizing such knowledge in the prevention of disease, the reduction of the death-rate and the prolongation of human life.

"3. The crystallizing of such educated public sentiment in necessary public health laws, regulations and ordinances, which will render possible a conservation of human life commensurate with our advancing knowledge and which will render such laws effective through the only force available in this country, namely, educated and enlightened public opinion."

Under the first head, namely, the investigation of the present public health situation, the Council emphasized the need for further knowledge in four main subjects, namely:

1. The need of a survey of the public health activities of the federal government in all its departments with a view to determining exactly what the federal government is doing for public health.

2. A similar survey of state public health activities.

3. A comprehensive survey of municipal public health work.

4. The collection of data on the work being done by voluntary public health organizations.

Under the second head the report continues:

"There is today, in every state in the Union, some form of public health organization. Owing to our form of government, each of these organizations is working independently. As the reports of the various state boards are not made on a uniform basis, a comparison of their various activities and a tabulation of the results secured by their efforts is difficult. It is therefore, practically impossible today to summarize the public health work which is being done by the different state boards of health, to compare one with another or to establish any standard by which their relative merits may be determined. The first necessity for such a comparative study of state public health activities is clearly a collection of authoritative, official data on the subject. Realizing the importance of this field of investigation, the Council has given the subject careful consideration and has been fortunate in securing the assistance of one of the leading public health authorities of the country in carrying on a study of state public health work. Beginning Jan. 1, 1914, Dr. Charles V. Chapin, Commissioner of Health of Providence, R. I., was appointed as special representative of the Council and directed to make a comparative study of the activities, equipment and accomplishments of the various State Boards of Health. During the past five months, in accordance with the plans formulated by Dr. Chapin and the Council, he has been visiting the various state boards, from time to time, and making a personal study of their condition. He plans to complete this study during the present year. The results of his observations will be presented later on in the form of a report on state public health work."

The publication and distribution of this report completes the first effort that has been made to carry on a comprehensive and comparative survey of the public health work of the various states and to undertake some kind of comparative rating of the work being done in the different states. The object of the Council in undertaking such a task is not in any sense due to a desire to be either critical or dictatorial, but rather to present in tabulated form the essential facts regarding state public health work as viewed by a recognized expert on this subject. It is hoped that the discussions of state public health work and the comparative tables will be of service to state boards of health and especially to executive secretaries of state boards of health in presenting to governors, legislators and legislative committees a clear statement of the facts regarding public health work in each state; that the rating sheet may be of value in pointing out the weak points in each state, by the strengthening of which the relative standing of the state may be raised; and that the collection and publication of the facts contained in the report may be of some service in increasing the effectiveness of state public health work.

TABLE OF CONTENTS

A SURVEY OF STATE PUBLIC
HEALTH WORK

To the Council on Health and Public Instruction of the American Medical Association:—

The following pages are the report of a brief survey of the principal public health activities of the different states, made in accordance with your request and suggestions. It might be expected that a fair idea could be obtained from an examination of the laws of each state and of the reports and other literature issued by the department of health. It is true that a great deal of the information here contained has been obtained from these sources, but, unfortunately, there are very few health departments which publish well arranged, clearly written and well analyzed accounts of their work. A day or two of conference with the officials of the department affords a better knowledge of local conditions than any amount of study of printed material. The Council, therefore, wisely decided that each state health office should be visited.

It was the desire of the Council to learn what is being done in the different states for the promotion of public health and in particular what is being done by the state department of health. An earnest desire was also expressed that the states should be grouped, or arranged, in accordance with the volume and effectiveness of their health work and that a score card should if possible be made for this purpose.

The report, therefore, is naturally divided into three parts; first, a summary of the conditions and needs of each state; second, a review of the health activities of the states; third, a score card rating.

The summaries are intended to show at a glance the principal accomplishments in health protection in the different states and what now seems necessary to be further done to better conditions. It sometimes happens that in a state which at present does very little, few recommendations are made, for it seems better to insist on the first essentials only, as too radical changes are likely to invite failure. On the other hand, in a state which has already made some progress, many things suggest themselves which seem almost within reach of the department and which could be secured with a little more effort.

The second portion of the report with its tables deals with the activities of state departments of health. The space given to each subject corresponds in a general way to the space which it occupies in the actual work of the departments rather than to its real importance in preventive medicine. The tables are designed to show in a more convenient form the organization and some of the principal lines of work in each state.

A review of state health work at first causes a feeling of discouragement. There is so much to be done and so little to do with, there are

so many technical problems to be solved and there are so many difficulties outside of the health department, in the way of efficient administration, that one fears that it will be a long time before the dreams of
the enthusiasts come true. Nevertheless, a great deal has been accomplished in many states. Progress in public health work is accelerating and
there is much to inspire a hope that it will be still more rapid in the
future. To have vastly improved public water supplies, to have made
the diagnostic laboratory accessible to all physicians, to have supplied
sera and vaccines to those who need them, to have rapidly initiated, or
improved, means for recording vital statistics, to have developed comprehensive plans of public health education, stand to the credit of many
states during the last few years. Two years ago West Virginia expended
only $2,500 on public health. There was no water control, no laboratories,
no distribution of antitoxin, no vital statistics, nor anything else. If her
neighbors on the east and west be compared with her, one is encouraged
with the progress they have made. Doubtless the health officials in Pennsylvania and Ohio find so much that ought to be done that they are often
discouraged but when it is remembered that it is not so very many years
ago that not much more was done in these, and in fact in most states,
than was done in West Virginia in 1913, there is certainly great hope
for the· future.

The purpose of this report is rather to discover lines along which
progress is most needed than it is to point out success already attained.
A review of public health conditions in the states today indicates that
by far the greatest hindrance to progress is the terrible incubus of politics. It seems incredible that the citizens of an otherwise progressive state
are perfectly content to see their health officers elected with no regard
for fitness or training, but simply because they, or their friends, were
helpful to the political party which was successful at the last election. Of
course, it is not only in the health office that the evils of politics are felt,
but nowhere else are the results so deadly. Until the people in such
politics-ridden communities experience a moral and intellectual revival
and insist that their governors select men for office because they are
qualified for it, it seems useless to talk about sanitary reform.

It is perfectly true that it is by no means easy to find men who are
properly qualified to take the position of state commissioner of health.
Such men should have a thorough scientific education, should have seriously studied public health problems and should have had practical experience in public health work. Under present conditions there is, in most
states, little to encourage a man to prepare himself for the position, or
to accept it if it were offered to him. If he proves deaf to the spoilsman,
he will be hampered in his work and he will lose his place on the first
political upheaval. Run through the states and note how very few men
were appointed because they were public health experts. It is true that
a number who were not such when appointed have since become leaders,
but it is an expensive and dangerous experiment for a state to try to
educate its high officials after it has placed them in office.

The health activities of the states are too often the result of haphazard
growth rather than well conceived plan. Some of the work is forced on
the department from without. Politicians order work which will make

a place for a friend. Persistent reformers get undue recognition for a cause, good, but not all important. The untrained health officer follows, not leads, and he often follows the wrong lead. The untrained man cannot initiate, so he copies. It is not easy to reorganize an illogical department and there are few able to do it, yet it is what is greatly needed in many states. Appropriations are never large enough to accomplish all that should be done. The money should be spent where it will do the most good. A wise apportionment of funds and activities along lines which will result in the greatest reduction in sickness and death is a necessary preface to the most efficient health administration. There are indications that more good planning can be expected in the future. This is recently illustrated by the divisions in the New York health department provided by statute and by the divisions of the Massachusetts department formed by the commissioner.

A review of the public health activities of the last fifteen or twenty years brings forcibly to mind the fact that sanitary science is still largely in the experimental stage. Many fundamental principles of profound importance have been established which will stand, but an immense number of subsidiary problems have of necessity arisen and wait for solution. If so many of the problems of the science remain to be worked out it cannot be expected that the sanitary laws and the organization of the health branch of the government can at once be fitted into a rigid mold. Ten years ago a hookworm campaign was unheard of, intensive work in typhoid fever was unknown, attention was focused on the sanatorium to combat tuberculosis, the milk station was the one means of reducing infant mortality, the first tuberculosis exhibit had just been held, pasteurized milk was frowned on by physicians and health officers. All of these matters are looked at very differently today. The hookworm campaign, in its original form, is over and has left those engaged with less certain ideas as to the best means of control. In the prevention of typhoid fever interest has shifted from the city water supply to the rural privy. The sanatorium is now given its proper place in tuberculosis work and more attention is given to the advanced case, the dispensary and the nurse. It is known that the personal guidance of the mother does more for the baby than does merely the furnishing of good milk. Methods of milk control are steadily changing. The plan of aggressive public health education was scarcely thought of ten years ago. It is now considered the corner stone of prevention. The organization of the health department, too, is changing. The old shotgun methods of doing a little of everything, and nothing effectively, are becoming obsolete. Definite lines of effective work are planned. Bureaus, or divisions, in the department have become necessary in all the larger states. The former scheme of an executive board has been found to work badly. A single executive is needed. Today we are told that he should be appointed by the governor. Tomorrow there may be some other plan. Some would have a legislative board with unlimited power and in some states such have been established. In other states the courts have decided that this could not be done. Local health organization will probably differ in county and township states. The peculiar problems of the South may require another type.

This state of flux in the science and art of preventive medicine, renders standardization difficult and undesirable except along a few limited lines. The principles of good registration are so well established that we can well have a "model" vital statistics law and standard forms. Even here conformity should not be too strongly insisted on, or there can be no progress. We are just beginning to learn how to control the communicable diseases, how to attack the tuberculosis problem and how to preserve infant life. To crystallize present day views by standardization would check experiment, and every science advances only by experiment. It is nature's plan to encourage variation and to select the best. There are those who believe that the variations in the organic world do not occur haphazard but proceed along certain lines only. It is fortunate that the nation consists of forty-eight commonwealths in which different experiments can be tried. It is well, however, that these should not be made blindly. If experiments are not to be costly and futile it is necessary to know what others have done and what are the results. A most essential preliminary to progress is for some central agency, as the American Medical Association, for instance, to collect and publish data as to what has been done, indicating if possible what lines of endeavor and what forms of organization give promise of the best results.

There are certain lines of state health work which have been shown by experience to be effective and practicable. Many of the conditions and details for their successful prosecution have also been provisionally determined. It is difficult to indicate numerically their relative importance though it appears that some are more important than others. The organization of the department, the collection of vital statistics, the diagnostic laboratory and systematic education are all necessary, though their value cannot be measured in terms of sickness prevented, or lives saved. The control of water and sewage disposal is a profitable field of effort and its value, in part at least, can be measured in deaths prevented. Some of the methods are so well established that they may even be standardized. The control of communicable disease, using the term in its broadest sense, must at the present be the most important and extensive of the state health department's activities. Each disease should have its due share of attention. One disease should not be neglected for another. It is just as important to prevent malaria as it is hookworm infection. A life saved from typhoid fever is just as much saved as one saved from tuberculosis. It is just as desirable to prevent deaths from measles as from smallpox. Every state health department should have a carefully planned and well balanced scheme for its communicable disease work. The diagnostic laboratory, the use of sera and vaccines and, to some extent, the direction and improvement of local health officials are only means for controlling these diseases. Every disease must be considered by itself. We know perfectly well how to control some, others we know little about.

Thus the control of the venereal diseases, so-called, is in the very first experimental stage. It is scarcely known where to begin. The last thing has not been said in regard to the prevention of tuberculosis but enough is known to warrant doing much more than is done.

The prevention of infant mortality is one of the most profitable lines of local health work. Effective means are well known, as are also the means by which the state health department can stimulate local effort. This again is an activity the efficiency of which can be easily measured. The importance of protecting the health of school children is very great. Effective methods are well established. That they are largely under the direction of school officials instead of health officials is due, in part at least, to the apathy of the latter. That the state health department can do much to stimulate local action is certain, and that in most states it does little, is also certain.

The proper protection of urban milk supplies is extremely difficult. We really do not know accurately what are the requisites for a safe milk. The technical difficulties in the way of improving milk are great and the legislative difficulties are often greater. The state health officials undoubtedly can, however, do more than is now being done.

Much attention is given to other foods by many health officials, especially to the prevention of adulteration. This is an economic problem, having little if any relation to health, but in some states it may be expedient to entrust it to the health department if it is not allowed to absorb energy which should be devoted to more important matters. The cleanliness of food is an important health matter, but it is as yet uncertain how much real cleanliness can be secured. This is another subject concerning which much observation and experiment are needed before we can be certain of the value of the methods employed. A somewhat similar activity is hotel inspection, which sometimes is a function of the health department.

The supervision of the health of factory workers and the prevention of occupational diseases are most important but their accomplishment by the health department is by no means easy. The tendency is to entrust such matters to the factory inspector, who is apt to give sanitary considerations a very subordinate place. To coordinate the work of the factory inspector, as it is ordinarily understood, and the sanitary supervision of the operatives, is one of the pressing problems.

The supervision of the construction of public buildings, especially schoolhouses, is occasionally a function of the state health department, and, particularly as concerns schoolhouses, may be very useful. Some of the older laws made the board of health supervise the management of various state institutions but it is to be feared that it was often perfunctory. It is very questionable whether it is desirable to force this duty on the health department.

The control of nuisances, especially those arising from slaughter houses and other offensive trades, is frequently taken up by state boards of health and they are also often given authority over all forms of nuisances. Much of this nuisance work has little relation to the public health but sometimes a central authority is needed and it may as well be the health department as any.

The examination and licensing of embalmers, nurses, optometrists, midwives, dentists, veterinarians, pharmacists, plumbers, and physicians is at times one of the duties of the state health department. Except in the case of midwives and physicians, this has little to do with the public health. Logically, the examination of physicians is properly a function of the health department but in practice it has been found to work especially well and it obtains in comparatively few states.

Among the miscellaneous activities of state health departments especially noted are "safety first" campaigns, mosquito control, education in sex hygiene, the inspection of plumbing, inspection of illuminating oils, enforcement of narcotic laws, supervision of pauper insane, campaigns against patent medicines, inspection of lodging houses, and the care of crippled children. Some of these have nothing to do with health, some are more properly functions of the local health department, while some have great possibility for good if developed with care and judgment.

The third portion of the report consists of the score and rating as shown in Table I. The writer has not the confidence of some in the marking system and very much fears that it has special limitations when applied to this particular subject. It is impossible to score the personal qualifications of officials, yet the future of every health department depends on this more than on anything else. Nevertheless, without funds, the best men can do nothing and their excellent character is even sometimes the cause of the small appropriation, as they cannot, and will not, stoop to the methods of the politician. It might be thought that the state should be given credit for the amount appropriated for public health but it is doubtful if this is so, unless the qualifications of the men who spend it are also taken into account. The freedom of a department from politics is of the greatest moment but the fact is difficult to determine and it seemed unwise to give it weight in the rating. There is very much in public health work for which it is very difficult to find any scheme of measurement. Without accurate measurement it is difficult or impossible to assign values, for they must depend on judgment, and men's judgments differ and are difficult to defend.

In the present scheme the intention has been to rate the states rather than the health department, for sometimes important matters, as water control, the diagnostic laboratory and certain phases of anti-tuberculosis work, are not under the control of the public health officials. It is also intended to rate function rather than organization. Only those activities are selected for rating which are either very generally found in state health departments or are of great importance.

It has not been learned that any previous attempt has been made to establish a system of rating for state health work. In preparing this scheme several persons have been consulted and they have expressed very decided differences of opinion. The writer's ideas have changed a good deal since it was first outlined and would probably be again modified after further thought and discussion. Perhaps some might think that the prevention of food adulteration should be recognized, but this does not seem to have much to do with health. Others would give more weight to the promotion of cleanliness of foods, and others to "sanitation." Some may think that instruction in sex hygiene, or the venereal diseases, should have recognition, but successful ways of teaching the one, and preventing the other, are so far from being standardized that it does not seem right to penalize a state for not experimenting. On the other hand, it may be objected that research does not save lives and should not be given credit, but there are so many problems to be solved that the department which takes no share in their solution should take a lower position than one which does.

The detailed report follows.

            Respectfully submitted,   CHAS. V. CHAPIN, M.D.

STATE SUMMARIES

ALABAMA

The most noticeable feature of public health affairs in this state is the provision that the State Medical Association shall be the State Board of Health and the county medical societies shall be the county boards of health. The same organization also controls the licensing of physicians.

This organization was adopted, partly to keep the department out of politics, and partly on the theory that medical men are the best qualified for controlling disease because of their knowledge of disease. In accordance with this theory one would expect especial excellence in vital statistics because mortality and birth returns depend on medical men and medical men ought especially to appreciate the value of such statistics. Yet, while some states have had good registration of deaths for fifty years and two thirds of the country is included in the "registration area" of the Census Bureau, Alabama has not yet been admitted to this area.

So, too, Alabama appears to be not at all progressive as regards its control of communicable diseases. The first requisite of this is notification and notification is poor, as indicated by a case fatality of 27 per cent. for diphtheria and 31 per cent. for typhoid fever, a percentage based on a still imperfect registration of deaths.

Nevertheless, like most of the southern states, Alabama has experienced a marked sanitary awakening in recent years. Most of this part of the country for a long time was little affected by modern sanitary science. To the outsider it appears that the work of the Rockefeller Sanitary Commission, bringing to the front young, active men, trained in scientific methods, has proved a great stimulus. The work of the Commission has been directed primarily against hookworm, but the men actually engaged in it have seen that the eradication of this disease is interwoven with sanitary progress in many lines and their campaign has involved preaching the general principles of sanitation and demonstrating that all sanitary progress must rest on a thoroughly scientific basis. While the work of the Commission has been far-reaching all sanitary progress in the South has by no means been dependent on its influence.

Tuberculosis is a notifiable disease but few cases are reported. A site for a sanatorium has been purchased.

In Alabama the establishment of the laboratory antedates hookworm work, dating as it does from 1908. There is an efficient staff and the work is well done, but it needs to be greatly extended, A total of 661 Widal examinations and 565 deaths from typhoid fever in the state in 1913 indicate that the physicians are not using the laboratory as they should.

Rabies has been prevalent and the laboratory has not only assisted in diagnosis, but has given the preventive treatment to a large number of persons. No provision is made for the distribution of other vaccines, or of antitoxin, except that arrangement is made for the sale of "board of health" diphtheria antitoxin at 170 stations.

The censors of the medical association are virtually the State Board of Health. As neither the people nor their representatives have a voice in the selection of the censors or in the management of medical associations we have a form of organization which does not commend itself to many persons outside of the state. It is dangerous to delegate so important a function and there is no evidence that it can be as well performed by a medical society as by a department of the state government as ordinarily established. Doubtless the time will come when Alabama will change to a more modern system.

Meanwhile there is no necessity for insisting on an immediate change if the existing organization will continue to develop scientific and effective lines of work under the immediate direction of capable men.

Unfortunately the collection of vital statistics is not satisfactory and Alabama is not reckoned a registration state. In this branch of its work the department ought to adopt modern, well tried methods which have proved efficient all over the country.

Local sanitation must be promoted by the appointment of efficient local health officers to be supervised by the state.

Probably the most important need is the establishment of a strong bureau which shall be devoted to the control, not only of hookworm infection, but typhoid fever, malaria, tuberculosis and the ordinary contagious diseases.

Better provision should be made for the distribution of antitoxins and vaccines.

A modern water and sewage law is needed and a competent engineer to enforce it. (As this was going to press an act was passed requiring the approval of plans for water supplies and an engineer has been appointed.)

An active campaign for infant mortality and child hygiene should be organized.

Educational work should be extended and systemized.

All this will take money but it will save lives, prevent sickness and increase efficiency. With the conditions existing in the South, a decided reduction in the death rate can be promised as the result of the wise expenditure along the lines named of a sum by no means burdensome.

ARIZONA

This state is large in area but has a small population, estimated as 247,299 in 1915, and of course sparsely distributed. It has a system of county and municipal health officers, some of them very good men. Vital statistics are being collected through the county health officers, a method not considered satisfactory, but which has given surprisingly good results. The state chemist and bacteriologist at the University at Tucson is charged with the enforcement of the pure food law under the direction of the State Board of Health. The laboratory also offers to do diagnostic work but practically none is done, which of itself, indicates a lax control of communicable diseases.

A quarterly bulletin is issued by the department.

What is needed first in this state is a full time superintendent of health who shall be a capable epidemiologist, and who will have charge of vital statistics and can develop the different lines of public health work as conditions in the state demand. Work will gradually develop as elsewhere, but in a small state much can be accomplished by a full time health officer and plans for the future be worked out by him.

The trouble is that the office has been considered one of the spoils of partisan success. To remove it from the domain of state politics is necessary. It would probably be a move in the right direction to establish a board of health appointed by the governor in the manner suggested elsewhere in this report and confer on this board legislative or rule making power and authority to choose the superintendent of health but with no other executive duties. Experience has shown that ex officio members of a board are rarely efficient, as their primary interests are elsewhere.

ARKANSAS

Previous to the entrance of the Rockefeller Sanitary Commission into Arkansas, practically nothing was done by the state to promote the public health. The first director of the hookworm work, Dr. Morgan Smith, was later elected secretary of the State Board of Health and to him is chiefly due the credit for the beginning of better things. The antihookworm campaign itself, here as elsewhere, has done much to stimulate an interest in public health work and a belief in its value.

The next step in sanitary progress was properly believed to be the registration of vital statistics and a law was passed and registration was begun February, 1914.

A diagnostic laboratory is another essential instrument of public sanitation and one was established in connection with the medical department of the state university in December, 1913.

This is little enough for a state of a million and a half of people, but it is a beginning. The health department fully realizes what must be done and that much more money will be needed.

First of all sufficient funds should be provided for the administration of the registration law.

Next it must be remembered that it will require the whole time of a high class man to direct much varied and important work and that the executive officer of the department should be paid a salary sufficient to secure such services. His tenure of office should be made secure. When convenient, the law which permits his election from the board should be changed, and it would be well if the continuity of the board should be rendered more certain by making the terms of the members seven years, one to expire each year.

Another important thing is the development of local health work. Some who are conversant with the situation believe that it is possible to educate and stimulate municipal and county health officers and to demonstrate to the cities and counties the necessity of expending more for public health purposes. It is thought that much can be accomplished along these lines without making any radical changes in organization, but this will require much active work by the state department of health.

Probably, however, the most pressing need is an expansion of the work of the Rockefeller Commission into a division of communicable diseases. To assist this division properly the laboratory must also be enlarged and later must come provision for the distribution of antitoxins and vaccines

This will naturally lead to the systematic development of public health education with a full time man in charge, for the men engaged in the technical work of the laboratory, disease prevention and vital statistics cannot find the necessary time to devote to exhibits, press work and the numerous other methods of popular education.

Doubtless, too, the need for an efficient law and effective methods of water control will be shown when the statistics of disease become available.

No progress can be made without an increase in funds and it is very unfortunate that the last legislature did not see fit to provide for any extension of the meagre health work of the state.

CALIFORNIA

The state department of health in California fell into disrepute owing to its failure to meet the bubonic plague emergency, but was later put on a better footing by Dr. Foster, and its work during the last few years has been greatly improved and extended by Dr. Snow. California now fully appreciates the importance of anti-plague measures and has recently strengthened the laws for the control of the disease and appropriated $25,000 a year for its eradication. Like other infected states California has given the execution of anti-plague measures to the United States Public Health Service and this service is now (1914) spending $15,000 a month in addition to the sum furnished by the state.

The registration of deaths is sufficiently accurate to place California among the registration states though there is still room for improvement. Birth registration remains quite defective.

The bacteriologic laboratory is doing excellent work but if the epidemiologic work were properly developed it ought to do a great deal more than it is doing now. Typhoid vaccine is made and sent out in considerable quantity and a large number of antirabic treatments are given. There are three branch laboratories.

There has recently been established a "Bureau of Tuberculosis" which is improving registration, encouraging and supervising hospitals and other local activities and doing some educational work. Seventy-five thousand dollars was appropriated by the 1915 legislature for the biennial period, $20,000 of which is to be used for education and $55,000 as subsidies to local hospitals and sanatoria.

The state has a fair water and sewerage law which was strengthened by the last legislature and an engineering bureau has just been organized in the department and is supported by an appropriation sufficient for good work.

The control of foods and drugs is placed in the health department and the laboratory is situated at the University at Berkeley. The prevention of adulteration is well done. The department also, to some extent, looks after the cleanliness of markets, bakeshops, slaughter houses, etc. It also administers the cold storage law.

A certain amount of sanitary inspection is done, particularly of camps of various kinds, of which there are large numbers in the state.

A large amount of educational work was done by Dr. Snow, who was the first to use a railroad car for transporting an exhibit. Not so much educational work has been carried on during the last year or two.

As in many other states, the improvement of local health administration is at present the most important sanitary need of California. Two plans are suggested. One is to have a considerable number of full time supervisors appointed by and paid by the state, and the other is to have them paid by the counties which make up the districts. Some such plan must be put in operation in order to make local health work really effective.

Even with the district supervisor the central department must do more or less epidemiologic work. A separate division for this should be organized and should be closely correlated with the bacteriologic laboratory.

More effort should be made to secure the administration of sera and vaccines, especially diphtheria antitoxin, and if necessary it should be furnished by the state.

Educational work should be better systemized and more money devoted to it. Perhaps for the present, until a better registration of birth accurately localizes the problem, the campaign for the prevention of infant mortality, as well as for the protection of child life, might be carried on by the bureau of education.

COLORADO

The health department of Colorado, from all accounts, suffers badly from the dictation of politics and from political methods within itself. The election of the executive officer from the board of health by the board has apparently been the cause of friction which has resulted in inefficiency and loss of influence. Although the department has an appropriation of about $25,000, very little is accomplished. Registration of vital statistics is complete enough to make Colorado a registration state for deaths, but the work might be very considerably improved. The only bacteriologic work is for the diagnosis of diphtheria. The food commissioner is an officer of the health department, but, though there is also employed a chemist of high standing connected with the University, very little effective work is done.

The department should be entirely reorganized along lines which shall best keep it free from politics. There should be public spirit enough in Colorado to demand that the care of the people's health shall be vested in an executive thoroughly trained in sanitary affairs and who shall give not only his whole time, but his whole energy, to the department. The work of county and local health officers must be improved and some sort of supervision by state appointed supervisors be provided for.

The work of the department must be extended and made effective. A modern bacteriologic laboratory is needed. An epidemiologist must be provided and the services of a sanitary engineer made available. Provision should be made for the distribution of vaccines and sera. A campaign of education should be carried on. If food control is to remain with the health department it must be better directed. It is useless, however, to expect good work along any of these lines unless the executive of the department is a man of high attainment in sanitary science and absolutely free from all political control.

CONNECTICUT

The Board of Health of this state is among the older organizations of the kind in the country and, perhaps because of the inertia of its inheritance, has not advanced as rapidly as it should. Nevertheless, the state has to its credit an excellent system of vital statistics which has placed it among the registration states for births[1] as well as for deaths. Free diphtheria antitoxin is distributed and the case fatality is low. Excellent diagnostic work is done by the State Board of Health at Wesleyan University and the laboratory is doing much to improve local milk supplies. Through it, too, studies are being made of public water supplies and the sewage pollution of streams.

Connecticut maintains four sanatoria for tuberculosis and expends between $300,000 and $400,000 for the control of this disease but these funds are expended by the State Tuberculosis Commission.

The State Board of Health is a licensing board for physicians but the examinations are conducted by committees of state medical societies nominally appointed by the State Board of Health.

The Board of Health should be given rule-making power. Members of the board should be ineligible for the position of executive officer.

The present system of county health officers, attorneys appointed by the judges of the supreme court, has proved ineffective or at times a hindrance, and should be abolished. In its place should be full time district supervisors, appointed by the state department of health.

There should be a full time epidemiologist in the department.

The work of the laboratory should be greatly extended and ample provision made for the chemical work needed by the proposed engineer.

A water and sewage law was enacted this year which is capable of yielding good results and the next step, and an essential one, is the organization of an engineering division within the department.

Educational work should be systemized and greatly enlarged.

DELAWARE

Delaware is peculiar in being a very small state with a small population, estimated as 211,598 in 1915, nearly half of which is in one city. Most of the problems which vex larger states do not exist in Delaware

---

1. The Census Bureau has not established a registration area for births, but in this report a state is considered in the birth registration area if it appears that 90 per cent. are reported.

'and an extensive and highly organized state health department is not needed. The state already has a very good system of vital statistics and an excellent hygienic laboratory. Provision is made for the distribution of diphtheria antitoxin. There is a pure food law but no provision for its enforcement.

The greatest improvement which could be made in sanitary matters in Delaware would be to provide for a whole time state health officer who could look after epidemiologic work and vital statistics and gradually develop such other lines of effort as may prove necessary.

FLORIDA

Florida holds a somewhat unique position among the states in public health matters. It is the only state in which no statutory provisions are found for the establishment of local health organizations, although they are required by the constitution. There are no county boards of health and such few municipal health departments, or health officers, as there are, are appointed under special charters or ordinances. Florida, also, is the only state in which the funds of the state health department are provided by a special tax. According to the statute, a tax of one-half mill on the assessed valuation of the state is to be set aside annually for the support of the State Board of Health. This sanitary tax yields a revenue of about $100,000. The original purpose of this plan was to put the state in a strong position as to finances and centralized administration so as to cope with yellow fever which was formerly such a constant and terrible menace. Owing to the dwindling danger from this source, and the transfer to the federal government of maritime quarantine, the activities of the department have undergone a progressive change, but like all the southern states, Florida needs a strong sanitary administration, well backed financially, to make the health of the people what it should be and what they can reasonably demand.

The registration of vital statistics has been most imperfect. Fortunately, the efforts of the department to secure a modern statute resulted last spring in the enactment by the legislature of the "model law."

There are very few efficient municipal health departments in Florida and in the cities, as well as in the rural districts, effective work, if done at all, must be done by the state. At one time the department had as many as thirty-two "county agents" but they were mostly part time men. At present there is an "assistant" health officer in each of the seven districts into which the state is divided, all full time men. These men are expected to look after all the details of local health work in a southern state with probably 750,000 people scattered over 54,000 square miles.

Almost no reports of communicable diseases are received except through laboratory specimens. The control of these diseases is left largely to the attending physician. The department did conduct an aggressive campaign against hookworm infection before the Rockefeller Commission began its work and the Florida methods were to a considerable extent followed by the Commission.

Tuberculosis is reportable but not well reported. The department has three social workers to visit cases of this disease. A sanatorium has been authorized but the department now feels that the money had better be spent in home instruction.

The department maintains four isolation hospitals for smallpox.

The State Board of Health maintains a central diagnostic laboratory at Jacksonville and five branch laboratories. A large amount of work is done.

Diphtheria and tetanus antitoxin and smallpox, typhoid and rabies vaccine are distributed. How adequate this distribution is it is impossible to determine in the absence of morbidity and mortality statistics.

The control of foods and of milk production is with the department of agriculture.

The monthly bulletin, which contains much effective material, is well known. There is a weekly press service covering about 225 papers. Films are sent out to the various moving picture houses. A traveling exhibit is being prepared.

There is a hotel law administered by a hotel commissioner—a separate department.

An unusual function for a state health department is the control of contagious diseases of animals. This includes the free distribution of hog cholera serum and the payment for slaughter of glandered animals. The total expense of this division was about $28,000 in 1914.

Another peculiar activity is providing hospital care for crippled children.

The last legislature provided that every schoolchild is to be examined by a medical inspector once each year under the direction of the State Board of Health and that the latter is to bear the expense.

It is now generally admitted that efficient local health administration is the key to sanitary progress. In Florida the state health department has peculiar responsibilities. No provision is made by statute for health officers in municipalities, or unorganized rural districts, while on the other hand the State Board of Health has full executive power and a considerable amount of money at its disposal. The department ought either to secure the appointment of efficient municipal and county health officers under the direction and pay of the local governments, or else appoint and pay a sufficient number of its own full time agents to cover the whole state. Some idea of the necessary number and pay of such officials can be obtained in North Carolina where there are already a number of full time county health officers, or in Kansas, where twenty-nine district health officers are proposed. There are some who are conversant with conditions in the South who believe that even a full time health officer in each county cannot do the work. Unless a still larger appropriation can be made available, it may be necessary both to require local communities to employ health officers and to provide a number of state supervisors according to the Massachusetts and New York plans.

After the mechanism for direct and continuous control is thus provided the reporting of communicable diseases should be insisted on and an epidemiologist appointed to direct local work. Doubtless under these conditions it would be found necessary to extend considerably the distribution of antitoxins and vaccines.

A division of public health education should be formed to carry on an energetic campaign for infant mortality, child hygiene and for the control of typhoid fever, malaria, hookworm infection and tuberculosis.

A chemist with engineering training would be a useful addition to the staff of the department.

GEORGIA

In 1905 a bacteriologic laboratory was established chiefly for diagnostic purposes.

In 1908 the production of antirabic virus and preventive treatment was begun.

In 1909 the department began the production and free distribution of diphtheria antitoxin. Several other sera and vaccines are now distributed, some of which are also manufactured. While the amount distributed is very considerable, these agents are certainly not used by the physicians of the state as freely as they should be.

In 1910 a chemist was employed to analyze water samples and inspect public water supplies.

The department has a publicity man who is chiefly engaged in lecturing and writing for the press. He also does some epidemiologic work.

A vital statistics law and a law for local sanitary organization have recently been passed but no money was appropriated for their administration.

The control of food supplies is under the Department of Agriculture.

The hookworm work, which as in other states, was only nominally under the state health department, and for which the state furnished merely office room and postage, was entirely abandoned after the withdrawal of the Rockefeller Commission.

Certainly the state should require the executive officer of its health department to give all his time to the administration of his office if it expects the work of the department to be properly coordinated and developed and of course should give a salary sufficient to warrant such a demand.

The most pressing need is the collection of accurate vital statistics, for without these it is impossible to determine just what the health needs of the state really are, or whether the preventive measures adopted are really accomplishing the desired ends. Thus with no knowledge as to the prevalence of diphtheria, tuberculosis and typhoid fever we cannot know with certainty whether enough antitoxin is distributed or the diagnostic laboratory is doing its duty or the water supplies of the state need better control.

There ought to be a strong bureau of communicable diseases in which the anti-hookworm work should be merged, but in which the other diseases should be given their proper attention. The diagnostic work of the laboratory is now very meagre. As effective epidemiologic work is developed, the work of the laboratory, as a part of it, is bound to develop also and the use of sera and vaccines is bound to increase.

Even with efficient and adequate epidemiologic work on the part of the state department of health it can only be partially successful until there is better local sanitary administration.

Educational work needs to be extended and all modern methods made use of, particularly exhibits. Definite campaigns should be organized for the prevention of malaria, typhoid fever and for the prevention of infant mortality and for child hygiene. Tuberculosis has apparently been much neglected in Georgia and should receive special attention.

A modern sewage and water law is needed and an engineer to enforce it.

IDAHO

Most of the work of the department of health is done by the dairy and food inspector who is also sanitary inspector, inspector of drugs, "humane officer" and sealer of weights and measures. Besides regular food and drug work, including milk and the scoring of dairies, he also examines local water supplies, enforces the hotel law, inspects slaughter houses, markets, groceries, restaurants and all places where food is handled and also barber shops and bathing places. He has five deputies, four clerks and a chemist. Although appointed by the board of health he works independently of it. The last incumbent did a good deal of publicity work and was a skilful advertiser. It has been alleged that politics has sadly interfered with the administration of this important office.

Outside of the food inspector's office the department does some educational work by means of press articles, exhibits and lantern lectures.

The state has adopted the model registration law somewhat modified, but has only one clerk to administer it.

There is a good diagnostic laboratory at Boise, with a branch at the State University at Moscow, but the latter needs another laboratory man.

More clerical force is needed for perfecting vital statistics.

There should be a better control of communicable diseases under a full time epidemiologist.

Provision should be made for the distribution of antitoxins and vaccines and the work of the diagnostic laboratory should be further developed.

A modern water and sewage law is needed and a full time engineer.

Educational work should be increased and specific campaigns carried on for child welfare and against tuberculosis and typhoid fever.

The department ought to be reorganized. The board is partly ex officio, which is not desirable. There should be a board of five or seven, one appointed each year for a term of five or seven years, and without executive power other than the election of an executive officer, who should not be a member of the board. The executive should be a full time man. The legislative power of the board, which is now somewhat uncertain, should be defined. The people of Idaho should demand that the whole department be kept absolutely free from politics of every kind.

ILLINOIS

Illinois is among the few states in which the State Board of Health is the Examining Board for Physicians. The plan has not seemed to work well here in the past as this function of the board has received undue attention as compared with its more strictly public health work. Perhaps, partly owing to this examining function, internal controversies in the state medical association seem to have involved the department and it must be recognized that medical politics as well as state politics may greatly hamper public health administration. Although the expenses of the department were something over $100,000 in 1914, about one quarter of this sum was expended for the examination and licensing of physicians, midwives and embalmers.

There is no satisfactory law for the registration of births, marriages and deaths and mortality statistics are in a more unsatisfactory condition in Illinois than in any of the states of the Middle West. [See below for supplementary statement.]

Local health organization throughout the state is generally poor. This is usually the case in rural communities, but it is said that very few, even of the cities, possess an active health organization and it is worthy of note that some of these departments are supported almost entirely by private endowment.

Communicable diseases are reported rather better than might be expected, but in the absence of mortality statistics it is difficult to determine just how complete notification really is, but outside of the large cities it is far from satisfactory. New regulations for morbidity reports have recently gone into effect which ought to enable the state department of health to exercise a more efficient control. The epidemiologic work of the department, as well as some sanitary inspection, is being attempted by three "medical inspectors" who give only a part of their time.

There is a diagnostic laboratory at Springfield, but compared with the amount of communicable disease it is not doing nearly enough work. The department is anxious to establish branch laboratories but probably the usefulness of the existing laboratory could be very considerably increased.

The department distributes diphtheria antitoxin freely to every one who needs it, at a cost last year of $29,000. Typhoid vaccine, also, is distributed and prophylactic packets for ophthalmia are now being sent out. Antirabic treatment is provided for the indigent at the Pasteur Institute in Chicago.

Tuberculosis has just been made reportable. There is no state sanatorium and few local hospitals, though there is a permissive law for hospitals in cities. The active state association is in cordial relation with the department.

Occupational diseases are reportable to the health department, under a law which does not appear to be very effective, but the sole function of the department seems to be to transmit them as soon as received to the factory inspector.

Illinois has no adequate water and sewage law, but the state water survey, in connection with the University, has done most excellent work in studying conditions and advising municipalities and private companies.

The State Food Commission has charge of the enforcement of the food laws, including the "sanitary food law," which relates to the cleanliness of places where food is handled. Some attention is given to the cleanliness of milk, especially through education. The state health department has a full time dairy inspector and four others during a part of the summer, who are occupied partly in seeing that milk excluded from one community does not go to another, and partly in helping cities, desiring it, to improve their milk supply by inspecting the farms from which it is derived.

Formerly the educational work was confined chiefly to special bulletins which as a rule are too bulky to be effective. At present there is a biweekly press service for about 375 papers. There is a traveling exhibit and the department has two films for "movies." Some lectures are given.

There is a hotel law containing several of the usual "sanitary" provisions which the State Board of Health is to enforce and under which it is to make rules, but practically nothing has been done and it is said that the law is likely to be repealed.

An attempt has been made at the inspection of summer resorts, construction camps and the like.

A peculiar activity of the department, and one which absorbs over $10,000 annually, is the purely local function of lodging-house inspection in Chicago.

While one may not consider the combination of medical and other professional and semiprofessional licensure with public health work desirable, it is not necessary to insist on the separation of the two. If for local reasons it is desirable to continue the combination in Illinois, it ought to be perfectly possible to carry on the work of the department effectively along modern lines if the Board of Health and its executive keep entirely aloof from medical as well as state politics and give to public health work proper, as distinguished from professional registration, the attention which it deserves and if the department is organized with these ends in view.

The first thing needed, of course, is a modern law for the registration of vital statistics with a sufficient appropriation to secure its administration.

Probably the next most important matter is the improvement of local health administration. At the present time the provision of a considerable number of well trained full time supervisors is the most practical measure.

The establishment of a division of epidemiology is also essential. This division may make use of the district supervisors, just referred to, for its field work, or may have field workers of its own. It is well to have the diagnostic laboratory and the distribution of antitoxins and vaccines in this division. It is hoped that the projected branch laboratories will be established.

An effective water and sewage law is needed. The difficulty will be in providing for its administration. It would be exceedingly unfortunate if the work of the water survey should be separated from the University and some plan should be devised for maintaining this union though the authority for executing the law might be conferred on the State Board of Health.

There should also be a division of education, for much of this needs to be done in connection with the prevention of infant mortality and with child hygiene as well as for the control of tuberculosis, typhoid fever and other diseases. Close cooperation should be provided for between this division and that of communicable diseases.

Although the above was written in March of this year, now, in September, it needs to be greatly modified. A great deal of important legislation was secured for which the department deserves the greatest credit.

The essentials of the model registration law were adopted and a division of vital statistics organized.

An epidemiologic division was provided for with a director and four assistants.

Two branch laboratories have been established.

Larger appropriations were made for sera and vaccines.

Counties may now provide sanatoria for tuberculosis and also dispensaries and nurses.

A division of engineering has been organized but the laboratory work is still to be done at the University.

INDIANA

The department of health in Indiana seems to have kept free from political interference and its efficient executive has remained in office for many years and has been able to follow a consistent policy.

A successful registration of deaths has been developed and that of births is rapidly improving and is doubtless over 90 per cent.

Contagious diseases are still not well reported though the bacteriologic laboratory has done a good amount of most excellent work.

A member of the laboratory staff administers antirabic treatment and the cost is defrayed by a portion of the dog tax. Typhoid vaccine is made and distributed and provision is made for the sale of diphtheria antitoxin at a low price.

Much educational work has been done in connection with tuberculosis. The state maintains a sanatorium of 100 beds and has a permissive hospital law for counties.

The bureau of foods and drugs is well known outside the state for its excellent work against adulteration. Good work has also been done in fighting fraudulent nostrums. A good deal of attention has been given to the sanitation of places where food is prepared and handled. The cold storage law is administered by this department. Some work is being done for the improvement of milk supplies.

Water and sewage control is under the bureau of food and drugs of this department. Much has been done in the way of inspection and surveys, and improvement in local water supplies has been brought about by advice and orders. The law however is not entirely satisfactory and it does not provide for the filing and approval of plans.

The educational work of the department is especially prominent and effective. Dr. Hurty has devised many new details which have been copied by others, such as the governor's letter presenting the "baby book" to mothers. It is possible, however, that carelessness is sometimes permitted as to subject matter.

The department has broad powers over the sanitary conditions of public buildings, especially schoolhouses, and during the past two years a large number of schoolhouses have been condemned and others renovated. It is estimated that nearly $4,000,000 has been expended in these improvements.

The department believes, and is doubtless correct, that the chief need at the present time is improvement in local health administration. A bill to secure this failed of passage at the present session of the legislature but effort should be continued to secure in one way or another the needed improvement in the service.

Meanwhile the State Board of Health could do much to improve the control of communicable diseases by developing and strengthening the epidemiologic work of the department. With sufficient state supervision, a great deal could be accomplished even with the present local health officials.

A better and more modern water and sewerage law is needed and it would be wise to establish a division of engineering entirely separate from the food and drugs division.

IOWA

Iowa has suffered from frequent changes in the secretaryship of the State Board of Health, and from friction with other branches of the government. Conditions are not satisfactory at the present time. The State Board of Health is appointed by an ex officio appointing board consisting of the Governor, Secretary of State and Auditor of State. The State Health Commissioner is also appointed by them. The finances of the department are controlled by the "Executive Council" consisting of the above-named appointing board together with the Treasurer of State, all of whom are ex officio members of the State Board of Health. The whole board meets only twice a year and meanwhile the state health officer has full executive authority, except as regards finances, and is in close touch with the "Executive Council" which seems to have much more to do with the management of the department than does the nominal board of health. Such a complicated organization suggests that it was not devised along broad lines but to meet some special exigency.

One member of the board is under pay as a full time engineer for the department, an amicable arrangement at present, but one likely to cause trouble. The four medical men on the board of health, together with the State Commissioner of Health, serve as the examining board for physicians. The provision that not more than three members of the board of health shall be of one political party suggests that other matters than fitness determine appointments.

Much of the time of the commissioner of health is taken by the examination of physicians, nurses, embalmers, optometrists and other clerical work, so that he has really little time for the study of important sanitary subjects.

The registration law is antiquated and deaths are not completely reported and birth statistics are still more defective.

Contagious diseases are not well reported and reports of typhoid fever are not required at all. It goes without saying that local sanitary administration is poor.

The bacteriologic laboratory is connected with the State University and is under joint control. The diagnostic work of this laboratory stands high and is greater in volume, and hence more useful, than in most states. As in other states, under similar conditions, friction has developed and last autumn the tension became acute. The University was desirous of undertaking epidemiologic work and the last legislature appropriated money for this purpose, but to this the board of health strenuously objected. Undoubtedly the University is at present better equipped to carry on such epidemiologic work, but it is dangerous for the University to be entrusted with such administrative duties and by no means to be recommended. Recently the epidemiologist has been appointed as provided.

The department is doing some educational work, chiefly through its quarterly and special bulletins, but it is not well done. The State Board of Control which manages the state sanatorium of 103 beds, was given $5,000 for educational work on tuberculosis. This seems unfortunate, for duplication, or antagonism, or contradiction, in educational work is bad, and the State Board of Health is the only department of the state logically to be intrusted with public health education.

The Board of Health is required to enforce the hotel law, and this with the control of water and sewerage, and other matters has been intrusted to the bureau of sanitary engineering. The water and sewerage control has apparently not been as efficient as could be desired and a new law is needed. At present control is exercised solely by means of rules.

Antitoxin is distributed at cost but the board does not know how much is used. The Pasteur treatment is given.

Iowa is far from taking its proper position in sanitary affairs. The department should be reorganized, having in mind solely the interests of public health. Probably a board which shall elect a commissioner, but which should have no other executive power, would be a good form. The positions should then be filled by the very best men attainable. If the department is such that the community has the highest confidence in it, the laboratory, epidemiological, educational and all other public health work should be placed directly under its control. This does not, however, mean that all connection with the University should be severed. It is very desirable that the laboratory be at the University if possible and that other University connections be established as well. Cooperation is equally important for the health department and for the University.

KANSAS

The department of health of Kansas seems to have kept out of political entanglement and been able for a number of years to devote itself earnestly to the promotion of the public health. A close alliance has grown up between it and the State University which has an excellent influence on and is most useful to the department. It is to be regretted that the University does not make more use of this valuable connection for the instruction of its students. Kansas has been admitted to the registration area for deaths and is making an earnest endeavor to perfect its entire system of registration. The department has a division of epidemiology an health organization which not only looks after communicable diseases but is undertaking a "sanitary survey" of the state by counties, probably to extend over a number of years.

Provision is made for the distribution of vaccines and antitoxins and the Pasteur treatment is given at the medical school. There is a diagnostic laboratory at Topeka. The department for three years, by means of a special appropriation of $10,000, carried on a vigorous antituberculosis campaign and is now supervising cases through the epidemiologic division. The department keeps in close touch with the state antituberculosis association. Much of the epidemiologic work has been begun only recently and needs to be greatly developed. The diagnostic laboratory particularly ought to be developed and more generally used, for without it the dangerous atypical cases can never be recognized. A division of child hygiene has recently been organized.

Excellent work is being done for the protection of water supplies and for solving problems of sewage disposal. The law seems to be very effective. There is a food and drug division in the department which not only looks after adulterations of foods and drugs, oils and seeds, but also devotes much time to the cleanliness of places where food is handled or prepared and enforces the weights and measures law. Hotel inspection was formerly under the health department but has been transferred to the hotel commissioner. The educational work is extensive and well known, but as with most educational work, a good deal more care should be given both to matter and form.

The department has developed to a considerable degree the more important fields of sanitary endeavor. As in other states which have reached this stage of sanitary effort, the most important present need in Kansas is such improvement in local health administration that, throughout the state, details of sanitary work shall be efficiently carried out. This is greatly desired by the department and is the most important matter under consideration by the Kansas commissioner of public health. It has been suggested that a desirable plan is the appointment of full time health officers for counties or groups of counties. It is not necessary here to urge the adoption of any specific scheme, but if Kansas is to progress, some effective plan must be adopted, and it must be kept in mind that no efficient local health work will ever be done unless it is adequately paid for. The reorganization of local health work and the strengthening of that of the state department along the lines now followed is what is needed. Since writing the above a law for the above purpose was framed but failed to pass.

KENTUCKY

The State Board of Health of Kentucky is organized on the plan, which has met with favor in several of the other southern states, by which the medical profession is given a share in its control. The members of the board, though appointed by the governor, are nominated by the state medical associations, regular, homeopathic, eclectic and osteopathic, and all are to be represented on the board. The avowed purpose is to remove the board from domination by politicians and secure the confidence and cooperation of the medical profession. Even if the expected benefits always resulted, the danger of thus conferring on private organizations the selection of state officials and the recognition of medical sects, is, as is pointed out elsewhere in this report, a dangerous practice. Furthermore, medical politics and medical bossism may be as pernicious as state politics. That a considerable degree of helpful cooperation has been secured in Kentucky is true. A willingness to adopt modern methods of treatment for hookworm, trachoma and diphtheria, the prompt reporting of cases of communicable disease and ready compliance with the vital statistics law are adduced as evidence, but these conditions do not seem to have been secured earlier, or to have more nearly reached the ideal, than in many other states where this form of organization does not prevail. With this form of organization it is logical that the licensing of physicians should be one of the functions of the board and it is considered a valuable asset.

The adoption of the model registration law in 1911 soon placed Kentucky in the registration area for deaths and the state is likely to be in the registration area for births about to be established.

The control of water and sewage is by rules of the board, the validity of which seems to be sustained by the courts. The aims of the department are excellent but its funds do not permit of a sufficiently systematized and close supervision.

Communicable diseases are well reported to the local officials but reports are sent to the state board only quarterly, which does not admit of effective control from the central office. The work of the Rockefeller Commission received the hearty support of the department and much attention is given to the eradication of hookworm, trachoma and typhoid fever, but funds for intensive work are not available. Preventive treatment for rabies is given.

The state has a special commission for the control of tuberculosis, which is carrying on the usual educational work. There is no state hospital and no county hospitals, though some have been voted.

The department distributes diphtheria antitoxin and many counties and towns furnish it free to the poor. Special effort is made to encourage its use but they have not been especially successful. Other sera and vaccines are distributed.

The diagnostic laboratory is doing a large amount of work in an economical manner, but hookworm infection occupies relatively too large a share of it.

The department did much to eliminate tuberculosis from milch cows and this work is now carried on by the Live Stock Board. The Food and Drug Commission does a good deal of dairy inspection. There is a hotel law and inspector, not in the health department. The educational work is of good quality and large in amount. The department has been very successful in securing the interest and cooperation of various agencies in the advancement of the public health.

Bureaus of nursing, of housing and of food and drugs have been established on paper, some work is being done, largely voluntary, by outside persons. It appears that in this and in some other directions the department is extending its efforts farther than its finances warrant.

One of the most important needs is a better control of communicable diseases. A full-time epidemiologist, doing nothing else, should be secured and assistants added as needed. The state is now spending $15,000 a year on its tuberculosis commission. It is difficult to see why the work of this commission is not properly work of the State Board of Health, and a part of these funds might be diverted to intensive campaigns against typhoid fever, malaria, etc. More active and continuous efforts along these lines will result in a greater use of the laboratory and of sera and vaccines.

As in most states better local health administration is needed and the department is working to secure full-time county health officers which would seem to be a reasonable possibility and well adapted to conditions in Kentucky.

The reduction of infant mortality has received practically no attention and almost nothing is known about conditions. In many states this has proved one of the most effective lines of health work and a bureau of child hygiene which will carry on intensive campaigns would seem to be far more important than bureaus of housing or food and drugs.

LOUISIANA

Politics are said to dictate appointments to the state board of health. If this is so permanency of tenure for the executive, and perhaps his subordinates, can never be secure and no matter how efficient an official may be, the whirligig of politics may displace him in a moment and reverse the policy of the department and destroy its influence. The incubus of easily preventable disease lies so heavy on the South that no southern state can afford to allow party or personal politics to exist in the department of health. The people should demand that no governor appoint to membership in the board of health any man who does not hold himself above all petty politics.

The registration of vital statistics has been very poor and until last year there was no effective law. Recently a special agent has been employed to secure its enforcement.

The food division does much more than attempt the control of adulterations. In fact that is rather a minor function. Considerable has been done to improve the character of local milk supplies and to encourage the use of tuberculin tested cows. A great deal of attention has been given to the cleanliness of markets, restaurants, hotels, bakeries, slaughter houses and all places where food is handled. Indeed the promotion of general municipal cleanliness seems to be one of the chief aims of the department and to secure it, it does a 'good deal of local executive work.

There is a division of engineering, but a large part of the engineer's time is occupied in inspection, examining plans for schoolhouses and public buildings and in lecturing. Though the control of water supplies is probably less important in Louisiana than some other states, it would seem that more attention should be given to it than at present.

The control of the sale of illuminating oils is an unusual function for a health department and has little to do with public health but brings to the department a substantial revenue.

A matter of fundamental importance is a local sanitary organization which can carry out the details of sanitary work. Some effective plan of full time parish health officers, or a system of local officials with state supervisors, or some other arrangement should be devised and put in operation.

In the advent of plague the State Board of Health joined in asking the United States Public Health Service to take charge of the situation, as was done in California, and during 1914 appropriated over $22,000 to assist in carrying on the work.

Since the cessation of the work of the Rockefeller Commission intensive work has been carried on in one county jointly by the State Board of Health and the International Health Commission.

Recently a beginning has been made in local supervision by the appointment of a district health officer in one of the parishes who is supported in part by the State Board of Health and is under its direction, though his support is partly derived from the county. Other district health officers overseeing the work in groups of counties are planned for.

As in some other southern states, general epidemiologic work has suffered, while relatively too much attention has been given to controlling hookworm disease. There should be a well organized and well supported bureau of communicable diseases and proper attention should be given to malaria, typhoid fever, tuberculosis and plague as well as to other diseases which are common to the whole country. The diagnostic laboratory is a most important factor in epidemiologic work and Louisiana should have a bacteriologic laboratory of its own, entirely independent of any other. So also the state should provide for the distribution of vaccines and antitoxins more effectively than it does at present. Louisiana, as is well known, has a difficult problem in leprosy, but the management of the leper hospital is not under the department of health.

The Louisiana health department has devoted a large part of its energies to general educational work. Its monthly bulletins are distributed in large numbers, many lectures are given, its portable exhibits are sent about the state and the "health train" is known to every one.

While births are so poorly reported it is impossible to learn the exact infantile death rate, the indications are that it is unduly high. Louisiana certainly ought to have a bureau of child hygiene in its department of health.

The principal criticism to be made of this department is that sufficient study has not been given to planning its activities or carrying out the details. Emphasis has not always been placed on the most important measures. Too much attention has been given to nuisances and general municipal sanitation and the attempt to render cleaner the handling of foods, and not enough to the direct control of malaria and typhoid fever, tuberculosis and the prevention of infant mortality. Effort needs to be concentrated.

MAINE

Maine, like the other New England states, has good registration of births, marriages and deaths and has had it for many years.

The department has an excellent laboratory which is doing a fairly large amount of diagnostic work. The director of the laboratory also makes inspections and advises as to water supplies and does chemical work for the department of agriculture which is in charge of food control.

For many years a considerable amount of educational work, but not of a sensational character, has been done by means of circulars, leaflets for schoolchildren, illustrated lectures, exhibits, etc.

Much educational work has been done in relation to school sanitation and plans of schoolhouses are examined and approved by the department.

The law requires that the townships furnish free diphtheria antitoxin to the poor and many of them do so under a contract with a manufacturer made by the state board of health.

The usefulness of the department could certainly be greatly increased by a very moderate and reasonable expenditure. The most important needs are:

Improvement in local health administration, which might be secured by the appointment of a supervisor and perhaps in other ways. The supervisor should of course first of all be a competent epidemiologist. More effective work could then be done in the control of contagious diseases. Better provision might also be made for the distribution and use of sera and vaccines.

The state is now taking over two sanatoria for tuberculosis formerly operated by the state association.

Educational work ought to be greatly extended and definite campaigns carried on for the protection of child life and for the prevention of tuberculosis. Either a special man is needed, or the secretary should be relieved of some of his routine work.

There are a very large number of labor and pleasure camps in Maine as well as numerous hotels and summer colonies and the state would do wisely to institute an effective supervision.

Although the public water supplies are not at present badly polluted, a modern water law is needed and a competent engineer to look after its enforcement, or perhaps a chemist with engineering training might prove the most useful at present.

MARYLAND

The Board of Health of Maryland is also the licensing board for physicians, a combination which is undesirable. The department is fortunate in having its own attorney, but is unfortunate, owing to a provision in the constitution, in not being able to pay its executive officer a proper salary.

Maryland is reckoned a registration state for deaths and the department is making a strong effort to improve the registration of births.

In 1910 a division of communicable diseases was established, but it has been occupied largely in office and statistical work and not enough field work has been done. Occupational diseases and tuberculosis are reported directly to the state department and the latter maintains more or less supervision over the cases of tuberculosis, but it is not very effective. No provision is made by the state for the distribution of curative sera, though typhoid vaccine is given out and antirabic treatment is provided and also smallpox vaccine is distributed by a state agent not in this department.

The diagnostic laboratory also is well managed and does a large amount of work. This laboratory makes many examinations for the engineering division.

An engineering division was established in 1912 and has been doing good work in the study of water and sewage problems, but at the time the state was visited, there was no law giving effective control. Since then one of the most complete laws in the country on this subject, and one which gives the department very great power, has been passed. It carries with it an appropriation of $25,000 annually and provides for four district engineers besides the force in the central office. This law has recently been sustained by the courts.

The division of food and drugs appears to be doing good work and some attention is paid to the cleanliness of places where food is sold. Since this was written a law has been passed giving the State Board of Health great power in relation to this, conferring at the same time authority to make additional rules.

The chemical laboratory is chiefly concerned with food and drug work, though many analyses are made for the engineering division.

The department has done much educational work in connection with tuberculosis but on the whole public health education has not received the attention it deserves.

It will thus be seen that the main lines of state sanitary work which have proved effective have been undertaken by the department. At the time the state was visited the greatest need appeared to be better local health administration. Since then there has been enacted a law giving the State Board of Health greater executive and legislative power and providing for sanitary districts with a deputy state health officer in each. The act carries an appropriation of $50,000 annually. Seven deputies have thus far been appointed.

Doubtless with the help of the district officers the division of communicable diseases will be strengthened, more field work done, better notification secured and more use made of the laboratory and of antitoxins and vaccines. Indeed it is proposed to bring about this result by making the district officers work under the direction of this division.

Educational work ought to be greatly extended and systemized, health officers educated and effective campaigns organized against infant mortality and tuberculosis.

MASSACHUSETTS

Massachusetts was, in 1869, the first state to establish a permanent board of health along modern lines and this department has had, during the intervening years, a greater volume of successful accomplishment than any other state department of health.

Undoubtedly the most important work of the department has been in connection with water supplies and sewage disposal and kindred matters. This division was organized in 1885, and so little was known of the subject that comprehensive investigations were needed, and were so well carried on, that the results for many years were considered authoritative, not only in this country, but abroad as well. Though the state has never had laws giving control over water and sewerage systems, such as are now found in many states, yet the health department succeeded in bringing about so many improvements in the water supplies of the state that the typhoid death rate soon began to decrease and for a quarter of a century Massachusetts has had less typhoid fever than any other state. The department has also been entrusted with the planning of many important works, such as the metropolitan sewerage system, the improvement of Charles River and the metropolitan water supply, and is now engaged in carrying out the improvement of the Neponset River, a drainage project costing about $200,000.

Diphtheria antitoxin was made and distributed as early as 1895 and smallpox vaccine has also been distributed. Recently the department has undertaken the preventive treatment of rabies and the vaccine and Wassermann laboratories have been united as a division of the department.

A diagnostic laboratory was established in 1895. It has now been made a part of the division of communicable diseases.

Massachusetts was the second state to enact a pure food and drug law (1882) and its administration by the state department of health has been eminently successful. Recently a cold storage law has been enacted and the department entrusted with its enforcement. A good deal of attention is given to the adulteration of milk by the pure food division and three inspectors under the veterinarian of the department until recently gave their time to the inspection of dairy farms. The state also controls slaughtering to some extent through locally appointed inspectors subject to its approval. It controls the taking of shell-fish from polluted beds.

The research work of the department has been extensive and varied and many valuable contributions to sanitary science have appeared in its reports.

Massachusetts was the first state to put in practice the modern idea of state-appointed inspectors as supervisors for which the state was, in 1907, divided into fifteen districts. An important part of the work of the inspectors in the beginning was the sanitation of industrial establishments which has recently, many believe unwisely, been transferred to another department. The state inspectors have certainly done much to unify and improve the work of local health officials.

The routine control of contagious diseases has not received the atten- tion it deserves, though such are fairly well reported. However, a division of communicable diseases has recently been organized on a broad basis and will doubtless do effective work. The state has a large sanatorium, and hospitals for advanced cases of tuberculosis, and the cities are required to furnish hospital accommodation for tuberculosis and for other contagious diseases, and the state department of health is to see that the law is enforced. The state also is to supervise tuberculosis dispensaries and has secured their establishment in all towns and cities of over 10,000. Ophthalmia has received more attention than in any other state. Perhaps the former neglect of routine epidemiologic work is due to the fact that the towns and cities of Massachusetts have done more of their own volition than have the cities in other states.

This department has been subjected to a good deal of criticism in recent years, but when one considers the honest criticism it appears that much of it refers to matters which in other states would be considered minor ones. Thus the writer has criticised the production of an unconcentrated diphtheria antitoxin, though it is well known that the state was the first to produce antitoxin and has distributed more than any other state. Because Massachusetts has done so well we expect her to do still better.

The reorganization of the department which went into effect on August 3, 1914, is not entirely ideal. Although the first selections are excellent, it is a question whether, under the present arrangement, the department will be able to keep out of politics during the next thirty-five years as it has during the past thirty-five. Executive power is not vested entirely in the commissioner, who is appointed by the governor for a term of five years, for all his appointments are subject to the approval of the public health council and salaries subject to approval by the "governor and council," thus bringing effective control within the sphere of state politics. The public health council is given legislative power but no penalty is provided. The state inspectors, though now made full time officials, are cut down to eight.

The collection of vital statistics, which is now in the hands of the Secretary of State, should be transferred to the health department.

Educational work, which has never received sufficient attention, should be developed and effective campaigns undertaken for specific purposes, such as child welfare. Since the above was written a division for this has been organized.

Legislation should be secured which would give the department a real control over water supplies and river pollution.

MICHIGAN

Michigan has a State Board of Health composed of representative men who take much interest in the work of the department and whose advice and assistance are of great value. Formerly the board elected its executive officer, but he was, a few years ago, made an appointee of the governor, which does not appear to be a wise change, but the last legislature provided that he is to be recommended by the board.

The state is fortunate in having had for some time excellent registration of births, marriages and deaths. It is unfortunate, however, that the collection of vital statistics is under the Secretary of State instead of the health department. There are only three other states in which this condition obtains. Registration should be where it can immediately be made use of for public health purposes.

Contagious diseases are not well reported, as shown by the case fatality (though physicians are paid for reports), and the present method of control is unsatisfactory as it is in most states. A full time epidemiologist is needed and some such supervision of local health work as the board has already tried to secure. A diagnostic laboratory is maintained at Lansing and another in the Upper Peninsula. Provision should be made so that vaccines and curative sera are made accessible to all. (The legislature of 1915 provided for a better distribution by municipalities.) The state has a small sanatorium of eighty beds for tuberculosis. The disease is reportable to the state board of health and the number of cases is about double the number of deaths. Literature is sent to the family. The state antituberculosis association is doing excellent work. The last legislature appropriated $100,000 for the biennial period for the prevention of tuberculosis to be expended at the discretion of the State Board of Health. The latter is undertaking extensive educational work and will try to organize associations and secure dispensaries and a hospital in every county.

The department maintains an engineering bureau which is doing good work in the supervision of water supplies and sewage disposal, though the law under which it acts might be improved. The work should be greatly extended and an increased appropriation made therefor.

The educational work of the department is extensive and in the main is very well done. It might well be strengthened, however, in several directions as in newspaper work, illustrated lectures and meetings for health officers, and there ought to be a man to devote all his time to it.

Little is done by the department for the protection of child life and an active campaign ought to be inaugurated.

The department feels that what is most needed at present is to improve local sanitary administration, and a bill was presented to the last legislature to provide for a system of supervisors to oversee the work of the local health officials, but it did not pass.

MINNESOTA

The state department of health is well organized and is doing excellent work with good plans for the future. It has had, and has now, many first class men on its staff. The registration of vital statistics is sufficiently accurate to permit of the inclusion of Minnesota as a registration state for both births and deaths. The division of sanitation and engineering has devoted its chief attention to the protection of water supplies. A partial survey of the state has been made and much accomplished in improving the public supplies of the state, of which there are some 500 or 600. This valuable work has been done without any adequate law, though the board has without success asked for such.

Attention has also been given to sewage problems, especially trade wastes. A follow up system is effectively in use to see that the recommendations of the division are complied with.

The most interesting division is that of preventable diseases, under which the diagnostic laboratory is now placed as a subsidiary bureau, an arrangement which is of great practical value as well as strictly logical. There are two branch laboratories and others are planned. This division seems to have done more and better work in the investigation and prevention of outbreaks than that of any other state. Moreover, a system of "follow up" and supervision from the central office is in force for the common infectious diseases. The diagnostic laboratory is doing excellent work and an unusually large amount of work. The Pasteur laboratory for the prevention of rabies has been very efficient and prepares its own virus. A good deal of typhoid vaccine is also made and used.

The state has a sanatorium for tuberculosis and there is a law providing for county hospitals with state aid, but the institutions are not under the control of the State Board of Health. The disease is reportable and the department follows up cases. The department has made some valuable county surveys.

The former method of distributing diphtheria antitoxin did not prove satisfactory and the last legislature provided $5,000 for this purpose and the department has now arranged for a sufficient number of stations for its distribution. A larger sum, however, than this is needed.

The department conducted an extensive tuberculosis campaign, partly in connection with the state antituberculosis association, and was afterward associated with the educational work of the Minnesota Public Health Association. An educational campaign for the medical inspection of schools was carried on for a while by Dr. Hoag, who was employed by the board.

There is a dairy and food commissioner and a hotel inspector, neither in the department of health.

It seems to be very desirable that this department should maintain its independence and present organization and that its immediate plans for extending its work should be supported by suitable appropriation and legislation. The engineering work should be extended and a suitable water and sewerage law secured. Educational work should be systemized and extended. It is probable that the registration of both deaths and births could be improved.

An aggressive child hygiene campaign should be carried on, including the prevention of infant mortality, and school inspection.

The most important matter just now is to secure a better sanitary administration in the smaller towns and rural districts. This is absolutely necessary if effective work is to be carried on against contagious diseases, infant mortality, impure water and bad milk. The department has plans for the effective supervision of local health work and it is most important to secure the legislation and appropriation necessary to put in operation some such method of control.

MISSISSIPPI

As in some other southern states the state medical society has a share in the control of the state health department, as, of the thirteen physicians of the board five, are nominated by the medical society. The board of health is also the licensing board for physicians.

The department appoints the county health officers, whose salaries are, however, fixed and paid by the county government. The sanitary inspector of the state board has supervision of these county health officers and they act as his deputies. He supervises the municipal health officers' work as well.

A registration law was passed in 1912 and the department is making earnest and successful endeavors to secure its enforcement.

The antihookworm work has been carried on along the usual lines, but more lectures have been given than in most states and more attention devoted to other subjects, as typhoid fever, and tuberculosis for Dr. Leathers believes that more permanent good is accomplished by broadening out the work than by restricting it too closely to one subject. Since the withdrawal of the Rockefeller Commission this state, like several others, has been carrying on a more intensive and somewhat broader work of rural sanitation by means of two "units" consisting of a director and three assistants. This is financed to a large extent by the International Health Commission.

Cases of tuberculosis are reported to the department and provided with literature and counties are authorized to established sanatoria, which when approved by the state department of health, are to receive an annual grant from the state. Only one has so far been built.

A good laboratory has been established, but its diagnostic work is not very extensive.

The state, through the county health officers, directs nuisance work, inspects slaughter houses, and pays particular attention to the cleanliness of all places where food is handled, as markets, bakeries, restaurants and hotels. Public institutions also are inspected. The milk supply is controlled by local licenses which are required by the state department of health, and the state has applied the tuberculin test to large numbers of milch cows and those reacting are required to be killed. The validity of this law has recently been affirmed by the supreme court. For the effort expended a great improvement has been effected in "sanitary conditions" throughout the state.

There has been a good deal of educational work. A monthly bulletin is published and there is an exhibit with lantern and "movies." Many lectures are given.

The department should be reorganized with a smaller board appointed according to modern ideas and with the elimination of the medical society. Neither medical politics nor state politics should have any place in the health department. The executive should be a full time man, thoroughly versed in sanitary science, and should be paid an adequate salary.

The local health service is, as elsewhere, in great need of improvement and those conversant with local conditions believe that full time county health officers could and must be provided by the counties. In failure of this, much could be done by a number of state supervisors to continually stimulate the work of the local officials.

The vital statistics division should have more clerical assistance.

Although the public water supplies of the state are not numerous a water and sewage law is needed and an engineer should be added to the staff of the department.

A division of epidemiology should be created which should include far more than "rural sanitation" and should wage effective campaigns against all infectious diseases.

The work of the diagnostic laboratory should be greatly extended.

Public health education should be increased in amount, systemized and specific campaigns carried on against malaria, typhoid fever, tuberculosis and for child welfare.

Better provision should be made for the free distribution of antitoxins and vaccines.

MISSOURI

Missouri is one of the states in which the State Board of Health is also the examining board for physicians. This is not a good arrangement, as the latter duty occupies time and energy which should be devoted to strictly public health matters. The mode of appointment of the board, by which the majority may be removed at one time, does not favor a strong policy and the election of the executive officer from the board, and by the board, does not favor selection of the best men and, with the mode of appointment of the board itself, gives ample opportunity for pernicious politics. The state does not appear to have taken its health department very seriously, for it has not given it much power nor placed many duties on it.

The "model" registration law was enacted in 1909 and the State Board of Health seems to have been very successful in securing records of deaths, so that Missouri is reckoned a registration state. The registration of births, too, is fairly good.

The board of health maintains a bacteriologic laboratory, with a capable man at the head, but the work has not been pushed.

Missouri has not a modern law for the registration and control of contagious diseases. Local health administration is especially poor. There is no effective law for the protection of water supplies and the supervision of public supplies has been delegated to the Public Service Commission, which seems unfortunate, as this commisson is burdened, and is likely to be so for some time, with many other very weighty matters.

The department ought to be reorganized along modern lines so as to discourage the interference of politics. Bureaus of vital statistics, epidemiology (including the laboratory), engineering, child hygiene and educational work should be established with first class men at their head who would have the entire confidence of the community. All the real public health work of the state, such as control of water supplies, and publicity, should be transferred to this department. With its advice the health laws need to be revised and local sanitary administration reorganized and the whole work maintained by suitable appropriations.

MONTANA

The state health department of Montana has made a beginning in those forms of sanitary endeavor which are considered most essential in the Mountain States, but the work is not as well planned as it should be and is not supported by a sufficient appropriation.

The state has a registration law which ought to secure complete returns but one clerk is not enough to secure proper enforcement.

Undue importance is attached to the food division, as of the total appropriation of about $15,000 there is set aside $5,000 for food inspection and $4,000 for the chemical laboratory, most of the work of which has been concerned with food analysis. It is true, however, that a good deal of the work of this division is directed to securing the cleanliness of hotels, restaurants, bakeries, markets, slaughterhouses and other places where food is handled. Moreover, milk dealers are required to be licensed by the State Board of Health and dairies are inspected and scored. All this is done chiefly by local health officers but under the rules and supervision of the State Board of Health.

The state has a diagnostic laboratory at Helena but it is doing very little work.

There is a water law which might yield better results if there were funds for its administration.

The department inspects many public buildings and institutions, as well as construction camps, and has to approve plans for schoolhouses.

The Montana board of health has done much in the study of Rocky Mountain tick fever and also in applying methods of control. In this it has worked in cooperation with the U. S. Public Health Service. At present there is a state commission of three, of which the secretary of the State Board of Health is a member, but which is now leaving most of the active work to the federal government.

The executive officer believes that the first need is the improvement of the local health service, and in this he is probably correct. It is his opinion that whole time health officers are entirely practicable provided some of the counties be united to form sanitary districts and the towns are placed under district supervision. The executive officer also believes that these health officers should be appointed by the State Board of Health. In any event the state board should supervise and control their work as fully as possible.

Another clerk is needed for vital statistics.

There should be an epidemiologist who could not only investigate outbreaks but could also develop a better system of control for contagious diseases. In this connection the work of the diagnostic laboratory should be greatly extended, perhaps by making the epidemiologist the head of the laboratory and giving him enough assistance. Provision should also be made for the distribution of antitoxins and vaccines.

The department needs a full time engineer who should devote a large part of his time to the control of the water supplies and sewage disposal. The typhoid death rate is high and a part of it is certainly due to water pollution, which should not be permitted. The engineer's advice would also be valuable for the sanitation of state buildings and schoolhouses. It is not improbable that a man could be found who could do both the engineering work and the water laboratory work as well. At present the chemical laboratory where the water and food analyses are made is at the agricultural college, and it seems desirable to maintain this connection.

A great deal more educational work is needed and a special man should be provided for this unless an assistant can relieve the executive officer of routine work so that the latter can devote the necessary time to it.

NEBRASKA

This state is not taking its proper position in sanitary work. The organization of the health department is bad and it is said that political influence makes itself felt. Local sanitary organization is generally poor throughout the state and diseases are not well reported. It is stated that in 1913, eighty-one cases and eighty-four deaths from scarlet fever were reported in a population of 1,200,000! Dr. Wilson, the state inspector, whose work is well spoken of, has to look after outbreaks of contagious diseases, as well as nuisances and vital statistics, and act as general agent of the department. He is the only full time man outside of the laboratory.

Although Nebraska has had since 1905 a registration law which ought to give good results, it has not been admitted as a registration state. The clerical force is not sufficient and the work is not well handled.

Practically nothing is done in the way of publicity and education, except an annual meeting of health officers. There is no systematic supervision of water supplies and no good law, though the laboratory has done some advisory work. No good provision is made for the distribution of antitoxins and vaccines. There is a small state sanatorium for tuberculosis, and the disease is reportable, but according to the bulletins only 17 cases were reported for the year ending December, 1913. The control of food, milk and dairies is in another department, as is hotel inspection. The department does practically nothing toward developing local activity in child hygiene. A little nitrate of silver is distributed for the prevention of ophthalmia and the law requires the licensing of boarding places for infants as well as maternity hospitals by the State Board of Health, though the secretary was not certain about this.

In October, 1913, a good bacteriologic and chemical laboratory was established which is making water examinations and giving advice, besides doing diagnostic work, all of which needs to be greatly extended.

The most important need is a reorganization of the department. The constitution forbids the establishment of a board of health, as it is usually constituted, so that the present exofficio board, consisting of the governor, the attorney general and the superintendent of public instruction, must continue. It would seem to be wise to allow the existing "board of secretaries" to remain and to continue as an examining board for physicians, which has hitherto been their chief function. All the executive power in regard to public health might be placed in the hands of a commissioner of public health to be appointed by the exofficio board of health, and who should be a man skilled in sanitary science and who would give his whole time to the work and who ought to be paid adequately therefor. He should be given full authority in appointments. When such a position is made and filled by an efficient man, he can best lay down specific plans for public health work, but it is safe to say that provision must be made for more efficient and better paid local health officers, for the enforcement of the vital statistics law and the law for reporting disease, for the services of an epidemiologist and for a water and sewage law and the services of an engineer, and for the distribution of antitoxin and vaccines as among the more immediate activities of the department.

NEVADA

State sanitation in Nevada is a very difficult problem, for the state is in population by far the smallest in the Union, the state having in 1910 but 81,875 persons, yet these are mostly in small communities, often difficult of access and scattered over more than 110,000 square miles. There are only five states with as large a land area. These conditions make public health work difficult and expensive while, of course, the revenue of the state must be comparatively small.

The state has a registration law which ought to give good results, though the details relating to local registrars and their fees might be improved.

There is a good bacteriologic laboratory in connection with the University at Reno, which not only does diagnostic work, but examines water and milk and does epidemiologic work and advises local communities as to various sanitary problems. The connection between this laboratory and the State Board of Health is slight and indefinite.

Food control is under another department.

The work of the laboratory might be greatly extended and a prospectus recently issued indicates this purpose. Educational work is needed which might well be carried on in connection with the laboratory. The epidemiologic work also should be extended and better reports of contagious diseases secured. The laboratory might also, on its own initiative, do more work in regard to water supplies. In all this there ought to be a close cooperation between the laboratory and the State Board of Health. Sufficient funds should be given the latter to enable the executive officer to travel where necessary in order to improve registration and stimulate the work of county health officers. More money is needed, and with a very little more money a great deal more work might be done.

NEW HAMPSHIRE

The New Hampshire department of health has been managed in a rather conservative manner but nevertheless has done much good.

The registration of vital statistics is excellent and places New Hampshire with the rest of New England among the registration states for births as well as deaths.

The state has had a pure food law for many years, administered by the health department, and much has been done, though of late more attention has wisely been devoted to the investigation of water supplies. A good deal of work has been done on milk for the smaller towns and, recently, under a new law, the department makes inspections and establishes rules for firms desiring to sell "inspected milk," an industry which the secretary expects to greatly increase. This state health department was also one of the first to adopt rules for the cleanliness of places where food is handled, but as there is only one inspector, who has other duties, not much executive work is done by the state.

The state has an effective water law and considerable work has been done but much more should be done.

There is a good bacteriologic laboratory which does much with water and milk and its diagnostic work is unusually good.

A recent act provides for the distribution of diphtheria antitoxin.

The department has certain duties concerning the indigent insane which require much clerical work

Among the important needs are an engineer, for, while the typhoid death rate is low, there are still polluted water supplies and sewage problems are numerous.

Although the laboratory is doing good work there should be a full time bacteriologist and more clerical assistance.

There should be much more, and more effective, educational work and a special man for this is needed who could carry on active campaigns for whatever sanitary need is most pressing.

It is not desirable that the state attend to the details of local inspection or control of contagious disease but should rather strive to instruct and supervise the local health officials. For this purpose two or three supervisors are needed working along the same lines as the supervisors in Massachusetts. These men should be, first of all, good epidemiologists.

NEW JERSEY

The health department of New Jersey, though not given to self-exploitation, has been doing excellent work for a number of years and is following most lines of effective sanitary administration.

The state has long had a registration law and its administration has steadily improved until the marriage and death record is practically complete, though birth registration needs to be improved.

There is a bureau of contagious diseases and sanitary inspection, which carries on the epidemiologic work as well as possible with its present force and under the defective local sanitary administration. Contagious diseases are not as well reported as they should be though the showing is better than in very many states.

The department has carried on a good deal of tuberculosis education and the state maintains a sanatorium under independent management and has a law requiring every county to provide hospital facilities for which the state may give aid. The state board of health is to see that this law is obeyed and expects soon that each county will be provided for. This state was the first to enact a compulsory isolation law for tuberculosis.

New Jersey formerly had a separate board to deal with water and sewerage problems but in 1908 this was consolidated with the state board of health and its work is continued by the division of food, drugs, water and sewerage. The state has a very good water and sewage law and it is well administered, as is indicated by the low typhoid death rate.

The diagnostic laboratory is under the above named division and does a large amount of work. The examinations for typhoid fever are especially numerous.

The food and drug division has done excellent work along the ordinary lines of preventing adulterations and of late has devoted an increasing amount of time to more strictly sanitary conditions. Much attention has been devoted to preventing the infection of clams and oysters and much has been accomplished. The cold storage law is administered by the department as is also the "broken egg law." Creameries and ice cream factories are supervised and canneries and slaughterhouses inspected.

The department seems to have done a good deal of effective education by its inspection of dairy farms which is usually done for the assistance, and with the cooperation, of local communities.

The state provides an inspector for maritime quarantine, appointed by the governor, but nominally acting under the State Board of Health. As the federal government maintains inspection at the same port this is an entirely needless expense.

New Jersey is one of the very few states which have a paid board of health. Each of the seven members, except the secretary, who receives $2,500, is paid $1,500 per annum. The board meets every week. The disadvantages of a paid board are elsewhere referred to, and also of having a board do executive work. Since the above was written the department has been reorganized by the legislature. The board of health is retained and it still possesses full executive power and has been given legislative power as well. The members serve without pay and elect the executive officer.

The divisions of the department should be rearranged, for certainly food control, engineering and the diagnostic laboratory do not belong together.

Local health administration needs to be decidedly improved. The present local expenditure of five cents per capita, permitted by the law, for health purposes is entirely inadequate. It is thought by the department that much improvement could be effected if the state board of health had authority, in cases of local inefficiency, to step in and charge the expense to the township and this power has just been granted. Adequate fees for local health officers might be fixed by law as in Vermont. Without doubt also the appointment of state supervisors as in Massachusetts and New York would prove useful, but in some way local health work should be made more efficient.

With an improvement in local health work doubtless contagious diseases would be better reported and the bureau having supervision over them would be in a position to do more and better work. Provision should be made for the distribution of antitoxins and vaccines.

The function which has received least attention is that of education. A division of public health education should be established to continue antituberculosis work and to develop local effort for the prevention of infant mortality.

Of course there are many details of legislation and administration which could be improved, but under a reorganized department, and with an improved local health service, these would be worked out by the staff and should be supported by an increasing appropriation.

NEW YORK

The health department of this state was entirely reorganized in January, 1914, and was enabled to undertake its new work with a greatly increased appropriation. Perhaps the most important features of the new organization are the "public health council," on which is conferred exceedingly broad legislative power concerning matters affecting the security of life or health, and the division of the state into sanitary districts, for each of which the commissioner of health appoints a sanitary supervisor. Provision is made in the organic law of the department for the organization of nine divisions, covering the main lines of sanitary work now deemed essential in this part of the country, but not all of these have yet been established.

The council has already framed a considerable body of legislation known as the "sanitary code" and covering such subjects as communicable diseases, milk, midwives, labor camps and nuisances. These rules are in the main far better, and show evidences of greater care in preparation, than similar regulations in most of the states.

Although New York has been reckoned a registration state for deaths and births, there is here, as elsewhere, room for improvement. The adoption of the model law and the appointment of Dr. Wilbur give assurance that effort will not be spared to make the records as nearly complete as is possible.

The state has been divided into twenty districts and supervisors appointed who, under the direction of the central office, are to supervise and unify the work of local officials, make epidemiologic studies and secure the enforcement of the sanitary code. In 1915 the number of supervisors was reduced to ten, entirely too small a number.

The division of communicable diseases has been organized and will operate largely through the supervisors who will do much of the field work.

Maritime quarantine in New York is not a function of the department of health but a separate department. It is carried on at a considerable cost to the state over and above the fees. It has been urged.

and with much reason, that maritime quarantine be transferred to the federal government, as has been done at nearly every port in the country, and it would seem desirable too that it be done here.

The division of laboratories and research does the work required by the engineering division, makes and distributes sera and vaccines, and does the usual diagnostic work.

The tuberculosis division has not been organized, owing to lack of appropriation, but the department is doing educational work, is preparing traveling exhibits, and has actively assisted in the campaign for the establishment of county hospitals.

The division of engineering, besides water and sewerage work, has among other duties, to inspect certain institutions, approve plans, investigate nuisances, inspect summer hotels, and study oyster pollution. Unfortunately the most important work of the division, the supervision of water supplies, is greatly hampered by the lack of proper legislation. A modern water and sewerage law seems to be needed to make this division as effective as it should be, a need of course which is well recognized by the department.

By statute the health department is charged with food control but as no appropriation has been made nothing has been done. The cold storage law is, however, enforced by this department.

The educational work is proceeding along sane and effective lines and is wisely avoiding some of the sensational and careless matter and methods which have found favor elsewhere.

The division of child hygiene has carried on vigorous campaigns for the purpose of organizing effective local work for the prevention of infant mortality, the success of which has already been shown by a lessened death rate.

The division of public health nursing, through its nurses, aims to establish, standardize and supervise the different lines of public health nursing throughout the state.

The state of New York is fortunate in having a department of health, not built up haphazard, but carefully planned by able men versed in sanitary affairs and it is equally fortunate in having it directed by exceedingly capable and earnest officials on whom has been conferred ample power. It remains for the state to appropriate sufficient funds to carry on the work according to the plans formulated.

NEW MEXICO

It is unfortunate that a state with a population which now probably numbers nearly half a million should do nothing whatever for public health. It is the only state of which this can be said. The State Board of Health has both legislative and executive power but no appropriation. It is also an examining board for physicians but it is said that at present the fees do not pay expenses. Surely the state is not so poor that it cannot afford sufficient salary for a full time executive trained in public health work. Such a man could do epidemiologic work, stimulate and supervise the local health officials, study the sanitary needs of the state, and with a suitable registration law establish a system of vital statistics. The people should demand that the office be absolutely free from politics. Such an officer would study local conditions and be able to develop the department along effective lines.

NORTH CAROLINA

The present activities and progressive attitude of the North Carolina department of health are largely due to the self sacrificing efforts of the former secretary, Dr. Lewis, who voluntarily resigned so that a full time executive might be appointed. Until 1909 the appropriation had been but $2,000.

The department was one of the first to recognize the paramount importance of improving local health administration and was one of the first to make a serious attempt to do so. In 1913 it secured a law permitting the appointment of full time county health officers and at present eleven counties have made such appointments. It is the belief of the department that such good results will be obtained from efficient work in these model counties that other counties will be led to adopt the same plan. This state, more markedly than most others, is attempting to place the responsibility for sanitation on the local governments.

Finding that the counties are slow to elect full time health officers the department has recently developed the "unit plan" for rural health work. Under this plan the counties pay for definite forms of work, such as vaccination or school inspection, and the work is actually done by the State Board of Health.

The "model" vital statistics law was enacted in 1913, though until 1915 burial permits were not required in places with less than 500 inhabitants. This law has been vigorously and wisely enforced.

Antihookworm work has been carried on, as in the other southern states, with some incidental, but important, education of the people along the lines of general sanitation, though it has perhaps deviated less from its original purpose than in some other states. Since the withdrawal of the Rockefeller Commission the department has abandoned this as a separate line of work.

In 1908 a bacteriologic laboratory was established which also gives antirabic treatment and acts as agent in the distribution of diphtheria antitoxin and makes and distributes typhoid vaccine. Authority has recently been given to manufacture antitoxin and the department is preparing to do so.

North Carolina has a sanatorium for tuberculosis, formerly under a separate board, but about two years ago it was placed under the management of the State Board of Health. Seventy-five thousand dollars was this year appropriated for enlarging the sanatorium and $10,000 for a "correspondence school" in connection with it, by which the department hopes to keep in advisory communication with the tuberculous population of the state.

The state has a good water and sewerage law but the engineer gives only a small part of his time to engineering work and consequently it has not received the attention it deserves.

The educational work is of excellent quality and is very extensive, particularly as regards press notices and bulletins.

Although much has already been accomplished, and in a short time, much more remains to be done. As in all other southern states the lines of work undertaken must be extended and appropriations increased.

The most important and urgent need is the formation of a division of communicable diseases which will give proper attention to malaria, typhoid fever, tuberculosis and the common contagious diseases. The diagnostic work of the laboratory should be greatly extended.

There should be a full time engineer to carry out the provisions of the water and sewerage law.

Educational work also ought to be greatly increased and new lines taken up, such as campaigns against malaria and for the reduction of infant mortality.

A most excellent beginning has been made in the prevention of disease, and if supported financially it is certain that the state department of health of North Carolina can make an enormous change in the health conditions of the state.

NORTH DAKOTA

The active force of the state department of health consists of the superintendent of health (part time only) with the addition of a clerk for two or three months in the year. A change in administration means a change in officials. Politics determines the election. The appropriation is $2,700 a year and has to cover the salary of the executive officer, clerk hire, travel and printing. Of course almost nothing can be accomplished under such conditions. Local health organization is about the same as in most states and of course needs supervision.

There is a small tuberculosis sanatorium and an active state anti-tuberculosis association is doing good educational work.

A registration law was enacted in 1907 but the appropriation of the department is insufficient for its administration.

The public health laboratories form an integral part of the State University and have no connection with the State Board of Health. The laboratories are doing excellent work in diagnosis and in water investigation.

The most important thing in this state is to secure a full time superintendent of health, experienced in public health work, and pay him sufficient salary to retain him, and with an indeterminate tenure of office. An unpaid board of health with legislative power, but with no executive authority except the election of the superintendent of health, is desirable. The appropriation must be greatly increased to afford a suitable salary for the superintendent of health and furnish enough clerical assistance for the registration of vital statistics, for increasing educational work, for a full time epidemiologist and for providing for the distribution of antitoxin and vaccines. A permanent office in the capitol, or some other accessible place, should be provided. When the department of health is thus strengthened and supported, some organic connection with the public health laboratory should be established, though it would be desirable to maintain the latter in connection with the University. The control of water and sewerage should be extended, either through the laboratory, or an engineering division of the department, and a modern law secured.

OHIO

The health department is unusually well organized and its work well systemized. It stands in close relation to the University and its offices and laboratories are situated on the campus. As the connection is entirely voluntary, not prescribed by the state, it is hoped that it will prove useful to both.

Contagious diseases are well reported as compared with the average state and the department has the services of an epidemiologist but, as in most states, real control cannot be obtained until local sanitary organization is improved.

The work of the diagnostic laboratory is good in amount but it could be still very considerably extended and improved.

Although, judging from the case fatality of diphtheria, antitoxin is quite freely used, and considerable typhoid vaccine is put out by the laboratory, the department ought to consider a freer distribution of these and other sera and vaccines. Since the above was written an appropriation has been made for the production of diphtheria antitoxin.

The bureau of public health education and tuberculosis is well organized and supported by a substantial appropriation, so that a great deal of educational work is being done by means of lectures, a traveling exhibit and by supervisory nurses and in other ways. Most of it is directed against tuberculosis as was intended. The state has a sanatorium of 140 beds and a district hospital law under which several hospitals have been built. Local antituberculosis activities of various kinds are being developed by the educational work.

Ohio has a good water and sewage law and the work of the engineering department has proved efficient in checking pollution and bringing about improvement in the water supplies of the state. A stricter supervision and more frequent inspection is desirable.

The department is making a survey of occupational diseases under a recent act of legislature and hopes that the work will be continued under a permanent bureau.

The state has a plumbing law which is applicable to the smaller municipalities, 751 of which are dependent on the State Board of Health for the inspection of the plumbing. As there is only one inspector with an assistant such inspection is impossible.

Comparatively little is done to promote child hygiene and probably the most important need of the department is the establishment of a special bureau for this purpose.

Without doubt the most important sanitary need of the state at the present time is better health administration in the small communities and rural districts. The recommendation of the department is that the state be divided into districts (excluding the cities) in each of which there would be a whole time health officer elected by the local officials with the approval of the State Board of Health and part time deputies appointed for each small health district into which the large district would be divided. Some plan which will secure efficient supervision of this sort ought to be adopted.

The registration of vital statistics is in the office of the secretary of state, which is an unfortunate arrangement, though the registration of deaths seems to be good. The registration of births is not so good but the law has been operative only five years. It is always better that registration should be under the health department and it is so in all but four states.

OKLAHOMA

For a state as populous, rich and progressive as Oklahoma comparatively little is done to protect the public health.

Vital statistics are being collected by the commissioner of health but registration will never be satisfactory without a modern law and a proper system of local registrars.

There is a laboratory at the State University but very little diagnostic work is done.

During 1914 the department had a fund of $7,500 for the free distribution of antitoxins and vaccines, but this is entirely inadequate for a state of this size.

A good deal of educational work is done in the way of press notices and an exhibit has been prepared relating chiefly to tuberculosis.

Since 1908 the supervision of food and drugs has been under the department of health. Though considerable effort is made to improve the "sanitary" conditions of markets and groceries, as well as to prevent adulteration, this food work is an unimportant health measure, yet it absorbs $12,500 of the $32,500 appropriation. There is a hotel law but it is supposed to be enforced by local health officers. It has been suggested that the food work be transferred to some other department of the state government. This is a matter of expediency but if it remains where it is, it should be remembered that its expenditures are not primarily for public health.

The department needs to be properly organized. While it is believed that a board of health, whose sole executive duty is to elect a state health officer, is the best form, yet if a commissioner of health, appointed by the governor, is preferred here, as it is in some other states, there ought certainly to be a legislative board as is provided for in New York.

It is of paramount importance that the department be kept absolutely free from all political entanglements. To mix in politics, either medical or civic, in the slightest degree, though it may, apparently for the moment, secure some sanitary advantage, is in the end always harmful. It goes without saying that the state should pay its commissioner of health a salary sufficient to retain his undivided services and should insist that these services be devoted solely to the scientific and administrative duties of his office. It is absurd to expect that $1,800 a year will do this.

The department should have definite divisions of work as follows:

A division of vital statistics operating under a modern registration law.

A division of engineering with a law giving effective control over water supplies and sewage disposal. This division should have ample laboratory facilities, preferably under its immediate control.

A division of communicable diseases with laboratory facilities for diagnostic purposes. The use of this laboratory should be greatly extended over what it now is. It is very desirable that the University connection be continued. The use of curative sera and vaccines also should be increased.

A division of public health education, which should carry on educational work along many lines, one of the most important of which in this state is for the prevention of tuberculosis.

A division of supervision of local health work. It would seem that with state appointed county health officers local sanitation might be greatly improved by the appointment of state inspectors or supervisors as has been done in other states.

The food and drug division could be retained by the department, or not, as might be thought best.

OREGON

The systematic work of the state health department is by no means extensive.

Vital statistics are collected but the method is defective and they are not complete. A modern law was, however, adopted in February of this year.

There is a bacteriologic laboratory which makes some examinations of water and does a moderate amount of diagnostic work.

There is a fund of $1,000 for furnishing diphtheria antitoxin and smallpox vaccine but very little of it is expended. Preventive treatment for rabies is given.

Tuberculosis is reportable to the department and literature is sent to the cases, but there is little real supervision and the disease is poorly reported. The state has a sanatorium of 70 beds.

There has been some inspection of construction and hop picking camps.

The department inspects and licenses institutions receiving state aid but there are only about half a dozen.

The general educational work has been moderate in amount. Special educational work for improving schoolhouse conditions and for the encouragement of medical inspection has been carried on by sending nurses well over the state to demonstrate methods.

The educational work in which the department has been most interested is that of "social hygiene," and in this it has cooperated closely with the Social Hygiene Association, which association receives a grant of $10,000 from the state for the biennial period ending Sept. 30, 1914. For the present period it is $7,500.

A water and sewage law was enacted last winter providing for the filing and approval of plans for new water supplies and the filing of plans for sewerage.

The work of the department needs to be better organized and carried on more aggressively along the most effective lines of modern health work.

The vital statistics law should be vigorously enforced.

A full time man is needed to look after the protection of water supplies and other engineering work.

A full time epidemiologist is required. It is suggested that he might well be a bacteriologist and have charge of the laboratory, which would seem to be a good arrangement, but he should in that case have ample assistance. It is to be expected that, with increased activity in communicable disease control, will come increased use of the diagnostic laboratory and a more extensive employment of sera and vaccines.

A general inspector is needed to investigate local conditions, stimulate and instruct local health officers and local registrars when the latter shall be appointed.

A man to conduct educational work also should be added to the staff as there is enough of this work of a general character to keep him busy, as well as specific campaigns against tuberculosis and for school inspection and infant hygiene.

___

PENNSYLVANIA

The health department of Pennsylvania does a larger volume of saitary work than does the corresponding department of any other state.

Perhaps the most distinctive feature of public health work in the state is the complete control by the central authority of local sanitation in a large portion of the less thickly settled regions of the commonwealth. There are 670 districts, including over 2,500,000 people, in which the health officer is appointed, paid and directed by the state department of health. Besides these local health officers there are county medical inspectors who act as supervisors and are also appointed by and paid by the state.

Vital statistics, which a few years ago were not worthy of the name, have been perfected to such an extent that Pennsylvania is now recognized as a registration state for births as well as for deaths.

The laboratory is at Philadelphia and, besides diagnostic work, makes bacteriologic, and some chemical examinations, for the engineering division, and also prepares several kinds of vaccines. The diagnostic work does not appear to have been pushed as it should have been and the laboratory is made use of by practicing physicians far less than is desirable.

The department distributes free to the poor diphtheria and tetanus antitoxins as well as tuberculins and typhoid and other vaccines.

The antituberculosis work of the department is very extensive and to it is devoted a large portion of the appropriation. Three large hospitals for all classes of cases are maintained. The department also has a system of dispensaries distributed through the state, 114 in number, administered by physicians and nurses in the employ of the department. Supervision of the patients is maintained and more or less supplies are furnished by the state. Besides this, a traveling exhibit is kept on the road and lectures and other educational work carried on.

A bureau of housing has recently been organized to look after tenement houses and boarding and lodging houses.

The division of engineering is larger than in any other state. The department is charged with complete control of water supplies and river pollution and keeps up a constant supervision of the waters of the state and is also making a most detailed survey of all watersheds. For this purpose it has a large force of inspectors, who also do most of the epidemiologic work for typhoid fever, and devote a considerable time to the abatement of local nuisances.

A traveling child welfare exhibit has been sent out to many places in the state and other educational work has been carried on by the department, but neither infant welfare work nor general educational work has been as extensively, or systematically, organized as would seem desirable.

Pennsylvania and Florida are the only states in which medical school inspection is avowedly made the duty of the state instead of the local government. Although the state does not inspect the schools in the larger communities there are nearly 12,000 rooms in the more sparsely settled portions of the state where inspection is made by nearly 900 medical men employed by the state department of health.

It is thus seen that in Pennsylvania the state takes an unusually large share in public health work, occupying itself extensively with local details and employing for this purpose a very large number of officials. Very much has been accomplished where little or nothing was done before. An active and uniform control of communicable diseases has been established in rural and village communities, antitoxins and vaccines have been freely distributed, local nuisances abated, large numbers of schoolchildren needing medical treatment have been sent to their physicians, much has been done to improve water supplies, an extensive campaign against tuberculosis is carried on and vital statistics have been vastly improved. The striking characteristic of the Pennsylvania system is the centralization of the work at Harrisburg, and it is doubtless true that, but for this entrance of the state into local work, large sections of the commonwealth most needing it would still show little sanitary progress.

The critics of such centralization in sanitary affairs believe that, though quick results may be obtained in this way, they are not so good, or so lasting, as when local communities are educated to look after their own affairs. It is pointed out that with so many to be appointed it is difficult to select from a central office the men best qualified. Without a strong and able administration, such as Dr. Dixon's assuredly is, it is impossible to carry on the system at all, but with it, individual initiative and responsbility is apt to degenerate into official routine. Moreover the administrative details of extensive organization are so burdensome and exacting that little opportunity remains for the critical study of sanitary problems without which success and progress are impossible. The employment of so many officials in one department makes its possible involvement in politics, which is the ruin of any health department, a very real danger, no matter how earnestly the head of the department may strive to avoid it. There are men, competent to judge, who claim that some of these very evils can be seen in Pennsylvania. However this may be, it does not appear that the success attained by such centralization, great though it be, is sufficient to induce other states which are making progress, though it may appear slow at times, by the development of local management of sanitary affairs, to abandon their methods for the dangers of frankly centralized control.

RHODE ISLAND

As Rhode Island has such a small area, with its 600,000 people mostly in quite sizable cities, the problems and duties of the state department of health are, in many ways, simpler than in most states.

Like the other New England states Rhode Island is a registration state for births as well as deaths. The statistical tables covering an exceptionally long period are considered of unusual value.

This was the first state health department to establish a diagnostic laboratory (Sept. 1, 1894) though not enough work is done in those parts of the state which need it most. With the recent appointment of a pathologist the laboratory expects to extend its activities along pathologic lines.

Rhode Island was also the first state to distribute free diphtheria antitoxin and has since included other sera as well as vaccines in the distribution. It was also the first to distribute preventive outfits for ophthalmia.

A water laboratory has been established for some years, a chemist with engineering training is employed, and much has been done by the department to improve the water supplies of the state, though there has been no adequate law.

The department has done quite a little educational work particularly by means of exhibits, lectures and "movies."

Tuberculosis is reportable to the State Board of Health and literature is sent out and sputum cups and paper napkins furnished. The state has a sanatorium of 130 beds for incipient cases and is about to build a hospital for advanced cases, neither however under the management of the department of health.

The state board of health is also the examining board for physicians.

There is a Food and Drug Commission, but with an entirely inadequate appropriation.

The Shell Fish Commission has done a great deal of excellent work in studying the conditions of the oyster industry and improving its output and the conditions under which the latter is handled.

The board has recently formed three bureaus which operate under the immediate direction of the board itself. An arrangement which, as will be referred to on another page, is bad in principle, and has worked poorly in New Jersey and can be expected to work poorly in most cases. A single strong executive officer is needed in every state.

Among the improvements to be recommended is a requirement that the executive officer be a full time man, which should of course carry with it an adequate salary.

In most of the towns, the local health work is quite inefficient, and one of the most important needs of the state department of health is a supervisor who shall instruct and direct the work of the local health officers and impress upon town officials its importance. Such a supervisor should be an expert epidemiologist.

The educational work of the department needs to be systemized and greatly extended, and might well supplant some of the effort of private organizations. A full time man is also needed for this.

The appropriation for antitoxin should be increased so that there may be enough for all who need it, both within institutions as well as without.

A modern water and sewage law is sorely needed, which will give the state department of health the same effective control, that obtains in many other states, over dangerous pollution.

SOUTH CAROLINA

Like the other southern states, South Carolina had in its state health department a Division of Rural Sanitation acting chiefly against hookworm and chiefly financed by the Rockefeller Commission.

The department also has an excellent bacteriological laboratory which is doing a good deal along some lines though little in others.

Some chemical and bacteriological tests of water supplies are made, but little supervision is exercised.

The department has distributed a good amount of diphtheria antitoxin and much typhoid vaccine, and has provided anti-rabic treatment.

A small sum has recently been appropriated for a sanatorium for tuberculosis, but little else has been done to control this disease.

Food control is under the Department of Commerce, Agriculture and Industry.

The "model" law for the registration of vital statistics was signed by the governor, Sept. 1, 1914, and has been vigorously enforced.

Since the vital statistics law has been put in operation, the most important need in South Carolina is better local sanitary administration. Whether this is brought about by the appointment of full time county health officers, or in some other way, the state department of health must exercise some efficient control and must have supervising officers.

The Division of Rural Sanitation should be extended so as to include all the communicable diseases, each of which should receive the share of attention to which its importance entitles it. With the active epi-. demiological work will come a great increase in the use of the diagnostic laboratory, and in the demand for antitoxins and vaccines.

Since the above was written, the exclusive antihookworm campaign together with the Division of Rural Sanitation, have been given up, and the department, with the help of the International Health Commission, is doing intensive sanitary work of a somewhat more general nature. Two sets of men, or "units," are employed, who spend about three months in each county.

Public health educational work should be put on a sound basis, and systemized, and specific campaigns inaugurated for the control of tuberculosis, malaria, and typhoid fever, and for the prevention of infant mortality and protection of child life.

A modern water law is needed, and a full time engineer should be employed.

SOUTH DAKOTA

Comparatively little health work is done by the state of South Dakota. The superintendent of health is a part time man, engaged in general practice in a small town in the northeastern part of the state. Politics enter into state appointments. With a change in administration, officials expect to hand in their resignations. The appropriation is small and the only assistance which the superintendent of health has is a stenographer and part time clerk. The board of health is also the examining board for physicians and this duty absorbs much of its interest. The state does little in the way of supervision of local health officers or in the control of contagious diseases. Little epidemiologic work is done. There is no distribution of antitoxins, no efficient publicity campaign, no control of water supplies, and no accurate knowledge of the prevalence of typhoid fever.

The state has a small sanatorium for tuberculosis and there is a food and drug commission at the state university at Vermilion, and also a health laboratory at the same place. The latter is doing good work, and is partly supported and directed by the State Board of Health, though, as a matter of fact, the latter really has little to do with it. The registration of vital statistics is in the department of history in the capitol in Pierre.

Here, as in North Dakota, the essential thing is to get the department out of politics, if possible. Probably a board of five with terms of five years, one member appointed each year, would be an improvement. This board should elect the superintendent of health, but not from its membership. The executive should be a full time officer and trained in public health work. He should be paid an adequate salary and supported with an adequate appropriation. When the department is properly established, the control of the health laboratory and the collection of vital statistics should be turned over to it. Instead of having the laboratory, the office of the registrar and the office of the superintendent of health, in different places, and the latter wherever the incumbent happens to live, the whole consolidated department should be together. Provision should then be made for a campaign of education, a better supervision of health officers, control of contagious disease, and investigation of outbreaks by a full time epidemiologist, or otherwise. Antitoxins and vaccines should in some way be made accessible to all. The water supplies of the state should be studied and probably a law for their control enacted.

TENNESSEE

It is unfortunate that the department is not free from political relations. It is true that the executive officer avers that he does not consider politics in the management of his office, but he admits that he is an active party man. It is certain that no executive officer can safely take any active part in political work, for it is sure ultimately to interfere with his efficiency, and perhaps cause his removal.

It is unfortunate, too, that the department has been unable to publish any reports since 1910.

The department has within a few years undertaken several new lines of work.

The "model" registration law became effective Jan. 1, 1914, and is apparently being well administered.

The department has, recently, with the liberal assistance of the International Health Commission, put in the field three "units" to carry on more intensive community work on somewhat broader lines than that of the former Division of Rural Sanitation.

Public health educational work is being carried on by means of lectures, exhibits at fairs, a traveling railroad exhibit, etc., but the work needs to be systemized and extended.

A diagnostic laboratory was started, January, 1914, but thus far very little has been accomplished. This very important work has apparently been neglected.

The department of food and drugs is supposed to be under the supervision of the department of health, but the connection is slight, as the chief inspector is appointed directly by the governor, and there is a special appropriation for the department. Six inspectors and two chemists are supposed not only to look after adulteration, including milk, but to enforce the "sanitary law" in regard to the cleanliness of hotels, restaurants, bakeries, stores, slaughterhouses, etc., the "hotel law," and the very important "anti-narcotic law," as well as to assist in the enforcement of the "weights and measures" law. Nevertheless, good work has been done by this small force.

The control of contagious disease is poor, and the state is doing little against tuberculosis. Local sanitary administration is unsatisfactory. There is no control of water supplies.

The most urgent needs of the state are:

The establishment of an efficient system of local administration, by the appointment of full time county health officers, by state supervisors, or by some other means.

The formation of a bureau of epidemiology, with a full time man at its head, and which should have charge of all the campaigns against contagious diseases, is one of the first needs of the department. It would probably be desirable to place the diagnostic laboratory in this bureau.

Provision should be made for placing curative sera and vaccines in the hands of all who need them.

A law for the control of water supplies and sewage disposal is needed, and a full time engineer to enforce it.

There should also be a full time man to take charge of educational work.

The promotion of child hygiene should be seriously taken up by the department and a systematic campaign carried on.

TEXAS

That Texas suffers from the doctrine that to the victor belongs the spoils is illustrated by the statement of the state health officer that a new governor would mean a new health officer, a prophecy of which he has since been the victim. The uncertainty of tenure in office of the head of the department precludes the carrying out of definite plans and a comprehensive development of public health work. Probably the safest plan of organization is a legislative board without executive power other than the election of a commissioner from outside its own membership, but no scheme is politics-proof. Public opinion must be awakened. Until the people of Texas realize the importance and value of public health work, and demand that the best qualified and capable men be appointed and kept in charge of the health department, and that offices be not used to pay political debts, or reward friends, it hardly seems worth while to waste time in the discussion of administrative details.

The state health officer should devote all his time to his office, and receive an adequate salary therefor.

The principal activity of the department is the maintenance of quarantine along the seaboard and the Rio Grande. This takes up a considerable part of the funds, and requires the investment of large sums in buildings, and it is difficult to find a reason why this function should not be turned over to the federal government, as has been done by nearly all cities and states in the country.

Within a few years, however, the department has taken up several new lines of activity.

There is a registration law, but it is not satisfactory and the results attained are poor. Less than the time of two persons is utilized in its enforcement, though in a new state the size of Texas probably ten or a dozen are needed.

Hookworm work has been carried on as elsewhere, but, as the infection is confined to about one third of the state's area, the educational influence of the campaign has not been as widespread as in other states. It has now been entirely abandoned.

In the spring of 1914, $25,000 was appropriated for the investigation and control of plague, and $4,000 for anthrax, but it has been impossible to learn how the money is expended.

The department has a bacteriologic laboratory, but the diagnostic work is very small in amount.

Antitoxins and vaccines are distributed, but the amount is not large. Antirabic treatment is given at the state asylum for the insane.

The state has provided a tuberculosis sanatorium of seventy beds under a separate commission, and has done some educational work but is doing little now.

Public health education has not been extensive but an exhibition car has recently been put on the road, which will doubtless prove an educational measure of value as it has in other states. A summer school for health officers has been provided.

A water and sewage law has been enacted but it was not drawn along modern lines and will not prove very effective.

The Pure Food and Drug Commission has done excellent work both on foods and milk.

The health department must be kept out of politics, and the executive made a full time health officer with an adequate salary.

There should be established a division of communicable diseases, provided with an adequate staff. It will be the duty of the division to see that the laboratory is brought into greater use and to see that sera and vaccines are supplied to all who need them. Maritime quarantine should be turned over to the federal government.

Local sanitary administration needs to be greatly improved and state supervisors of local health officers appointed, and an earnest and continued effort made to bring about a steady improvement in the work of these officers and to secure for them an adequate compensation.

The vital statistics law should be improved and a sufficient appropriation provided for its administration.

A really modern and effective water law should be enacted, and an engineering staff and laboratory provided for.

Educational work needs to be thoroughly systemized and well directed campaigns carried on against various diseases, and for child hygiene and the prevention of infant mortality, as well as to acquaint the public with the needs and value of the department and with progress in the art of sanitation.

UTAH

The sanitary activities of the state in Utah are limited.

There is a registration law and the collection of vital statistics is improving so that Utah has, by the federal census bureau, been considered a registration state for deaths.

The department employs two inspectors, who are not physicians, at salaries of $900 and $1,320 a year, respectively. They not only look up nuisances but represent the state department of health with advice and assistance in local sanitary affairs.

There is a bacteriologic laboratory in connection with the university, but the state health department spends only a small amount each year ($500) on it for printing, etc. As is usual when the epidemiologic work of the health department is neglected, the laboratory is comparatively little used.

Very little has been done to control tuberculosis, except the testing of cows and the slaughter of those infected. The testing was done by the federal government.

There is a State Dairy and Food Bureau, a department separate from the State Board of Health, which not only looks after adulterations, but inspects dairy farms, slaughterhouses, and all places where food is handled, as well as enforces the hotel law and the weights and measures law.

The state chemist not only analyzes foods for the above bureau, but also analyzes some water specimens for the health department.

It is thus seen that the state health department does very little really effective work. It should be reorganized and the executive made a full time man with adequate salary. This has recently been done.

There is needed a full time skilled epidemiologist. The diagnostic laboratory should be brought under direct control of the department and perhaps the epidemiologist might be made director with a competent assistant as bacteriologist. Ample provision should be made for the distribution of antitoxins and vaccines to all who need them.

Educational work should be systemized and greatly extended, and a full time man is needed for this.

It might be that the executive officer and the two officials above referred to could find time to systematically visit and supervise local health officers, or it might develop that a special man for this is needed.

The state needs a good water and sewage law, and a chemist with engineering training to enforce it.

VERMONT

Vermont is to be numbered among the more progressive states as regards public sanitation. The department of health has been free'from politics, and the board itself has been composed of men of high character and professional standing and greatly interested in public health.

Vital statistics have been well collected for many years.

The department has felt that the most essential thing was to improve the local health service, and to this end secured a law by which all the local health officers are appointed by the State Board of Health. Though appointed by the state, they are paid by the towns. The next step was the training of the health officers, which is attempted by means of an annual "school," the cost of which is borne by the state. The local health officers, as a result, seem to be superior to those of the other New England states.

The diagnostic laboratory does most excellent work.

The only antitoxin distributed is that for diphtheria, but the low death rate from this disease indicates that it is made good use of.

A good deal of educational work has been done with exhibits, lectures, and "movies," particularly in connection with tuberculosis. There is no sanatorium and, though the state appropriates a small amount for the care of advanced cases, not much is accomplished.

There has been no very systematic control of water supplies, but in many ways the department has been able to bring about improvement, so that the supplies are in pretty good condition, as indicated by the fairly low typhoid death rate, but continued supervision will be necessary.

The department does excellent work in the prevention of food adulteration, including milk. The chemical laboratory is well conducted and, besides the usual food and water work, makes medicolegal analyses and tests liquors and paints.

The department also exercises an effective control over the sanitation of school houses and other public buildings, and has done much to improve the condition of the former throughout the state. The dean of the engineering department of the university gives a good part of his services to the health department, advising as to public buildings, as well as to water and sewage problems.

Recently the department has been given $25,000 from private sources for the prevention of poliomyelitis and its sequelae.

The activities now carried on by the department need to be extended and additional appropriations will be required.

A better control of contagious diseases is needed, and a full time epidemiologist should be added to the staff. Besides diphtheria antitoxin, other sera and vaccines should be distributed.

Educational work should be increased and will require the whole time of a capable man.

The department also needs a full time engineer and a modern water and sewage law should be enacted.

VIRGINIA

This state has, during the last few years, shown a remarkable sanitary development. The department is kept free from political entanglements and has a very efficient staff.

In 1912 an amended form of the model registration law went into effect and has been vigorously enforced with excellent results.

The Bureau of Rural Sanitation is in large part an epidemiologic department, and, under the guidance of Dr. Freeman, markedly reduced the incidence of typhoid fever and wisely and effectively directed the work of the Rockefeller Commission in the state.

Since the withdrawal of the Rockefeller Commission, the department has put in the field four "units," of three or four trained men each, to carry on intensive work in the rural districts along somewhat broader lines than the former scheme of rural sanitation. This is financed chiefly by the International Health Commission.

The work of the district health officers, or general inspectors, has been increased and much time is devoted to school inspection.

A trachoma hospital is being maintained jointly by the State Board of Health, the U. S. Public Health Service, and the town in which it is situated.

The Bureau of Education has been a leader in popular education, and as regards the matter put out, is one of the best in the country.

The engineer is doing good work, but an up-to-date water and sewage law is needed.

There is a good laboratory, but the diagnostic work needs to be pushed.

Hotel inspection is under the board of health, but the inspector often assists the other bureaus.

The state sanatorium for tuberculosis, with 160 beds, is managed by the State Board of Health. The disease is reportable.

Food and dairy work is carried on by the dairy and food commissioner, and considerable attention is given to sanitary conditions.

The work of the state department of health, though well organized should be extended. The appropriations must be correspondingly increased. Additional employees will be required in the bureaus. There should be a better local sanitary organization, the details of which can best be worked out by the department. Ample provision should be made for the distribution of vaccines and antitoxins. Little has been done to lower infant mortality and an aggressive campaign is needed. Ophthalmia neonatorum has not received due attention and in fact the whole subject of child hygiene should be given a more important place.

WASHINGTON

It is important that a state department of health which has such clear ideas as to its duties and such definite plans for carrying them out cannot secure the necessary legislation and funds. With an appropriation of only about $15,000, nearly a third of which is for vital statistics, the department has been able to do very little to protect the lives of about 1,500,000 people spread over 66,836 square miles of territory.

Very rightly the registration of vital statistics has been considered of primary importance, and though the death rate is surprisingly low it appears that returns are made with a fair degree of accuracy and Washington has consequently been considered a registration state for deaths.

The department maintains a bacteriological laboratory but the number of examinations made is small, as it probably will be, until epidemiological work is seriously undertaken.

A good deal of typhoid vaccine is made and distributed and antirabic treatment is given.

Some educational work has been done, particularly in connection with tuberculosis, but some of this has been discontinued. Tuberculosis is poorly reported. The state gives assistance to counties and municipalities which establish hospitals and some are taking advantage of it. Plans and sites are to be approved by the state department of health.

The state takes little part in anti-plague work as this is carried on by the cities and the Federal Public Health Service, chiefly by the latter. The officials of the latter are however made state inspectors.

The department has investigated water supplies in a limited way, but so far as it was able, and enough to demonstrate the need of more effective control.

A very efficient inspector has done much to improve the sanitary condition of the many industrial camps in the state and has also assisted in solving other local sanitary problems.

The State Board of Health has investigated the conditions of oyster growing and has shown the need for a law to prevent pollution.

Food and milk control is placed in the department of agriculture.

The important needs of the department are:

Perfection of vital statistics, especially the returns of births.

An adequate water and sewage law with an engineer and necessary assistants to properly enforce it.

The systemization and development of education, with specific campaigns against tuberculosis, for the prevention of infant mortality and for the development of school inspection.

A division of communicable diseases should be established with trained epidemiologists who should have ample laboratory facilities at their disposal. Provision should be made for the distribution of vaccines and antitoxins of various kinds.

Probably the most important need is the development of the local health service. Doubtless the department can best determine just what arrangement of municipal or county health officers is most feasible, but a primary need, with any form of local health service, is direct supervision by the state department of health through its own inspectors.

The department is desirous of developing a division of industrial hygiene and if local conditions are favorable for placing this in the health department it would be advantageous to do so.

WEST VIRGINIA

Until 1914 the State Board of Health was little more than an examining board for physicians. Although a rich state with a population of 1,250,000 only $2,500 a year was appropriated for the state department of health. In 1914 this was raised to $15,000. The form of organization is not the best, as the appointment of the executive officer by the governor and the terms of the board, which are such that half expire at one time, tend to throw this department into politics. The board has no executive power and very little and illy defined legislative power.

Since this was written a law has been enacted which provides for a Commissioner of Health and a Public Health Council. The latter is given great legislative power. Both the Council and the Commissioner have very considerable executive power.

Local sanitary organization is not effective. Consequently control of nuisances and contagious diseases is poor. The latter are imperfectly reported. The state has done little supervisory work. A bacteriological and chemical laboratory has, however, recently been established in connection with the State University. The work of this laboratory should be pushed, and if its geographical location is not accessible enough it should be moved, though a University connection is desirable if possible. The department has established a school for health officers and started a bulletin but this educational work needs to be greatly expanded. There is no adequate control of water supplies and sewage disposal, though according to the executive, typhoid fever is prevalent. Vital statistics are very defective and the model law should be adopted and sufficient money appropriated to properly enforce it. If the present law providing for the free distribution of antitoxin and vaccines cannot be made effective ample provision should be made in some other way. (This also is authorized by the new law.) The state has a sanatorium for tuberculosis of about sixty beds. $10,000 was appropriated especially for educational work in this disease and an exhibition car with exhibit and lecturers traversed the state during the season of 1913-1914.

There is a hotel law and an inspector, but not under the board of health, though the latter can make rules. There is a law requiring certain schools to provide medical inspection and making it permissive for others, but the state board of health is taking no action.

The very limited activities of the department ought to be greatly extended, and perhaps the most important things to be done at present are:

The enactment of the model registration law, with an appropriation sufficient to administer it.

The enactment of a modern water and sewage law and the employment of a full time engineer.

The employment of a full time epidemiologist.

(Both the engineer and the epidemiologist have recently been appointed.)

More efficient organization of local health organizations.

WISCONSIN

The present organization of the department is good and favors aloofness from political entanglements though the recent service of the executive officer in the legislature was unwise and dangerous. The salary of the executive should certainly be made sufficient for him to devote all his time to the duties of his office.

The department has appreciated the importance of better local sanitary work and has secured the services of five Deputy State Health Officers who carry on advisory and educational work in their districts.

The state has a very good water and sewage law which requires the approval of plans by the state department of health and allows the department considerable power in ordering changes. The department through its chemist and consulting engineer has done a good deal of inspecting and analyzing water and in approving plans, but to properly control the waters of the state more work, and systematic work, in the way of supervision and inspection should be done, requiring more employees and a full time engineer.

The registration of births, marriages and deaths is properly in this department. The latter seem to be well recorded and Wisconsin is reckoned a registration state for deaths by the Census Bureau. The registration of births has improved so that probably over 90 per cent. of these are now reported.

Contagious diseases are not well reported. An apparent case fatality of 14.5 for diphtheria, and 30.7 for typhoid fever shows that something is wrong. This is not any worse than is found in many other states, but Wisconsin, with its Deputy State Health Officers, is prepared to exercise a better control and should insist on the report of cases. One way is to develop the diagnostic laboratory. It is decidedly unfortunate when the laboratory is not directly controlled by the department of health. A closer connection than in the past has been arranged for and the diagnostic work ought to be greatly increased.

The Pasteur treatment for rabies is given by the department at a charge of $25. Diphtheria antitoxin is distributed under an arrangement made with the manufacturer and in the case of the indigent is paid for by the municipality. Its use does not seem to have been sufficiently pushed. The laboratory is making and sending out a good amount of typhoid vaccine.

The state has a tuberculosis sanatorium of 200 beds. There is also a law under which counties with the aid of the state may provide for advanced cases. Eight counties have built, or are building, hospitals for this purpose.

Among other work of the department may be mentioned the inspection of hotels and camps under two inspectors. Lumber, construction and pleasure camps are important in this state and this control, if effective, should be productive of good results. The department has made elaborate rules for slaughter houses and for the care of school houses. It has also recently been authorized to prepare a uniform plumbing code for the state and expects soon to have eight inspectors to enforce the code in the smaller cities and supervise its enforcement in the larger.

The most important lines of progress at the present time seem to be:

The strengthening of the state inspection service (deputy health officers) by the appointment of more men and the improvement in local health organization.

Development of water and sewage control.

Extension of diagnostic laboratory work and insistence on morbidity reports and a full time epidemiologist.

A better distribution of sera and vaccines.

Systematic educational work with a special man for that purpose.

WYOMING

Wyoming has next to the smallest population of any state, but an area about equal to that of New York, New Jersey and Pennsylvania combined. This makes state health work difficult and expensive. With an appropriation of $2,100 a year little can be done.

The vital statistics law while not ideal could be made, with sufficient clerical assistance, to give good results.

There is a Dairy, Food and Oil Department which looks after adulteration and also enforces the "sanitary law" relating to the cleanliness of foods.

There is a state chemist who analyzes food and water.

While Wyoming does not need as extensive a department of health as is necessary in other states, it should take the preservation of health as a serious state affair. The state can at least appoint a full time health officer and pay a salary sufficient to retain the services of a capable and efficient man. Such a man, through the control of local health officers which now obtains could greatly improve sanitary conditions.

A laboratory should be provided where diagnostic, as well as chemical work, can be done. Either the laboratory man or the health officer should have some knowledge of water problems.

It is believed that when the health department is put on a more substantial basis the present chemical laboratory should be joined with it. Unless a hygienic and diagnostic laboratory is controlled by the department of health it rarely attains its greatest usefulness.

A good water and sewage law should be enacted, for, in a growing state, water pollution, with its attendant evils, is sure to increase, unless efficiently controlled.

ORGANIZATION OF THE DEPARTMENT OF HEALTH

HISTORY OF PUBLIC HEALTH ORGANIZATION IN THE UNITED STATES

In the United States, public health work began in the towns long before it was undertaken by the states. The usual reason for official sanitary activity was the presence of some serious epidemic. Under such conditions it was natural that a committee of prominent citizens should be appointed to take charge of affairs. Usually these committees would be discharged from their duties as soon as the emergency had passed. Later on, it was seen that much could be done to improve the public health at all times and hence permanent committees were appointed. This was the origin of the board of health as distinguished from the single sanitary executive whom we now call the health officer. In the absence of men trained in public health work a committee of citizens, who could consult together, was the only logical means of carrying on sanitary work. It is probably largely for the reason that trained men have not been available that the board of health has persisted, though doubtless its continuance has also been largely the result of custom.

Apparently there was a state board of health established in Louisiana in 1855, but it had to do solely with quarantine. The report of the Massachusetts Sanitary Commission, headed by Lemuel Shattuck, in 1850 strongly urged the establishment of a state board of health, but it took a long time to develop public sentiment and it was not until 1869 that such a board was established, the first state board to be organized for the general purpose of promoting the public health. The example of Massachusetts has been followed until, at the present time, every state is provided with a central sanitary organization, which in all but Oklahoma, consists in part at least of a board of health, and in this state, although it is not provided for in the statute, the commissioner of health has formed an advisory board of four persons. Kansas also has an advisory board besides the regular board.

It is now generally recognized that, whether in civil government, business enterprise, or social activity, it is very difficult to get good team work from boards, or committees. One or two men do most of the work. Public health work at the present time requires men who have been especially trained and who have a wide knowledge, which can only be secured by years of study or experience. It is impossible to have a state or municipal board of health composed of such men, hence has come about the evolution of the health officer who devotes his whole time to public health work and is trained for it. Even before there was any training for public health, boards of health usually selected one of their own number, or some one from outside, who had paid more or less attention to these matters and who could, and would, devote considerable time to, and who ultimately performed, most of the work of the board.

Most state boards of health have such an executive officer, often called the secretary, who is really the head of the public health work of the state. There have been some exceptions to this, notably in Massachusetts, where, owing to the exceptional character and ability of the members of that board and the time which they were able to give to the work, the plan for many years yielded most excellent results The Massachusetts State Board of Health itself has almost always taken the initiative and immediately directed its employees. The almost unique success of the Massachusetts board can rarely be hoped for under usual conditions and, in fact, successful team work has been attained in few if in any other states. On the other hand, the desire of boards of health to control the policies and details of administration, have, in some states, resulted disastrously. Thus the New Jersey board of health before its recent reorganization met every week and naturally had much to say about the detailed work of the department. This is believed by many thoughtful people in New Jersey to be a hindrance to the best work and has led to the introduction of a bill to substitute a single commissioner as the executive of the department. This failed of passage, but the department was reorganized with a full time executive.

The fact that the state boards of health generally do not do much executive work and that success in state sanitation has been, in most instances, due to the efforts of the secretary, state health officer, or whatever he may be called, has led many to advocate the abolition of the board and the substitution of a single state commissioner of health. This is in accord with the ideas of students of government who believe, not only that efficiency is thus secured, but that responsibility is thus fixed. Although this has been strongly urged, Oklahoma is, as was stated above, the only state in which a board of health is not provided for by law. Texas formerly had merely a state health officer, but a board was established in 1907. Probably the reason why the idea of a single executive has not gained ground is that the legislatures realize the great powers which are usually conferred on the health department and hesitate to trust them to one man. A real objection to a single executive is that he would have to be appointed by the governor and experience teaches that it is more difficult under such conditions to keep the office out of politics than when the executive is elected by a board of health.

INFLUENCE OF POLITICS IN PUBLIC HEALTH WORK

Politics is the greatest hindrance to efficient health work in the United States, both in states and municipalities. It is impossible to get good service unless the best men are secured and there are altogether too few good men. A man must remain in office for some time to do the best work. The theory of the politicians that to the victors belong the spoils absolutely prevents good public health work. No first-class man is likely to take a position from which he would be removed at the first change in administration. We are likely to find this political theory put in practice in any part of the country, but conditions seem to be rather worse west of the Mississippi. In the mountain states, in the Dakotas, in Nebraska, Oklahoma, Texas and Louisiana the officials of the health department expect to go with a change in administration, at times handing in their resignations as a matter of course, and at times waiting to have them asked for.

Since writing the above, the expected has happened in Oklahoma and Texas. Occasionally, too, personal as well as partisan politics, brings about the removal of efficient men. Politics has had its influence on the Pacific coast but these states seem to be improving. Often the health officials deprecate these conditions and try to stem the tide, but often, they too, are believers in the pernicious doctrine and, owing their position to the principle that office is a reward for party work are little inclined to reform. In one state where the executive officer has done his best to keep free from political entanglements, his assistant criticised this position and said that he "ought to get into the game and then he could get something done." It is certain that all executive officers should keep absolutely free from all political activity. When the offices in the health department are used to pay off political debts there is an end of efficient work. If we are to have progress in state sanitation it is necessary to have a single executive who is reasonably secure in his position and who has full executive power and cannot be dictated to from the outside. Let us consider how such an executive may be obtained.

METHODS OF SELECTING STATE HEALTH OFFICERS

Two methods are in vogue, one is appointment by the governor and the other is election by the state board of health. The first is followed in Arizona, Louisiana, Massachusetts, under the new law, Michigan (is recommended by state board of health), Nevada, New York, under the new law, North Dakota, Oklahoma, Pennsylvania, South Carolina (is recommended by the executive committee of the state board of health), South Dakota, Texas, Virginia, West Virginia and Wyoming (when there is only one physician on the board he is to be the secretary and is appointed by the governor. When all the members are physicians, as at present, they must of necessity choose the secretary). Although the present gubernatorial appointments made in New York and Massachusetts, necessarily in the full light of publicity, are exceptionally good, there is little in the history of health conditions in the states named to encourage a belief that improvement in the character of the state's sanitary executive can best be secured by appointment by the governor. On the other hand the freedom from pernicious politics for long years, and the success of such state health departments as those of Indiana, Kansas, Maryland, Massachusetts, Minnesota, New Jersey, North Carolina, Ohio, Rhode Island and Vermont in which the board of health chooses the executive, or did so during a long period of usefulness, suggest that this method is the safer one and for the present is likely to yield better results.

This method of selecting an executive, by election by the board of health, is the oldest method and, as has been stated, was a natural evolution from the original plan which conceived the board itself as doing most of the executive work. In thirty-three states, viz., Alabama, Arkansas, California, Colorado, Connecticut, Delaware, Florida, Georgia, Idaho,

Illinois, Indiana, Iowa,[1] Kansas, Kentucky, Maine, Maryland, Minnesota, Mississippi, Missouri, Montana, Nebraska,[2] New Hampshire, New Jersey, New Mexico, North Carolina, Ohio, Oregon, Rhode Island, Tennessee, Utah, Vermont, Washington, and Wisconsin the executive officer is elected by the board.

The only reason that is advanced in favor of appointment by the governor is the somewhat theoretical one that all executive power should be lodged in the chief executive so as to fix responsibility. To offset this we have the fact that the governor is a partisan and often too much at home in the pernicious methods of practical politics. The board of health is, as a matter of fact, very frequently, though unfortunately not always, free from political entanglements and often unfamiliar with the political spirit and methods. Furthermore the selection of a public health executive is no easy task and scarcely any one would claim that the governor is as well qualified to select a competent health officer as are the members of the board of health who are usually far more familiar with the needs of such an office than is the governor. When the utopian day arrives in which the governor, in his appointments, will ignore all claims to office, except fitness, it may be well to transfer to him all executive appointments, but until then the states in which the state health officer is selected by the board of health had better cling to this method. It is unfortunate when it is felt necessary to change the method simply as a means of getting rid of an undesirable official. The general organization of the state health departments is shown in Table 2.

THE BOARD OF HEALTH

There are probably very few who would do away entirely with the board of health and even these must admit that in many states its abolition is highly improbable. Those who would have the board shorn of all executive power would still retain it as a legislative body, and those who believe that it affords the means for 'choosing a public health executive, would, of course, retain it. It is therefore worth while to consider how to obtain the best board possible. In this connection certain matters are much more important than others. Among the former are:

1. **Appointment.**—The oldest and most common method is appointment by the governor. It is followed in twenty-seven states, viz., California, Colorado, Delaware, Florida, Georgia, Illinois, Kansas, Louisiana, Massachusetts, Minnesota, Mississippi (five of the thirteen members appointed on recommendation State Medical Society), Missouri, Nevada, New Jersey, New Mexico, New York, North Carolina (four of the nine members are elected by the medical society), Pennsylvania, Rhode Island, South Dakota, Texas, Utah, Vermont, Virginia, West Virginia, Wisconsin and Wyoming. In nine, Arkansas, Connecticut, Kentucky, Maine, Michigan, Oregon, Idaho, Maryland, Montana and in addition to the members appointed by the governor, there is added an executive officer elected by the board. In eleven, Arizona, Idaho, Maryland, Montana,

---

1. By board of appointment.
2. By board of secretaries.

Nebraska, New Hampshire, North Dakota, Ohio, South Carolina (seven members recommended by State Medical Association), Tennessee and Washington, the governor appoints a part of the members and some are members exofficio. Among the officials so serving are the governor who is a member in several states, Arizona, Iowa, Nebraska, New Hampshire, North Dakota, Ohio, Tennessee and Washington; the attorney general in quite a number, Arizona, Idaho, Iowa, Maryland, Montana, Nebraska, New Hampshire and South Carolina, the state veterinarian in one, Montana; the commissioner of agriculture in one, Tennessee; the superintendent of public instruction in one, Nebraska; while in Maryland the commissioner of health of Baltimore is one of the exofficio members of the board. Generally exofficio members are not of much value as they are not inclined to take much time from their principal duties to devote to the department of health. There are exceptions, however, and occasionally services of such members are highly appreciated.

In the South, the medical profession seems to hold a relatively more important position than in other portions of the country and its influence is less impaired by sects and various forms of medical delusion and organized quackery. Perhaps, as a consequence, we find that in several southern states the state medical society has much to do with state public health work.

In Alabama and South Carolina the state medical society is the State Board of Health. In Alabama the board of censors acts as a committee on public health. In South Carolina the society recommends seven members to the governor who is to appoint them to act with the attorney general and comptroller general as an executive committee.

In North Carolina four of the nine members are elected by the medical society.

In Mississippi five of the thirteen members are nominated by the medical society.

Kentucky is one of the few states in which different "schools" of medicine are recognized in the composition of the board. In this state each one of the three "schools" which is represented is to present a list of three names to the governor from which he is to make his selection.

While it is of the utmost importance that the medical profession should take a most active interest in public health work, it does not seem to be wise to attempt to secure it by transferring to an organization entirely outside of the state government a most important department of executive work. This method does not, in the states mentioned, seem to have produced results so much better than those attained under the more common form of organization, as to warrant such a dangerous delegation of power. It is especially dangerous at the present time, for osteopaths, eclectics, Christian Scientists, and similar sects, are pressing for, and obtaining, legislative recognition and it would be sad indeed for the future of public health work if it should be delegated to persons entirely untrained in, and even actually hostile, to science.

Indiana, Iowa, and Nebraska have methods of their own for the selection of a state board of health. In Indiana the board is elected by an exofficio commission consisting of the governor, the secretary of state and the state auditor. In Nebraska the State Board of Health consists of the governor, the attorney general and the superintendent of public instruction, but they meet rarely, and delegate most of the work to a "board of secretaries," four in number, appointed by them. In Iowa the appointive members are appointed by a "board of appointment" consisting of the governor, the secretary of state and the auditor of state.

2. Terms.—It is highly desirable that the board of health should not have a change of its entire membership, or even of a majority, at any one time. To guard against this most states have provided for long terms, two to seven years, mostly four years, and that only a part of the membership can be changed in the same year. The only objection to this is that it is a slow process to remove an inefficient board, but it is of the utmost importance that the board be kept out of politics and the above method of appointment renders it more difficult for the politician to use the board for political purposes. A few states, however, make the terms of members expire at the same time, namely, Arizona, Arkansas, California, Florida, Mississippi, Nevada, New Hampshire, North Carolina, North Dakota, Pennsylvania, South Carolina, Texas and Wyoming.

3. Salaries.—It is important that the board of health should be an unpaid board. If salaries are paid the office is sure to attract the politicans and be used to pay political debts. The only states in which a salary is paid are, Iowa, where it is $900 for each member per annum, in New York $1,000, and Wyoming $200.

In nearly all the states the members receive mileage and other traveling expenses. In Colorado, Nebraska and South Carolina the members receive compensation as examiners. In most states they have from $3 to $20 per day while attending meetings, or performing other duties. Although the various activities of the board and the department will be further discussed, the main lines may be mentioned here.

4. Duties.—(a) The principal business of the department of health is to execute the laws. This executive power can be better exercised by one than by many, hence it should be conferred on the executive of the board rather than on the board itself. The executive officer should appoint all his subordinates and the board should have nothing to do with the appointments. Its only appointments should be that of the executive officer.

(b) The board alone should have legislative power.

(c) The legislature sometimes considers it necessary to confer quasi-judicial power on the board of health concerning nuisances, offensive trades, river pollution, food adulteration and the like, giving it authority to hold hearings and summon witnesses.

MINOR QUESTIONS OF ORGANIZATION

Among minor matters of organization may be mentioned:

1. Number.—The number of members of the board of health varies from three to thirteen, in a large proportion of states it is seven. If too large it is difficult to get the board together and meetings are expensive. On the other hand, it is well, sometimes, to have representatives of the board well scattered over the state and, with a large board, a sudden change of policy is less likely. Seven members with terms of seven years, one to be appointed each year is a good number.

2. Appointment.—The desirability of having different parts of the state represented has been referred to. This is sometimes provided for by law. Thus there must be one member from each congressional district in Mississippi, Virginia and West Virginia, one from each county in Delaware and Rhode Island, and one from each "grand division of the state" in Tennessee.

3. Qualifications.—In former times, when the board of health was supposed to administer all the affairs of the department, it was thought desirable that its members should have special qualifications, should be men with a knowledge of sanitary affairs. Hence it was often specified that the members should be physicians or engineers. Various exofficio members have been referred to on a preceding page and a similar idea doubtless led to their selection. Besides these, Connecticut requires a lawyer, and Iowa, Maryland, New Hampshire, New Jersey, New York, North Carolina, Pennsylvania and Utah require an engineer. In fourteen states the members must all be physicians, in fourteen, a majority, and in six others one or more members must be physicians. The question as to the representation of physicians and engineers on the state board of health has aroused a good deal of discussion, which, at times, has been quite lively. This arises from a misapprehension as to the true functions of the board. These are no longer administrative, so that technical knowledge is no longer required. The board is to advise with the executive and help to keep him in touch with the community. What is wanted is men of sound judgment and with an interest in public health work. They do not need to have technical knowledge, in fact it is much better that they should not have it. The health commissioner is to have that and there should be no friction. Physicians are very desirable, because they help to keep the department in touch with the medical profession, which is most necessary, but they should not be men who are professional sanitarians, or there is likely to be trouble at once. So too engineers, practicing along sanitary lines, are not desirable for a similar reason. Another objection to a sanitary engineer is that the department will try to get advice from him for nothing when an engineer ought to be employed for that purpose. Some health officials state that they have found a legal member of the board of great assistance, but if they use an unpaid member to do work which should be done by the attorney general they are not doing the right thing. If the governor is to appoint the state board of health and assume full responsibility therefor, it would seem only right to give free rein and not hamper him by any restrictions as to qualifications.

4. The Executive Officer as a Member.—In some thirty of the states as shown in Table 3, the executive officer of the board is by virtue of his office a member of the board. In Iowa, Indiana, Kansas, North Carolina, Ohio, Pennsylvania, Rhode Island, South Carolina, Tennessee and Virginia it is specified that he is not to be a member. In Alabama, Dela-

aware, Florida, Illinois, Minnesota, New Hampshire, Vermont and
Washington it is not specified whether the executive officer shall be a
member of the board. If elected from its membership he retains his
membership, if elected from outside he does not become a member.
At the present time he is not a member in Florida, Illinois, Minnesota,
South Carolina and Vermont. It seems not to be a matter of any very
great importance whether the executive officer is, or is not, a member
of the board.

THE EXECUTIVE OFFICER

The executive officer of the department is commonly the secretary of
the board of health, more rarely its president. In a few states he is
called the state health officer, in three, the superintendent of health, in
one, director of health, and in six, the commissioner of health. Various
data relating to him as his appointment, salary, term, etc., are shown
in Table 3.

1. **Mode of Election.**—This has already been referred to. The best
way to keep the office out of politics seems to be to have the board
of health elect the executive and this is important enough to demand a
board of health, even if the latter fulfilled no other purpose.

2. **Qualifications.**—It is of importance that provision be made by
statute that the executive officer be not elected from the membership of
the board. Experience has shown that in the absence of such provision
there is at times scrambling among the members for the position and
then follows antagonism between the executive and the defeated coterie
of the board. Of course this decidedly makes for inefficiency. Moreover it often happens that no member of the board is well qualified, for
they usually are not selected, and should not be selected, for their technical
knowledge of sanitation.

It is most essential, that the executive should have this technical
knowledge. No man should be elected to the important position of
state health officer who has not had good training in sanitation, not
necessarily university training, but certainly training in some subordinate position in the department, or in municipal work. The man should
be thoroughly interested in both the art and the science of sanitation.
It goes without saying that he should be a good administrator, but
above all he must have the scientific discernment to select the most
efficient means for promoting the public health. It is worse to waste the
state's money in fruitless lines of endeavor than it is to dissipate it by
poor administration. Gorgas succeeded in Havana and Panama because
he had the discernment to devote his attention wholly to work that bore
fruit, even more than to the fact that he was a good administrator.

It is not a qualification for holding such an office that a man is a
party worker or can manipulate his medical society, or poll a majority of
the state board of health.

One of the most ridiculous, antiquated and mischievous of provisions
is one found in the statutes, or even constitutions, of some states, that
the incumbents of public office must be residents of the state and even

voters, for it frequently happens that the most suitable person for a position like this cannot be found within the confines of the state.

3. Term.—The term of office of the executive as provided by law varies from one to six years, the average being four years, and only six states making it six years. In Alabama, California, Connecticut, Delaware, Idaho, Illinois, Kansas, Maine, Maryland, Minnesota, New Hampshire, Ohio, Oregon, Rhode Island, South Carolina, Utah, Vermont and Wisconsin the term is during good behavior, with, of course, power of removal. This would seem to be the best arrangement.

4. Full Time.—The state health officer should in every instance be a full time man. There is no state so small that this is not necessary. The best results can almost never be attained by a part time man with divided interests.

5. Salary.—The salary of the state health officer varies from $200 in Wyoming to $10,000 in Pennsylvania. Salaries naturally vary in different parts of the country. They are rather higher in the far West and lower in the South than they are in the East or Middle West. The average state of this latter region should in the future expect to pay not less than $5,000 or $6,000 to retain permanently the services of the best man.

POWERS

POWERS OF THE DEPARTMENT OF HEALTH

Except in some of the southern states, when the administration of quarantine was an important feature, state boards of health were originally intended to be chiefly investigative and advisory bodies. Their duties have, however, rapidly increased so that now, in many states, there is scarcely a branch of the state government with functions so numerous and varied.

The three great lines of activity of civil government, as they are commonly grouped, are judicial, legislative and executive. All three are represented in state health work.

QUASI-JUDICIAL FUNCTIONS

It is often necessary for the health department to act in a sort of judicial capacity. In the case of certain nuisances, especially offensive trades, the state board of health may be authorized, or directed, to hold hearings and to listen to the evidence presented by opposing parties and to render a decision. Similar action may have to be taken in regard to the pollution of streams, in regard to food adulteration, or in regard to violations of the medical practice act. Of course, it is perfectly legitimate for boards of health, without any statutory authority, to hold such hearings and doubtless they at times do so, but in a number of states such hearings are provided for. They are provided for in connection with food control in Colorado, Idaho, Kansas, New Hampshire and Oklahoma; in connection with water control in California, Connecticut, Idaho, Indiana, Massachusetts, Minnesota, New York, Ohio, Texas and Vermont; in connection with the medical practice act in Illinois and Montana. Other states in which judicial hearings are provided for are Kentucky, Maryland, Nebraska, Pennsylvania, South Carolina and Wisconsin. It is not unlikely that they may be in others still, for the laws have not been systematically searched and the executive himself may not be aware of the existence of a provision of the law only rarely made use of. In Connecticut, Nebraska, New York, Pennsylvania and Texas, authority is granted to summon witnesses and make them testify.

LEGISLATIVE POWER

Most state boards of health are, by the statutes, given authority to make health regulations. Sometimes this power is very broad and sometimes it is quite restricted. A very broad grant, such as to make "rules for the protection of the public health" is virtually conferring on the board of health great legislative power and a power which may profoundly affect the lives and property of the citizens.

While there seems to be no doubt that the legislature is competent to confer this broad rule making power on municipalities, either on the elective council, or on an appointive board like a local board of health, it has been held by some courts that such legislative power cannot, by the state legislature, be delegated to a state appointive board like the state board of health. Decisions affirming this doctrine have been handed down by the courts in Wisconsin (State v. Burdge, 95 Wis., 390), and Illinois (Potts v. Brun, 167 Ill., 67), and perhaps in other states. In Texas, the attorney general considered such a grant of power unconstitutional and the section of the act which conferred it on the State Board of Health was repealed. In other states, too, various attorney generals have expressed similar views though they have not in all cases been accepted by the state board of health. On the other hand, some recent decisions (State v. Snyder, No. 19, 418, Sup. Ct. La., 1912, and Pierce v. Doolittle, 130 Ia., 333) affirm the authority of the state board of health to exercise what is virtually legislative power. It is to be feared that the statutes granting to state boards of health rule-making power, have usually been enacted without giving this matter any thought, but it was far otherwise with the recent public health law in New York. The constitutionality of the provision conferring extensive legislative authority on the public health council in New York was carefully considered by the lawyers who were interested in drawing the bill and while it was recognized that there was a possibility of this provision not being sustained by the courts it was felt that this was not sufficiently probable to warrant abandoning this feature of the measure. In framing any new legislation concerning the powers of the state department of health this matter should receive careful consideration.

While a broad grant of legislative power to a state board of health may not be considered constitutional in some states, there seems to be no objection to the board making administrative rules for the purpose of defining and carrying out the details of measures authorized by the legislature. Thus it is probably always permissible to authorize a state health department to declare what diseases are to be considered communicable and how they shall be reported, to determine the manner and period of isolation, to prescribe exactly methods of disinfection, to make rules to prevent water supplies from receiving pollution, to make regulations for the cleanliness of hotels, bakeries and slaughter houses, to fix chemical and bacterial standards for milk and other foods and to prescribe a great number of similar details of public health administration which the legislature cannot conveniently or properly consider and the rules for which, moreover, oftentimes, need to be flexible enough to be easily changed.

The state health department of every state except Connecticut, at one time or another, has adopted rules relating to some phase of public health work, though in Texas they have been repealed and reenacted by the legislature as a statute. In Colorado, too, the "code" has been declared a dead letter by the law department of the state. Colorado, Connecticut and Texas, then, are the only states in which the health department exercises no legislative function.

In Arkansas, Delaware, Florida, Georgia, Illinois, Iowa, Louisiana, Minnesota, Mississippi, Montana, Nebraska, New Mexico, New Jersey, New York, Oregon, Pennsylvania, South Dakota, Vermont, Washington and West Virginia, the grant of legislative authority is couched in the most general terms. It is scarcely possible, however, to find exactly the same terms in any two states. In Iowa, the expression reads "for the preservation and the improvement of the public health." The violation of a rule made under this provision, and requiring the reporting of scarlet fever, gave rise to a case which was carried to the supreme court and resulted in establishing the validity of the act and the rule.

The most recent enactment of this kind was in New York, where much care was given to the wording of the clause which reads as follows: "The sanitary code may deal with any matters affecting the security of life and health or the preservation and improvement of public health. . . ."

In some of the states which have a broad and general grant of legislative power, special subjects of legislation are also named. Among such are Arkansas, Delaware, Florida, Georgia, Louisiana, Minnesota, New Mexico, New York and Utah.

In the remaining states there is no general provision, but one or more subjects are specified, concerning which the state health department is to make regulations. Naturally the most common of these is communicable disease. This is named in Arizona, California, Delaware, Idaho, Kansas, Kentucky, Maine, Maryland, Michigan, Missouri, Nevada, North Dakota, Ohio, Oklahoma, Rhode Island, South Carolina, Tennessee, Utah, Virginia, West Virginia, Wisconsin and Wyoming. It is the only subject named in Kentucky, Maine, Missouri, Nevada, Rhode Island and Wyoming. Unfortunately, in some states, the authority is granted only for use in time of threatened invasion, as in Idaho, Maryland and West Virginia. In Delaware, Indiana, and Oregon, "quarantine" is mentioned as a subject for regulation but what is intended by the term is doubtful. Probably it means the prevention of the introduction of a disease into a community. This was formerly its exclusive meaning, but of late years it has been applied to the seclusion of infected persons within a dwelling. Isolation, the term which was formerly used for this procedure, is now often restricted to the isolation of a person within the house from other members of the family. Years ago, while this change in the use of the word quarantine was slowly coming about, the writer called attention to the legal confusion which would surely result.

Among other subjects for legislation mentioned, are water, ice, sewage, midwives, garbage, nuisances, public buildings, baths, cold storage, food, vital statistics and the disposal or transportation of dead bodies. The latter is referred to in at least a dozen states and reflects popular ideas of a few years ago when great importance was attached to this really negligible -source of infection. In several states, the state board of health has authority to make rules in regard to the adulteration or sanitation of foods, and in other states this power is granted the board or commissioner having control of foods, but the food laws have not been especially examined for this.

There are quite a number of states in which no broad grant of legislative power has been given the state department of health, but in which the legislature has nevertheless conferred the right to make rules on quite a variety of subjects. Among such states are California, Indiana, Maryland, Massachusetts, New Jersey (previous to 1915), South Carolina, and Virginia. Apparently, in these states, the legislature has thought it unwise, or perhaps unconstitutional, to confer broad legislative power, but has determined that there are a good many matters which need regulation, but the details of the regulation the legislature has been unwilling to consider, recognizing that the preparation of administrative rules requires much technical knowledge. This has been particularly true in Massachusetts and New Jersey. In the former state, the state board of health is authorized to make rules in regard to water, ice, cold storage, slaughtering, cremation, jails and lodging houses, while in New Jersey the subjects specified were, food, canneries, slaughter-houses, cold storage, egg-breaking, oysters, tuberculous persons and dead bodies. It is perhaps worthy of note that in Massachusetts, while the new law confers on the Public Health Council authority to "make and promulgate rules and regulations" there is no penalty. In the original bill the phrase was "rules and regulations under the public health laws, the enforcement of which devolves on the state department of health," and a penalty was provided for. The legislature was evidently chary about giving a free hand in legislation.

In Maine the regulations of the board must be approved by the governor and council and in Minnesota, South Dakota and West Virginia by the attorney general, though in Minnesota one attorney general has held that it was not constitutional for him to do so.

In Connecticut the State Board of Health must approve the sanitary rules adopted by the townships before they can become effective.

In New Hampshire the peculiar provision is found that the State Board of Health may make additions to local regulations. This has been done, but the curious condition exists that if a township has no sanitary rules, the state board can do nothing to improve matters, as there are no rules to be added to.

In Minnesota and South Dakota, if the regulations made by the state board of health conflict with the charter or ordinances of cities of the first class, the latter have the precedence. In New York the "code" adopted by the public health council does not apply to the City of New York.

Regulations without penalties which can be enforced are of little value. Of course, in most states a penalty is provided, but there appear to be none in Alabama, Massachusetts (for rules made under general grant oi authority), Michigan (for communicable diseases), New Jersey (for some rules) and Utah (for rules made under general grant of authority). In Delaware and Georgia the validity of the penalty clause is doubtful. In Kentucky there is a penalty for common carriers, but for no others, for the violation of quarantine rules, the only kind the State Board of Health is especially authorized to make.

With the exception of a few of the more conservative, almost all state health officials believe that the state department of health should have as broad legislative power as possible. They feel that it is only in this way that important matters relating to the public health can adequately be dealt with. Most of the regulations dealing with communicable disease, disinfection, the purity of milk and foods, the protection of water, the construction of buildings, the disposal of refuse, and similar matters, require a large technical knowledge on the part of the framers. Their framing, also, requires much careful thought. The legislature can furnish neither the technical knowledge nor the time, so it is claimed. This view was very strongly held by the men who framed the recent public health law in New York and the broad grant of legislative power to the public health council was considered one of the most important features of the plan. It must be confessed, however, that some of the "codes" and regulations adopted by the various state health departments have not come up to the high standards which one would expect from experts. Indeed, they often are not the work of experts. Political appointees, with little or no training, or scientific knowledge, do not even know where to go for expert advice, and still less how to draft public health regulations. Much of this rule making is of a very crude character and does not show any improvement over statute law. One trouble with these codes is that the attempt is made to cover at one time, by regulation, almost every conceivable sanitary subject. This is an unwise plan. Better results are obtained when subjects are considered one at a time and carefully. Some of the best examples of rule making are to be found in the new sanitary code of New York. During the first year of the public health council the subjects legislated on were communicable disease, milk, midwives and labor camps. The regulations are unusually well thought out, and what is especially unusual, are closely in accord with the best scientific knowledge of the time.

CENTRAL CONTROL OF LOCAL AFFAIRS

While, at first, it was not intended that the state board of health should take charge of local sanitary work except, perhaps, in some states, in quarantine, there has been an increasing tendency to place more and more of this duty on the state health department, until many have come to think this the ideal place. At the present time, in most states, the central sanitary authority has more or less executive control of local affairs. Sometimes this control is not very extensive, and sometimes it is complete.

As one would naturally expect, it is in connection with the communicable diseases that the state department of health authority. As is shown in Table 4, the control of quarantine, using the word in its older sense as a restriction of intercourse between communities, is, in all states, vested in the state health department except in Connecticut, Nevada and North Carolina. Other lines of local communicable disease work in which the state health department takes a share, are referred to on another page, but it is here sufficient to note that the only states in which the department has no such authority are Alabama, Connecticut, New Hampshire, New York, Rhode Island and Wyoming. In Arkansas, Maryland, Missouri, Nevada and Texas the authority is doubtful, or very limited. In Colorado, Delaware, Michigan, Nebraska, New Jersey, North Carolina and Tennessee executive control of communicable diseases in the local government can only be exercised when the local governments fail to appoint sanitary officials, or when these do not act and neglect to enforce the law. In Massachusetts, New Jersey and Ohio the state department of health has certain executive authority over nuisances. As will be seen when considering engineering, in a number of states, the health department is given executive authority in regard to the control of water and sewerage. In other directions, too, it will be found that in one state or another special executive duties are imposed.

Besides the more or less limited executive powers in local matters, which have been referred to, as conferred on state health departments, what appears to be complete executive authority is granted in twenty-five states, namely, Arizona, California, Florida, Idaho, Indiana, Iowa, Kansas, Kentucky, Louisiana, Minnesota, Mississippi, Montana, New Mexico, North Dakota, Oklahoma, Oregon, Pennsylvania, South Carolina, South Dakota, Utah, Vermont, Virginia, Washington, West Virginia and Wisconsin. It perhaps ought not to be affirmed positively that they all have this power, for it is not always clear from the laws, and they have rarely been tested in the courts. It was apparently, however, the intention in these states that these important powers should be thus delegated. Executive officers themselves do not feel sure what their powers really are. Many state health officials do not believe that the state ought to take charge in local affairs and they make no effort to do so, or to determine whether they have the authority. Others are deterred from taking action because of lack of funds, for it is only in a few states, and under special circumstances, where the cost of the executive work by the state can be charged to the local community. Such action as a temporary measure, is reported to have been occasionally taken in Delaware, Illinois, Indiana, Kansas, Maryland, Massachusetts, Mississippi, Oregon and Wisconsin. In Maryland the department was once enjoined, but the case was not fought out.

This matter of the state health department taking entire charge of local affairs, thereby displacing local officials, is one of the greatest importance, concerning which there are wide differences of opinion. Many officials believe that it is entirely wrong in principle. While it is admitted, perhaps by the majority, that the present status of sanitary administration in the country, especially in the smaller communities, is so poor that a change to state control would in many states result in an immediate improvement, it is believed by the opponents of this plan that ultimately the best results cannot be obtained in this way. They point out the difficulty of selecting, from a central office, the best men for all parts of the state, and the difficulty of directing the details of their work from a distance. With a large organization red tape is necessary, and red tape deadens energy, initiative, personal responsibility, enthusiasm and ambition. The whole mechanism tends to become inflexible and scientific progress is hindered. Above all the greatest danger is, that, in the present state of morals and intelligence, the department, enlarged by many scattered representatives in all parts of the state, in constant touch with many people, will become a political machine. Even if the head of the department is utterly opposed to this, and many are not thus fortified, pressure will be brought to bear, and if the surrender is made, failure is certain. Most students of a political science agree that the principle of home rule is one to be fostered. It encourages the interest of the individual citizen in his local government and his feeling of responsibility for it. Everything, they say, is bad which tends to take away this responsibility from him and place it on state officials. It is admitted that the progress of the town or the county, in public health work, will be slow, but sanitation will in the end be on a surer foundation than if control is transferred to the state. It is the part of wisdom to assist and encourage the local health official, and much more of this should be done in the future than in the past, but it should not be the policy of the state to take over this work. It is believed that much of the advantage gained by central administration can be secured by this sort of state supervision, not using supervision in the sense of control, but in the sense of teaching, advising and assisting. However poor sanitary administration has been in small places, it will probably be admitted that it has been much better in our larger cities. Most of the real improvements that have been made in the control of communicable diseases, in the prevention of nuisances, in school inspection and in the reduction of infant mortality have been made by municipal, not state health officials. It is not surprising that it should be so, for the former has had the direct responsibility and what is more important has been brought into direct contact with the people and knows the practical difficulties of public health work. To supplant the municipal health officer by state appointed officials would be under present conditions a grave mistake, and in many cities a decided backward step. To exempt such cties from direct state control would seem to be wise, and has been done, but the city taxpayer would soon resent, it is feared, being taxed for the benefit of rural sanitation while still called upon to pay for the sanitary administration of his own city.

A very practical obstacle to the plan of complete state control is the attitude of the local communities. In many sections of the country the great body of the citizens are opposed to the state usurping any more of the functions of their town or their county. It would be difficult in these states, where home rule is a fetish, to displace the local health official by the state health official. Of course, in many other states the feeling for home government is not especially strong and the change would be easier.

Those who advocate central control, show that, thus far, local communities have been extremely slow to take advantage of the progress of sanitary science. They claim that the central government can introduce sanitary reform over the whole state at once, that under state supervision, uniform conditions can be secured over the whole state, and that far greater efficiency will result than now obtains. Every part of the state will have its due share of the funds, while under existing conditions many communities, which need it most, will, for a long time, have to get along with little, or nothing. It is claimed that a strong central health department, with an efficient corps of field workers, can accomplish more in actual life saving in two or three years, than the present haphazard ways of local health administration can in twenty. It is claimed, also, that the aggregate cost of state work will be less than for local work of the same quality.

Turning now from the theoretical, it may be said that many of the state health departments have been taking on, occasionally, during recent years, one executive function after another, and that there has been a growing sentiment in favor of the state taking exclusive control. A considerable number of health officials desire to see their state appoint local health officers, and through them do all the executive work and let the state bear the burden of the cost. Yet thus far there has not been much progress in this direction. Appointment of local health officers by the state cannot be relied on to accomplish much of itself. If the salary comes from the home community, the allegiance of the official is divided. If the salary is inadequate, no amount of control by the state will get more work out of the man than he is paid for. The appointment of local officials by the state will later be referred to. Real control of local health officers' appointments obtains only in Arkansas. Florida, Mississippi, Oklahoma, Pennsylvania, South Dakota, Vermont and Wyoming. In Mississippi the county fixes and pays the salary of the county health officer, but there are only two full time officers in the state. In Oklahoma, South Dakota, and Vermont the fees or salaries of the health officers are fixed by law and there is not a full time officer in any one of the three states. It would appear that the state appointment of local health officers in Mississippi and Vermont has resulted in a better condition of affairs than is found in neighboring states, where this condition does not prevail. The work through the state is more uniform, much more seems to be done and work of a more effective character. It may be, too, that state appointments are giving good results in Oklahoma and South Dakota, but in those states frequent changes in the state health department, insufficient funds and poor organization as well as political considerations make it impossible to draw any satisfactory conclusions.

It is possible for a state health department to do a great deal of local executive work, even if it does not appoint local officers and does not take formal charge. By means of state inspectors much can be accomplished, doubtless, even when the state health department has no authority at all to intervene in local affairs. Inspectors and field workers, with tact and judgment, can gain the good will of the local officials and do a great deal without any authority. If they have a right to intervene, as they have in a very considerable number of states, their position is still more secure. Not many state health departments have attempted much along these lines. Minnesota is rapidly developing central control of communicable diseases by means of field workers and a supervision of cases from the office. In Louisiana the state inspectors have done much in improving the sanitation of public buildings and places where food is handled. The hookworm work in the South is an example of how much may be accomplished without formal control.

It is also an illustration of the value of central supervision and organized effort.

In various parts of this report reference is made to different lines of work such as food sanitation, dairy inspection, schoolhouse supervision, plumbing inspection, river inspection, etc., carried on by inspectors working under the state health department, entirely independent of the local officials. It may well be that a large amount of state control will be developed, gradually, in this way, without formally taking over the appointment and payment of local health officers. It is not unlikely that the "supervisors," appointed in some states, may develop into true executive officers.

There are really only two states in which formal provision has been made for carrying on all sanitary work by the state health department and where sufficient funds have been provided to do this. These are Florida and Pennsylvania.

In Florida the state health department has complete executive power in all parts of the state. There is little local health work done outside of Jacksonville. The department has an appropriation amounting to about $100,000 per annum. Nevertheless, the state maintains a force totally inadequate, according to the views of those most conversant with health conditions in the South, to cope with prevailing diseases. It is impossible to show by figures the health conditions of the state, as there are no mortality statistics and no morbidity statistics. No systematic epidemiologic work is done. With the exception of the hookworm work which has been mostly abandoned, and tuberculosis work which is just beginning, no intensive campaigns have been conducted against disease. That such are needed, and would be successful, is indicated by the example of Jacksonville, where well directed efforts of an efficient department reduced to a minimum a typhoid death rate, very excessive, but probably not greater than prevails in the rest of the state. Nevertheless the state's health appropriation is by no means all expended. The department has accomplished much in some directions, particularly with its diagnostic laboratories, but the general sanitary condition of Florida, to say the least, is not markedly superior to that of other states without strong central control and with small appropriations. State administration of itself does not necessarily ensure the best results.

In Pennsylvania, too, the State Department of Health is authorized to take full control of sanitary work in every community. Although the cost may, in some, be made a charge on the local government, this is not done, and where the state does exercise its executive power, it pays the bills. The commissioner states that it is the policy of the department to encourage communities to administer their own sanitary affairs and that, if this is well done, the state has no desire to intervene. Nevertheless, owing to the general failure of local sanitary work in the country and in the smaller towns, the State Health Department does, at its own cost, and with its own officials, carry on general public health work in the rural districts and small towns all over the state. For this purpose the department employs, outside of its special work in tuberculosis, school inspection and the like, a medical inspector in each county except Philadelphia, and 670 local health officers. These look after the sanitary needs of nearly 2,500,000 people. The cost of this general executive work, as distinct from school inspection, and some other activities, is not separated in the reports, but appears to be between $300,000 and $400,000 annually. The results of this system of state control have been briefly considered in another part of the report dealing specifically with health conditions in that state. It is certainly true that these conditions have vastly improved since the state took up this work, but whether, on the whole, the results justify the cost and the methods, could not be determined except by a careful and detailed study and the ultimate results might not be apparent until after the lapse of years and after changes in the administration.

SPECIFIC ADMINISTRATIVE FUNCTIONS

The remainder of the report will be occupied with a consideration of the various duties which are now performed by the state health departments of the country. The old conception of a state board of health as a body of estimable medical gentlemen with some special interest in communicable diseases, who, without pay, would consent to advise the legislature on public health matters and write voluminous reports dealing in glittering generalities, has generally become obsolete, though it is to be feared that it may still persist in some unprogressive localities. In most states the protection of the public health is considered a serious matter. Sanitation, which formerly consisted of empirical attempts at nuisance prevention, quarantine and disinfection, has now developed into a real science, though still with many lamentable limitations. Much definite knowledge has accumulated as to what the state can do to save lives and prevent sickness and we seem on the eve of learning much more. "Public health is purchasable," we are told. It is the business of the state health department to see that the people get their money's worth.

LOCAL HEALTH ADMINISTRATION
AND THE STATE

In England and the United States, the sanitary administration of the larger cities has been fully up to that of the state government, in the adoption of progressive methods, in the amount of work done and in the results accomplished. The cities have often set the example which the state has followed and recently our largest state has selected an executive of its largest city to carry out a comprehensive state plan of sanitary reform. While the sanitation of our larger cities is far from perfect, it is far superior to what is found in the smaller municipalities where public health is usually sadly neglected. In the rural portions of the country, conditions are still more unsatisfactory. While the death rate was reduced 21.2 per cent. in the cities of the registration states from 1900 to 1912, in the rural sections of those states it was reduced only 8.6 per cent. Yet in 1910 over half the population of the United States lived in the country, or in towns of less than 2,500, and the sanitary administration of most towns of 2,500 is wretched. While experience has shown that the larger cities can for the most part be left to care for their health themselves, the country and the small towns, left to themselves, have, with rare exceptions, done little or nothing. It is now the general and well founded belief that the sanitary progress of these communities must be stimulated, directed and perhaps controlled, by the state.

Although for the most part quite ineffective, yet a nominal local sanitary organization is provided for in practically the whole of our country's area, rural as well as urban. There are four classes of communities which at present serve as local health units which differ much in character and conditions, though the first class merges gradually into the second. These classes are:

LOCAL HEALTH ORGANIZATION

1. The larger cities, with 50,000 inhabitants or over.
2. The smaller cities, towns and villages.
3. Townships.
4. Counties.

1. The larger cities can, and often do, have an efficient local health department. Every city of 50,000 ought to have a full time health officer, and well defined lines of sanitary work. Many cities much smaller are cared for efficiently, sometimes remarkably so, by part time men. Many more could do it if properly directed and stimulated. The organization of cities is provided for by general laws, or charters, and varies a good deal. These are two general types of health service in cities, the board of health and the single commissioner, or health officer, responsible either to the council or the mayor, this latter type being now the most popular. It is not, as a rule, in this class of communities that

state supervision and control are needed, though in many of the smaller ones it is.

2. The smaller cities, towns and villages, including those ranging in size down to 150 inhabitants. While in New England urban communities with 25,000 inhabitants or more, still retaining their township form of government, are not unknown, in other parts of the country it is the custom to incorporate exceedingly small collections of people, and cities of 150 persons are not rare on the Pacific coast. Sanitation in these communities is usually as bad as it is in purely rural regions and the need for it is greater. It is practically impossible for them to secure it by their own independent action. While the statutes provide for the appointment of village and town boards of health and health officers, the communities are too small to furnish enough pay, or enough work, to secure the services of a capable man or keep him interested if they could.

3. Townships. While townships are found in a large number of states, this political division varies greatly in meaning and in importance in different parts of the country. In New England, the townships form the primary political units which make up the state. The counties often are of comparatively little importance. In Rhode Island, there is no county government at all. In a number of other states, particularly those settled directly from New England, the township, while not holding the same place in the affections of the inhabitants as in New England, is still the real unit of government, though its importance is less in some states than in others. Where it is of importance, the township has to be reckoned with in any scheme of state control, for the township is loathe to give up its powers and its rights, one of which is to have its own board of health or health officer. Township boards of health are found in Illinois, Iowa, Maine, Massachusetts, Michigan, Minnesota, New Hampshire, New Jersey, New York, North Dakota, Ohio, Oklahoma, Pennsylvania, Rhode Island, South Dakota and Wisconsin, and township health officers in Connecticut and Vermont. In the Dakotas and Oklahoma, the township boards do not appear to be of any importance. While the tendency of the day is towards single officials instead of boards, the conservatism of those states in which the township is important, has preserved the board. Some persons, as the state health executive of New Hampshire, and one of the state inspectors in Massachusetts, consider a board the better type, the former because there are then three chances to one (in a board of three) that a good man will be secured, and the latter because by appointing men from different parts of the township, these parts can be more easily and quickly served. In many of the above named states the appointment of health officers in addition to the board of health is obligatory, and in most it is customary.

The township, in the older and more populous states, serves as an excellent primary sanitary district, its size, population and the ideas of the people all favoring this. The standard township of many states in the Middle West is, however, only six miles square, and if it is chiefly agricultural it has rather too small a population for this purpose.

4. In most of the states the county is the political unit, and in every one of these, except Delaware and South Carolina, we find some sort of county health officials. County boards of health are provided for in Alabama, Arizona, Colorado, Idaho, Illinois,[1] Kansas, Kentucky, Louisiana (parish), Maryland, Minnesota, Missouri, Montana, Nebraska, Nevada, North Carolina, North Dakota, Oregon, South Dakota, Tennessee, Utah, Virginia, Washington and West Virginia. Minnesota, North Dakota, Oklahoma and South Dakota have both county and township boards of health. In Minnesota, the former are of little importance, as they only have jurisdiction over the unincorporated territory, and most of the counties are organized into townships, there being over 2,000 township boards of health. In the other three states, the township board is of little consequence. In a few states there are no county boards of health, but county health officers. These are Arkansas, California, Connecticut, Indiana, Mississippi, New Mexico, Oklahoma, Texas and Wyoming. In Florida, the state health officer formerly appointed an agent in many of the counties who was practically a county health officer. Now, however, the state is divided into seven sanitary districts with an assistant state health officer in each. In Pennsylvania, the medical inspector appointed in each county by the state commissioner of health, actually performs the duties of county health officer.

Some of the men who have been actively engaged in intensive local health work in the South, notably Dr. Ferrell and Dr. Freeman, believe that the county is too large a unit for effective health administration in that portion of the country. In the absence of strong township government artificial divisions are suggested. In 1913 an act (Ch. 154) was passed in North Carolina providing for such districts. The county commissioners are authorized to establish such, on petition of a majority of the freeholders residing in the proposed district. A special district tax for sanitary purposes is provided for. The district is to have a health committee appointed by the county commissioners. This committee is virtually a board of health and is authorized to make rules and elect a health officer.

Many of the details of local sanitary organization are interesting and important and can be learned elsewhere (Municipal Sanitation in the U. S., Chapin, Providence, 1901; U. S. Public Health Service, Bull. 54, 1912), but there is no need of considering them here, as our only interest in local health organization is to learn if possible, to what extent it has been, or can be made use of by the state health department in promoting the health of the people. It would be difficult to find any one who would claim that existing agencies outside of the larger cities, if left to themselves, are capable of accomplishing very much. They have been tried and have failed. The health officer in the small community at the best abates a few nuisances, placards some cases of contagious disease and fumigates after their recovery. If he is left to himself there will be no tracing of typhoid fever cases, no campaign against malaria, no attempt to control hookworm, no hospital for the poor consumptive no cutting down of infant mortality and no inspection of

---

1. Only for counties with no township organization.

schoolchildren. How to get effective service from the officials who come directly in touch with the people in the rural districts and smaller municipalities is now recognized by every one as the foremost practical public health problem of the day.

It is often said that all public health problems lead back to just one thing, and that is money. We can generally, "within natural limitations," get what we want to pay for in health as in commodities. If communities were willing to pay for efficient health service they could get it. That they do not at present want to do this is shown by facts from many places. In Louisiana, out of 195 municipalities, seventy-three pay no salary to the health officer. The average is $191. Omitting the three or four larger cities, the average total expenditure for health purposes is $310. In Vermont the average fees received by the health officers in place of salary is about $100. In New Hampshire many of the health officers receive only $10 to $25 a year. In North Carolina the salaries of county health officers average from $250 to $300, in Mississippi about $200. In 1910 one city of 10,000 in Iowa paid its health officer $100, another of 5,000, nothing. In California the county health officers receive $60 to $600; in Oklahoma, $300 to $700. In Tennessee, some of the county health officers receive only $50 and do jail work besides. In some of the mountain states, they are somewhat higher, as in Montana, where they average about $1,000, varying from $240 to $3,000. Very many county health officers, however, have to do jail or poor-house work as well as public health work.

Attempts have been made to fix the compensation of local health officers by statute, but this has not been very successful. Legislatures have not appreciated the importance of public health work and have been slow to fix a decent compensation. The poorer communities, in such legislative attempts, usually make their views felt by their representatives. Thus, in Indiana and Oregon, the compensation for county health officers is fixed at 1½ cents per capita, which in counties of 20,000 would yield a salary of only $300. In Indiana, city health officers are to receive 2 cents and in Oregon 1½ cents per capita. In Alabama, it is 2 cents per capita in counties under 10,000 inhabitants, and less in larger counties, and in Maryland, it is $150 per annum in counties of less than 15,000 inhabitants. In New Jersey, the township boards of health are authorized to expend a maximum of 5 cents per capita for all health purposes. Ridiculously low minima are fixed for salaries in some states, as $10 in Indiana. The legislatures seem more fearful that health officers shall be overpaid and a maximum is more often fixed, as $300 for county health officers in Arizona, and $1,500 in Indiana and Oklahoma. It is evident that, in these states, great difficulty will be experienced in improving the service under the statutes.

STATE CONTROL OF LOCAL AFFAIRS

It has long been felt that the state health department might bring about improvement by means of some control over the local health officials. Various attempts have been made, from time to time, and in various places, to secure such control. Most of these attempts have been made without any very careful forethought and most of them have accomplished very little.

1. Control by Direct Authority.—In a number of states provision is made by the statutes for the supervision or direction of local boards of health or health officers. In most cases the provision is of a general nature, and so worded that it would be uncertain how far the state could go in this supervision unless the meaning of the law is more clearly defined by court decisions. Such expressions as "supervisory control," "general supervision," "subsidiary to," "to superintend," "subordinate to" are found in Alabama, Arizona, Louisiana, Minnesota, Montana, Missouri, Nevada, New York, North Dakota, Oklahoma, South Carolina, South Dakota and Wyoming.

In Colorado the local health officer must act in cooperation with and under the advice of the state board of health.

In some states control by the state health department is more clearly expressed in the statutes. Thus, in Oregon the county boards of health are to protect the public health "as directed or approved by the state board of health," and are to "perform such other duties as may from time to time be required of them by the state board of health." In Iowa, "local boards of health shall obey and enforce the rules and regulations of the state board of health." In Kansas, the county health officer is "to perform such other duties as . . . the state board of health may require of him." In Texas, "In all matters in which the state board of health may be clothed with authority, said county health officer shall at all times be under its direction." Refusal to obey reasonable commands shall subject the health officer to removal. In New Jersey, the state board of health can require the local board to take any action deemed necessary in regard to contagious disease and can apply to the court for a mandamus.

Another way in which the state department of health can control local health officials is by means of the legislative, or rule making power, which is often conferred on the former, and the scope and nature of which has been previously considered. Thus, by means of such rules the state department of health may prescribe what shall be done by the local health officials in controlling infectious diseases, in disinfecting, in inspecting schools, or dairy farms, or abating nuisances, or in enforcing fly screening, or in all similar matters. The state, in this way, exercises very great power in controlling and compelling actions of local health officials, and this, too, when no specific mention is made in the statute of the use of the regulations for any such purpose. This is possible whenever broad legislative power is conferred on the state health department, as is very often the case, and provided also a penalty is affixed.

Sometimes, the statutes specifically prescribe that the state department of health is to control local boards through its rules. Thus, in Wiscon "The board (state) shall have power to adopt and enforce rules and regulations governing the duties of all health officers and health boards and any violations of said rules shall be punished by a fine of not less than ten, nor more than one hundred dollars for each offence." In Texas, the county and city health officer is to perform such duties as may "be prescribed for him under the rules and regulations and requirements of the Texas state board of health," though in this state the attorney general has considered this grant of legislative power as unconstitutional. Among other states in which control over local affairs by means of rules of the state health department are prescribed by statute are Indiana and Tennessee.

2. Control by Taking Temporary Charge of Local Affairs.—An important means of control of local boards of health is the provision found in a number of states that the state health department may, when it deems that local sanitary affairs are not being properly managed, take matters into its own hands, execute the laws and take such other action as may be necessary to preserve the public health. Such a means of control is far more effective, if it is also provided, that the expense incurred shall be a charge on the local community. Most townships, municipalities and counties seriously object to having state health officers thus usurp local functions and run up bills which the local authorities have to pay. Such a provision is found in the laws of California, Colorado, Delaware, Idaho, Indiana, Iowa, Kansas, Michigan, Minnesota, Mississippi, Nebraska, New Jersey, Oregon, Pennsylvania (for certain boroughs and townships), South Carolina, South Dakota, Tennessee, Virginia, Washington and Wisconsin. This action is occasionally, though rarely taken by the state. More often it is threatened and this usually brings the negligent officials to time. There seems to be little doubt that a knowledge that the state can and will thus take charge of local affairs encourages local health officers to do their duty and makes them ready to take the advice or follow the directions of the state department.

In other states it is provided that the state may take charge of local affairs but no provision is made for the payment of expenses by the local government, so that if the state steps in, the state will have to bear the expense. This is true in Georgia, Florida, Louisiana, Montana, New Mexico, North Dakota, Oklahoma and Pennsylvania (in certain places), and in West Virginia, so far as communicable diseases are concerned. This does not have the compelling effect on local health officers that the provision previously referred to, has, indeed it sometimes has the opposite effect, as is said to be the case in some Pennsylvania communities, but on the whole, most communities believe strongly enough in home rule to prefer to manage their own affairs in their own way rather than have the state step in. In Massachusetts and Utah practically the same relation exists by virtue of a provision of the law which gives the state and local officials coordinate powers.

3. Control by Prescribing Qualifications of Local Officials.—While some of the methods of control just referred to certainly accomplish something, it is believed by many that the chief reason for the failure of local sanitation is the failure of local authorities to elect or appoint capable men to public health positions. This is due partly to the dominance of that great American evil, the spoils system, and partly to the fact that town councils, county boards and mayors do not know the proper qualifications of a health officer. Hence it is proposed that the state in some way control local appointments.

One plan is that adopted in New Jersey, where health officials and inspectors must be selected from those who have passed an examination set by the state board of health. The results of this law have not equaled the anticipation. The compensation of health officers is low, and there is no opportunity for the education of health officers in the state, so that there is little encouragement for men to prepare themselves properly. Nevertheless, it is said that a considerable number present themselves for examination and the character of the applicants is improving.

A somewhat different provision of the new New York law is that the Public Health Council shall have the power to prescribe the qualifications of local health officers.

4. Control by Appointment and Removal.—It is doubtless the belief of the great majority of state health officials that one of the most important means of improving local health administration is for the state department to appoint the local health officers. This, of course, is contrary to the principle of local self government which is so dear to the hearts of Americans, but much public health work is police work, and all police power is vested in the state, and only delegated by the state, when deemed best, to the local units of government. Moreover, in the more ordinary lines of police work, the state in numerous instances sees fit to exercise this power itself, and hence we find state police and state constabulary. In certain kinds of sanitary work, as in collecting vital statistics, receiving and forwarding reports of disease, the local health officer acts really as the agent of the state department of health and hence there is some argument for his appointment by the state. There seems to be no theoretical reason why the state should not appoint local health officers, though there are some practical ones. However, a number of states have seen fit to provide for this form of appointment.

In a number of states, while the local health officials are not usually appointed by the state, they may be under certain circumstances, namely, on failure of the local government to appoint. It is often provided that in such cases the appointments shall be made by the state department of health. Such a provision is found in Arkansas, California, Maine, Minnesota, Montana, Nebraska, North Carolina, Ohio, South Carolina, and Wisconsin. It does not appear that this is often done, for in communities which take too little interest to elect a health officer the mere appointment of one by outside authority would usually amount to little.

Many states go further than this and provide for the appointment of local officials by the central health department as a fixed policy. In Kentucky three of five members of the county boards of health are appointed by the state department, in South Dakota two of three, in Virginia three of four, and in West Virginia one of three. In Arkansas, Mississippi, Oklahoma and Wyoming the county health officer is so appointed, and in New Hampshire the townshiy health officer.

In Vermont township health officials (including health officials in cities) are appointed by the State Board of Health. In Arkansas, however, the appointment is to be with the approval of the county judge, and the attorney general has ruled that his approval must be secured first, which results in the virtual appointment by the judge. In West Virginia, too, the member appointed by the State Board of Health is first chosen by the county commissioner and, in one case, where this man was not appointed by the State Board of Health, the county refused to make another choice. In New Hampshire, he is to be recommended by the selectmen.

In South Dakota one of the appointees of the State Board of Health, though a member of the County Board of Health, is the county superintendent of health, that is, county health officer.

In Connecticut the township health officers are appointed by the county health officer who in turn is appointed by the judges of the superior court.

In South Carolina the State Board of Health appoints boards of health for unincorporated places.

In Ohio the appointment of health officials in villages must be approved by the state board of health.

The appointment of local health officials by the state, where they are paid by the local communities, is naturally likely to raise local opposition, which is still more accentuated, if the compensation is fixed by the state. These conditions have given rise to much opposition in South Dakota and Vermont, and in the latter state, it is said, it would now be impossible to secure the passage of the law vesting appointment in the state and attempts are at times made to secure its repeal. In Wyoming, however, the state health officer says that there has been little objection to this arrangement. In Virginia, in all but eleven charter cities, the State Board of Health appoints three of the four members of municipal boards of health.

Power of removal should go with power of appointment and doubtless does in the states just named. In others the state department of health has power to remove incompetent officials, though their appointment is not the general policy. This is so in Idaho, Indiana, Kansas, Maryland, Nevada, New York, North Dakota, Oregon, Washington and Wisconsin. In Iowa the removal is to be made by the Attorney General. In a number of these states such removals are from time to time made. In Texas and Utah the state health department may file complaints for the removal of local officers.

The public health organization in Alabama is unique and dates back nearly half a century. It is said to be the result of an effort to unify sanitary practice throughout the state and to take it out of politics, though it was perhaps forgotten that politics can be as rampant in a medical society as elsewhere. The state medical association is the State Board of Health. The association elects from its "councilors," 100 in number, a board of censors of ten, which acts as a committee on health. The censors nominate and the association elects the state health officer. The county medical societies are boards of health for their respective counties and elect a county health officer and health officials for incorporated places.

5. Control by State Supervision.—The mere appointment of local health officials by the state does not of itself necessarily involve any really effective control or direction. Some means of practical supervision and education must be devised. This would probably always be necessary, but is absolutely essential, at the present time, when there are so few men trained in public health work and it is impossible, even at the best, to get health officials who have more than the vaguest superficial knowledge of their duties.

Connecticut, over twenty years ago, devised the plan of coordinating and improving public health work by appointing a health officer for each county who should in turn appoint the local health officials and "cooperate with and supervise their doings." The peculiarity of this scheme is that the county health officials are attorneys at law and of course have only a very superficial knowledge of public health work. Naturally the system has proved valueless, or, as might be expected, in some instances, worse.

A recent act in Maryland provides that the State Board of Health shall, with the exclusion of Baltimore, divide the state into ten sanitary districts and shall appoint on the nomination of the secretary, a deputy state health officer for each district. The deputy is a full time man and is to receive a salary, fixed by the State Board of Health, not to exceed $2,500, together with necessary expenses. Deputies may be moved from one district to another. While they are to assist and supervise local health officials, they are clothed with large executive power and it is the apparent intention of the law that they shall exercise it. Nurses and other assistants may be provided by the State Board of Health. The act carries an annual appropriation of $50,000. At present there are seven deputies.

In 1907 the state of Massachusetts was divided into fifteen health districts, later reduced to fourteen and again to twelve, and a state inspector was appointed for each district. The appointments were made by the governor with the advice and consent of his council. The governor and council were also to fix the salaries. The state inspectors besides supervising and advising local health officials had a great deal of executive work in connection with the sanitation of factories and mercantile establishments, with the occupations of minors, with tenement houses where clothing is made, as well as with other matters. In 1912 many of these duties were transferred to the State Board of Labor and Industries. Under the new law (1914) there are to be but eight districts and the inspectors are full time men appointed by the commissioner of health with the approval of the public health council. The salary is not to exceed $3,500 per annum. Their work will now be that of supervisors and directors of local work, to secure the enforcement of law and to perform such other duties as the commissioner may direct. A full account of the past work of these inspectors may be found in the annual reports of the Massachusetts State Board of Health.

The new law in New York, which went into effect in January, 1914, contains as one of its essential features, provision for a similar division of the state (the city of New York excepted) into sanitary districts, with a supervisor for each district, appointed by the commissioner of health. At first there were twenty districts, each with a medical man as supervisor at a salary of $4,000, including traveling expenses. A number of these supervisors also act as health officer of some large city in the district and receive another salary for this. In 1915, owing to lack of funds, the supervisors were cut down to ten.

The duties of the supervisors are specified in the act as follows:

1. Keep himself informed as to the work of each local health officer within his sanitary district.

2. Aid each local health officer within his sanitary district in the performance of his duties, and particularly on the appearance of any contagious disease.

3. Assist each local health officer within his sanitary district in making an annual sanitary survey of the territory within his jurisdiction, and in maintaining therein a continuous sanitary supervision.

4. Call together the local health officers within his district or any portion of it from time to time for conference.

5. Adjust questions of jurisdiction arising between local health officers within his district.

6. Study the causes of excessive mortality from any disease in any portion of his district.

7. Promote efficient registration of births and deaths.

8. Inspect from time to time all labor camps within his district and enforce the regulations of the public health council in relation thereto.

9. Inspect from time to time all Indian reservations and enforce all provisions of the sanitary code relating thereto.

10. Endeavor to enlist the cooperation of all the organizations of physicians within his district in .the improvement of the public health therein.

11. Promote the information of the general public in all matters pertaining to the public health.

12. Act as the representative of the state commissioner of health, and under his direction, in securing the enforcement within his district of the provisions of the public health law and the sanitary code.

In Wisconsin there are five deputy state health officers each having his own district. They are full time men, under civil service rules, with a salary of $2,250 and expenses. Their duties are specified in Section 4, Chapter 674 of 1913. One of these is to develop and supervise the work of local officers. They have many other things to do and supervision of local officials does not as yet appear to have been their chief activity.

In North Carolina the attempt is being made through the initiative and under the guidance of the state health department to improve local conditions by inducing the counties to appoint full time health officials. Already eleven counties have done this, and to coordinate their activities the state department established a bureau of county health work. (This has recently been merged in a bureau of rural sanitation.) It is the purpose here to very actively assist the counties in establishing a full time health service and to put men from the central office into the counties for a time until the work is fairly started. More counties are proposing full time officers than the state department is able, with its present force, to set up in this way. The executive of the state department is firmly convinced that more permanent results can be obtained in this way than where the state makes the appointments and permanently directs from the central office. Moreover public sentiment in North Carolina is decidedly opposed, it is said, to such centralization.

In Virginia there are three district health officers partly engaged in supervisory work.

In Illinois there are four district health officers at a salary of $1,800.

Of course, there are many other states where the executive officer, or perhaps some inspector, or other employee of the department, does more or less in the way of bettering local health work by personal visits, advice and assistance, as well as by correspondence. Massachusetts, North Carolina and New York seem to be the only states which have adopted a comprehensive method of control by means of personal visits by supervisors. Pennsylvania relies more on printed rules and forms and correspondence direct from the central office. Wisconsin has a nucleus in its deputy health officers which may easily be developed into a system of personal supervision. All these are, with the exception of North Carolina, township states, with a large number of local health officers. North Carolina is a county state with fewer health officers, and their supervision by the central office may perhaps ultimately require a smaller central force than is needed in township states. In Massachusetts the supervisors themselves have hitherto been directed by the assistant to the secretary, and in New York there is a bureau in the department for this purpose.

6. The "Unit Plan."—The state department of health of North Carolina has recently put in effect what it calls the "unit plan" for the state direction of local health work. This must not be confused with the "unit work" of the International Health Commission. In the latter the "unit" refers to the staff engaged in the intensive local health work which it is the purpose of the commission to promote. In the North Carolina plan the "unit" refers to the kind of health work which the state proposes to undertake.

The advocates of the North Carolina plan are strongly convinced that it is very important that local governments should be made to feel their responsibility in sanitary matters and that they should bear the cost of improving the health of the people. They believe that where the counties or other rural divisions cannot afford to maintain a full time health officer and carry on all the important lines of health work they can be induced to take up, one at a time, the more important lines of endeavor and pay the state health department to do the work selected. This would be the "unit" of work and the county might pay for one, two, three or more units, as it should see fit. It could spend as much or little as it liked, and in any event, could be assured of having the work done well, as the state department of health would do it. The state could always keep in its employ trained men who would do in an efficient and economical manner whatever they might be called on to do. In the summer of 1915 a contract was entered into with ten counties in North Carolina for free immunization against typhoid fever. Each county appropriated $500, and in some counties as many as one third of the people were immunized. Another unit is school inspection. For $10 per school the department will engage to examine the children and the building, and to arrange the proper exercises for a "health day" in each school district, which will interest the parents as well as the children, and be the beginning of better things in sanitation.

7. All Local Work Done by State.—Only two states have adopted this principle, Florida, for practically the whole state, and Pennsylvania, for about one quarter of the population scattered over the rural and less densely settled portions.

In Florida there is no county health organization and no municipal health department, worthy the name, except in Jacksonville. The State Board of Health has full authority, and assumes full responsibility, for health conditions throughout the state. For purposes of sanitary control the state is divided into seven districts and an assistant health officer is employed by the State Board of Health for each district. These are full time men. There are in addition two "county agents," and four sanitary policemen to look after the details in the principal cities.

In Pennsylvania the State Department of Health, ever since its reorganization in 1905, has pursued a policy of controlling from the central office as far as possible, health work over large areas of the state. For this purpose a medical inspector is appointed by the commissioner of health in each county and also local health officers who have jurisdiction over unincorporated territory as well as over many incorporated places. The state's county medical officers, who are largely occupied with communicable diseases, frequently advise the local health officers. All of the work of these officers is directed by the "medical division" of the department in much detail by rules, forms, reports, directions and correspondence. The department also has a "general inspector" and an assistant, but apparently they do not do much supervisory work, as that is understood in Massachusetts and New York. Local health organization has been very backward in Pennsylvania. This was even true of Harrisburg, the capital city, with a population of about 60,000, which had no health department until 1909. The state health department has made earnest effort to secure the establishment of boards of health in all incorporated places of any considerable size.

8. Supervision by Conferences.—An obviously useful way of coordinating and improving local public health work is by means of meetings of health officers, at which matters relating to public health can be discussed. In some of the states as New Jersey, New York and Massachusetts the need of such meetings was felt twenty-five or thirty years ago and voluntary associations of health officers and others were formed for this purpose. Whether or not the association was or was not organized by the state health department, the latter usually took much interest in promoting its prosperity and usefulness. Such associations are found in Arizona, Connecticut, Kansas, Massachusetts, Michigan, New York, North Carolina, Oklahoma, South Dakota, Utah and Virginia. In some of these voluntary associations, particularly the older ones, the membership is by no means confined to health officers, but many other persons interested in public health work are members.

A somewhat different and later type of meeting, and one more frankly official, is the "conference" of public health officials, which is called by the state health department for purposes of instruction. Some of these conferences are called "schools for health officers,"   as in Indiana, Kansas, Kentucky, Oregon, Texas, West Virginia and Vermont. At times, as in Kansas and Texas, these meetings are more in the nature of a school, for didactic instruction, as well as laboratory work is given. More often the "conference" or school is like the meetings of medical or other scientific bodies in which papers are read and discussed with occasionally a symposium or round table discussion, or a question box. The speakers at these conferences are often local health officers, or men connected with the state health department, but usually some speakers from other states are invited. Such conferences, or schools, are required by law in Arkansas, Indiana, Kentucky, New Hampshire, New Jersey, New York, Ohio, Utah, Vermont, Washington and Wisconsin. They are held also in California, Louisiana, Minnesota, Mississippi, Montana, Nebraska, Oregon, Rhode Island, Tennessee, Texas and West Virginia. In Pennsylvania the commissioner of health calls conferences of his own health officers who number many hundred. In Kansas, New Jersey and New York, besides these official conferences held under the auspices of the state department of health, there are voluntary associations of persons interested in public health. In Kansas the official "school" is held jointly by the state board of health and the state university, and the physicians of the state are invited to attend. In Texas it was organized by the university, with the cooperation of the state department of health.

Sometimes these conferences are held at the time of the meeting of the state medical society, but more often they are entirely independent Sometimes the meetings last for one day only, or they may be longer, as two days in Oregon, Utah, Tennessee, Texas and Wisconsin, three days in Indiana, Kentucky, New York, Ohio, Washington and Vermont, a week in Kansas and three weeks in Texas. Usually the meetings are held annually, but in Connecticut and Wisconsin biennially. The health officers' association in Massachusetts and New Jersey hold quarterly meetings. In order the better to accommodate the members, Vermont last year hold four "schools" in different parts of the state. In California, where the conference meets with the state medical society, there are also southern and northern conferences which meet with the southern and northern branches of the medical society. In Montana three distinct meetings are held, and in West Virginia two. In Indiana, besides the general meeting, there is one held by the northern counties. In Ohio a northern and a southern meeting are held. In New York there are frequent conferences of the health officers in one or two counties and in Connecticut there are some county conferences and in Massachustts some of the state inspectors hold local conferences. It is believed by many that some of the most effective educational work among local health officers can be done in these small district conferences, and it seems likely that these will be held a great deal more in the immediate future.

One of the great difficulties with the conferences is that they are usually not very well attended and the men who need them most do not go. The difficulty is largely a financial one. A health officer with a meagre salary does not feel that he can afford to leave his practice and pay his expenses to one of these conferences. Of course, some communities pay the expenses of their health officers and some more can be induced to when urged by the state health department. A few states have passed laws requiring the health officers to attend and also requiring their communities to pay their expenses. This is the case in Indiana, Kentucky, New Hampshire, New Jersey, New York, Ohio, Utah, Washington, West Virginia and Wisconsin. Even then the attendance is far less than it should be. In Arkansas and Texas the counties may or may not pay. Vermont has gone further and not only requires attendance, but the state pays the health officer $4 a day and expenses. The cost of the school, when only one was held, was about $6,000, and when four district schools were held, about half that sum. About 80 per cent. of the health officers attend.

Realizing the difficulty of getting attendance at conferences a prominent official has recently suggested that a practical way of improving local health service would be to establish correspondence courses for health officers, and at least one state department has been seriously considering the plan.

PLANS FOR THE IMPROVEMENT OF LOCAL HEALTH WORK

Probably during the last four or five years no subject has received more consideration from state health officials than the improvement of local health service. Very little has so far been accomplished, but there has been much discussion and various plans have been evolved and bills drawn.

Comparatively few approve the plan of having the state appoint all local officers and some, who would like to see this done, recognize that it is impossible.

A dozen or more state officials are in favor of supervisors after the Massachusetts and New York plans. About half of this number are in states where township government is fairly strong and where supervisors would seem to be the most natural step in the evolution of a better service.

Almost an equal number are in favor of county health officers. In many states, however, it is recognized that some of the counties are too small and that provision would have to be made for a combination of counties in some cases. This has been done in some recent bills, as in Kansas and Ohio. The township, too, even in those states with large townships with a strong government, is too small for a full time health officer and voluntary combinations of townships have been formed in Massachusetts and New Jersey and of small cities in Illinois. In Ohio the compulsory combination of townships to furnish an area sufficiently large for the deputy health officer is provided for in the pending bill. Acts just passed in New York and West Virginia authorize, but do not compel, combinations of towns in New York and counties in West Virginia.

On the other hand, some believe that in the South, with its many pressing sanitary problems, a county is too large and, as was previously mentioned, the formation of artificial sanitary districts within the county has been provided for in North Carolina.

One cannot say, at present, what is the best plan of organization for securing more effective health work in the county and in the smaller municipalities. Little success has been attained in the past, and the newer schemes have not been tried, or have been tried too short a time, to determine their value.

The ideal plan in the minds of not a few is for the state to appoint and pay its local health officers. This has been done only in Florida and a portion of Pennsylvania, and it is doubtful whether, at present, it could be done over the whole of any other state.

There are still more who would have the state appoint local health officers, but have their salaries come from the communities they serve. This is done for township health officers in Vermont and for county health officers in Arkansas, Mississippi and Oklahoma.

It is realized that there is not much use in appointing a health officer unless he is paid an adequate salary and so, in many states, attempts have been made to fix the salary paid by the local authorities, but legislatures are loath to provide large salaries for health officials, and in no state has it been made sufficient.

In about a dozen states, where the township form of government is most highly developed, including New England, New York, New Jersey and some states of the Middle West, the township health officer is likely to remain a fixture. Under these circumstances there is general agreement that supervisors appointed by, and paid by, the state, can do a great deal to improve the situation.

Over the remainder of the country, where the county system prevails, two plans seem to find favor.

One plan is that of the full time county health officer who will do all of the health work of the county himself. This meets approval where the really rural population is fairly dense. In some states the county seems to make such a unit. The executive officer of the State Board of Health in North Carolina believes it to be so in his state. where the counties average something less than 25,000 in population, and something less than 500 square miles in area. In that state it is proposed that candidates for the position of county health officer shall spend from six to eight months with the State Board of Health studying the methods to be followed in their future work. The bill recently defeated in Kansas provided for districts, usually containing several counties, and with a population averaging about 55,000. The average size of the districts was about 1,200 square miles. The state health officials believed that, in view of the character of the population, the topography and the prevalent diseases, one whole time officer could, with an automobile, cover such a district. In other states, especially in the Rocky Mountains and on the Pacific Coast, the counties often have a very large area, though the population may be comparatively scanty, and here the county health officer must certainly be provided with deputies. In some of the more sparsely settled states, like the Dakotas, where the counties have a smaller area than in the mountain states, it is suggested that a number of counties should be combined to provide for a full time health officer who would then have deputies.

Several carefully prepared bills were introduced in the 1915 legislatures which are worthy of consideration in this connection. The proposed act in Indiana provided for the appointment of a health commissioner in every county, and in all cities of over 20,000 inhabitants, to be appointed by a special board in each county, consisting of the county superintendent of schools, the county auditor and the president of the county, and to serve for four years. The appointments were to be made from: 1. Physicians of four years' recent public health experience in Indiana. 2. Physicians who have passed an examination satisfactory to the State Board of Health, and 3. Persons holding a degree of doctor of public health from a reputable school. The health commissioners were to be full time men and to have large executive power, but were to be entirely subordinate to the State Board of Health and the latter could remove them for cause. Salaries were fixed, varying from $1,200 to $2,500 in counties, according to the size of the county.

The bill in Kansas provided that the State Board of Health should divide the state into thirty districts. Each district was to have a board of health formed from the county commissioners and representatives from cities, this board to elect a full time health officer for a term of four years from an eligible list furnished by a special examining board. The health officer's salary was to be fixed by the board of health, but to be not less than $2,000. The county health officer was given full executive power, except over cities electing to maintain a health department, and the board of health was to have legislative power.

The proposed acts in Michigan and Ohio, unlike those just referred to, had to recognize the townships, and in Michigan it was not thought advisable to interfere with the township boards of health and health officers. The bill authorized the State Board of Health to divide the state into thirty districts, with a health commissioner in each, to be appointed for four years by an appointing board to consist of the judges of the probate and the county school commissioners of the counties in the district, the appointment to be from a list of physicians who had passed an examination by the State Board of Health as provided. The commissioners were to be full time men and receive a salary of $3,500 and traveling expenses up to $1,000, to be paid by the state, and were given large executive power and were to act as agents of the State Board of Health. Detroit was to be exempt from the provisions of the bill, but its health officer was to be agent of the State Board of Health. The existing local health officers were to be deputies of the district health commissioners.

In Ohio the State Board of Health was to divide the state into districts of one or more counties, as it should determine, with subdistricts, consisting of one or more townships. The county commissioners of the counties were to elect a district health officer, subject to the approval of the State Board of Health, from a list certified to by the civil service commission after examination, the candidates to be physicians or holders of the degree of doctor of public health. Each subdistrict was to have a deputy district health officer appointed by the district health officer, from a list certified to, after examination, by the civil service commission. Both the district health officers and the deputies were to serve until removal or resignation. The salary of the district health officers was to be not less than $2,000, and be fixed by the county commissioners, with the approval of the State Board of Health, and paid by the counties comprising the districts. The salary of the deputies was to be fixed by the trustees with the approval of the district health officer and paid by the townships. Local boards of health would be done away with by the act, and the health officers succeed to their powers, except as regards the making of regulations; the health officers to have large executive powers, acting under the instructions of the State Board of Health.

None of these bills was enacted into law.

In Vermont it has been proposed to do away with the local health officers and for the State Board of Health to appoint ten full time district officers in their place.

COMMUNICABLE DISEASES

The primary object of the establishment of boards of health was the prevention of communicable diseases, particularly the more serious and spectacular outbreaks, and though the modern health department is far from considering this its sole function, it is still its most important one. In our present scheme of public health administration most of the daily routine work in managing the ordinary communicable diseases falls on the local health officials. Some one near the spot must visit the infected premises, investigate, get the history, establish isolation, placard, disinfect or do whatever else is considered necessary. Nevertheless, the state department can, and should, do a great deal, and it sometimes keeps in close touch with all the details. Some of the principal features of the relation of each state health department to communicable diseases are shown in Table 4.

REPORTS OF COMMUNICABLE DISEASES

The first step, and the most essential step, in the control of communicable disease, is its proper registration, and here the state department can do much. First of all, a morbidity registration law is necessary, and this the department should secure. Every state in the Union has some sort of law of this kind, though they vary greatly in many respects. In many of these details we have little interest in this connection. They may be found compiled in a recent bulletin of the Public Health Service (U. S. Public Health Service, Bulletins 45 and 63). Several things are, however, of interest. One of these is uniformity. To encourage uniformity a model morbidity law was approved June 16, 1913, by a conference of the state health authorities and the United States public health service. This has been adopted as "rules" of the state board of health of Florida, Kansas and South Carolina, and many of its provisions in Mississippi and Ohio.

While it is readily admitted that, for the convenience of everybody concerned, there should be uniform procedures for the control of communicable diseases over the whole of each state, it is very undesirable, at the present time, that we should have uniform laws on this subject over the whole country. Our knowledge of these diseases and the best means for their control is too limited to warrant any such uniformity. While we do not desire forty-eight different laws, we should do nothing to discourage experimentation on the part of different states. Until our knowledge becomes exact it is best that one state try one plan, and one another, and let the best survive. All of us need to be kept posted as to what is being done and what are the results, and this should be one of the most important functions of the federal government, but it would be a great mistake for any body, or organization, to urge too persistently the premature crystallization into law of the experiments so many are now making in the control of communicable diseases.

There are two types of laws relating to morbidity reports. In one the statute itself specifies the diseases which are to be reported. This is unfortunate, for, with the advance of science, new diseases are sure to be added and it might happen that others may be removed. To be be able to alter such details only by statutory amendment is unwise. The addition to the statute of a blanket clause such as "or other contagious, infectious or communicable disease" is of little value as the question is then left to the courts. The majority of the laws have wisely provided that the state health department may add to the list of notifiable diseases, or is to specify those which are to be so considered. Sometimes, as, recently in Arkansas and New York, the notification of disease is required by regulations of the state department of health made under its broad authority to make rules for the protection of the public health. The best way is for the state department of health to specify the diseases, for no matter what opinion one may have as to the constitutionality or advisibility of delegating to the state department of health unlimited legislative power in regard to public health, probably all will agree that it is both proper and desirable that the department should be given authority to make purely administrative rules specifying what diseases are to be reported, how long isolation is to be maintained, when children may return to school or how a house shall be disinfected.

In Delaware, Florida and Louisiana reports are made directly by the physician to the state health department. In Georgia and in South Carolina, where there is no local health officer, cases are reported to the state department of health, and in New Jersey when they are on dairy farms. In Texas "pestilential" diseases are to be reported by telegraph. In Maine, Maryland, Minnesota (where not reportable to local board), Mississippi, Nebraska, New Hampshire, Oregon, Rhode Island, Utah and Vermont tuberculosis is to be reported to the state health department, and in Rhode Island poliomyelitis and cerebrospinal meningitis. Elsewhere communicable diseases are reportable to the local health department, township, municipal or county. If the state department is to exercise any direct routine control, or is to keep in close touch with the course of the disease, reports must quickly be sent by the local health officials to the state department. In a number of states it is required that this be done "daily," or "immediately," as in Arizona, California, Connecticut, Illinois (first case in locality), Iowa (first case), Kansas, Maryland (outside of Baltimore), Massachusetts, Michigan, Minnesota, Missouri, Montana (typhoid and Rocky Mountain fever), New Hampshire (first case), New York, South Dakota, Utah (typhoid fever) and Wyoming. While the statute requires this, it is by no means always done, and in several of the above named states the reports are made only monthly and poorly at that. Florida, Delaware, Maryland, Massachusetts, Michigan, Minnesota, New York and Pennsylvania (in portions controlled by state health officers) are the only states in which daily reports are received by the state department. In Maine, New Jersey, Pennsylvania, Vermont, Virginia and Wisconsin weekly reports are required, but in most states they are to be made only monthly, though in Ohio they are to be made twice a month, and in West Virginia quarterly

It is perfectly evident that, except for statistical purposes, anything but weekly reports to the state department of health are entirely worthless and that even weekly reports will do little except to call the attention of the department to outbreaks which have already gained a foothold. For the state to exercise any direct and effective control, immediate reports are necessary, and the fact that they are rarely made, shows that the state rarely intends to attempt such direct management of the cases. That monthly reports satisfy most of the states indicates that their state officials are not active in this line of work. The "model" morbidity law requires that reports shall be made "within seven days." It should require either immediate reports, or reports at the end of each calendar week.

If one examines the morbidity reports of the different states it becomes apparent that diseases are poorly reported. Very many states furnish no figures at all and in others they are exceedingly incomplete. The United States Public Health Service included only twenty-seven states in its reports for 1914. It is difficult to measure the accuracy of returns but something can be judged from the case fatality, but it must be remembered that in the states with the poorest morbidity returns the mortality statistics are also incomplete, so that conditions are really worse than they appear on the face. It is evident that much remains to be done by the states to secure good morbidity returns, especially outside of the larger cities.

The state can do much to improve morbidity reports.

1. It can strive to see that some use is made of them. The local officials to whom they are reported should do something besides placing them on file. If that is all that happens physicians should scarcely be blamed if they fail to report. While people may object to being inspected and isolated and disinfected, everything that is done advertises to the public that reports are required, and if physicians forget, the neighbors will remember. But the greater use that is made of reports the less likely the physician will be to forget. Develop and render effective control of communicable diseases and their notification will steadily improve.

2. One reason why cases of communicable diseases are not reported is because they are not recognized. As will be referred to again, the diagnostic laboratory, if properly utilized, is one of the most important aids to effective morbidity registration.

3. The state health department can, through its educational bureau, do much, directly and indirectly, to stimulate notification. It can also, by correspondence and personal visits, stimulate the local officers to see to the enforcement of the law.

4. Notification should be made as easy and simple as possible. A long list of diseases, the reports of which are never made us of, are discouraging. If a state wishes to seriously study the incidence of cancer, then it is proper to make it a notifiable disease, but there is no sense in putting it in the morbidity law of every state, when it is known beforehand that the reports will merely "be placed on file." Reports by telephone, or by sending laboratory specimens, should be encouraged. When written, the simplest forms should be used. It is for

the health official, not the physician, to obtain administrative or statistical data.

The state health department also has other duties in connection with morbidity reports. Such reports should be transmitted promptly to the United States Public Health Service. This service should be our great sanitary clearing house, where all kinds of information are exchanged. It is of the utmost importance that this service should publish at the earliest possible moment complete morbidity and mortality statistics of the different states and principal cities. This it is attempting to do, but it has to depend on state and local health officials and these, particularly the former, are in duty bound to make every effort to facilitate the compilation made by this service.

Another, and very proper function of the state department of health, is the notification of communities outside its jurisdiction when it has knowledge that cases of communicable disease or infected persons are leaving, or have left for such communities. This reciprocal notification has received special attention in Minnesota.

ADMINISTRATIVE CONTROL

1. **Supervision of All Cases.**—As has been referred to, in only a very few states does the state department of health assume direct management of cases of communicable diseases as routine practice.

In Florida there are scarcely any local health officers, and the State Board of Health assumes direct control of disease practically all over the state except in Jacksonville. For this purpose it has seven full time assistant health officers, two part time agents and four patrolmen.

In Pennsylvania, of course, the state department of health has the entire and direct control of communicable diseases among the 2,500,000 people living in the districts over which the department health officers preside. The department makes the administrative rules to carry out the statutes relating to this subject and issues its orders to its health officer. Every case is immediately reported to the state department, as is also its terminal disinfection, as well as every detail of the health officer's work. All supplies are furnished from the central office which is, by correspondence and otherwise, kept informed as to unusual features or the general progress of the disease.

In Minnesota the division of communicable diseases of the state health department has gradually developed a system of "follow up" which probably results in a more effective control than is found in any other state. This follow up work is not concerned with the cities of Minneapolis, St. Paul, or Duluth, but does apply to about 1,500,000 persons. The local health officers send immediately to the state health department the report cards received from physicians and these, and the report cards accompanying the laboratory specimens, are at once placed on the desk of the director who is thus enabled to keep in close touch with the course of disease. Deaths of unreported cases are at once looked up.

All cases of poliomyelitis and cerebrospinal meningitis are personally visited by an inspector from the department.

In other diseases, except tuberculosis, requests are sent out to the attending physician for additional epidemiologic data which are then filed with the original report. Circulars in regard to the management of the disease are sent to the family in scarlet fever and to the physician in diphtheria and typhoid fever. Release cultures are required in diphtheria in municipalities and within two miles thereof, and are supposed to be taken by the health officer who also placards and supervises disinfection and cleansing, the last of which is insisted on. The health officers are obliged to report to the central office at the termination of each case and in this way the department learns whether the case has been properly managed. In tuberculosis increasing effort is made to secure reports, especially from institutions. The health officer is asked to look up families. Literature is sent to families. Discharged cases are looked up. This follow up work was begun in 1912 and has become increasingly effective.

In Delaware, the physicians report direct to the state health officer who looks after all the details of control either himself or by a deputy, but in a state the size of Delaware the state health officer stands in about the position of a county health officer in other states.

In Massachusetts the local health officer, on receipt of a notification from a physician, not only sends it at once to the State Board of Health, but also notifies the state inspector for that district. The latter thus keeps in touch with the disease and, in many instances, at once advises with the physician or the health officer.

2. Control of Outbreaks.—While only two or three states make any pretense of directly controlling the management of all cases of communicable diseases as reported, there is probably not a state department of health which does not consider it one of its duties to assist and advise local authorities, and even to take entire charge of local outbreaks which are of sufficient extent to attract public attention. It is impossible to define to every one's satisfaction what an outbreak, or an epidemic, is, but we all know perfectly what is meant as these terms are popularly employed.

A very considerable number of state health departments make no particular effort to discover, or to intervene, in these outbreaks but only take action, and that advisory only, when they are called on by local officials, or citizens, or when the conditions chance to be brought to their notice. Among states which do more than this and really seek to discover outbreaks by a study of reports, of the daily press, and in other ways, may be mentioned California, Indiana, Kansas, Massachusetts, Minnesota, New Jersey, New York, Ohio, Pennsylvania, Virginia and Wisconsin. Of these perhaps Minnesota, Ohio, Virginia and Pennsylvania have done the most. The epidemiologic investigations of the Minnesota department have been especially thorough and successful. The methods of this department will repay careful study by all who are contemplating an extension of epidemiologic work. Massachusetts has also made exceedingly valuable epidemiologic studies of cerebrospinal meningitis and poliomyelitis.

When the state health department undertakes the investigation of local outbreaks this is as far as its activities usually go. The local officers are glad to have the advice and assistance of the state officials and proceed to carry out their directions. Sometimes, however, friction arises and, as has been shown on another page, the state department in many states is authorized to take charge of local affairs, sometimes collecting the cost from the community and sometimes not. This, however, is in practice a very unusual procedure. Even to threaten to do so is unusual, and the threat usually brings the local officials to a sense of their duties.

Practically all the state health departments are authorized to investigate outbreaks of disease and study its causes. As is the case with a number of other laws, the Massachusetts statute of 1869 has been copied sometimes exactly, and sometimes with variations, by many other states. It reads as follows:

"Said board shall , . . make sanitary investigations, and inquiries relative to the causes of disease and especially of epidemics. . . ."

In some states as Kansas, Louisiana, Maryland, Minnesota, New Jersey, New York and Texas, the state officials are authorized to enter premises, or to require information from corporations and others as in Kansas, or to settle questions of diagnosis, as in Alabama, Louisiana, Maryland, New Hampshire, Wisconsin and Washington.

The authority for the intervention of the state in the local investigation and control of communicable diseases, is to be found in the general grant of executive power to the state health department, in its rule making power, and in specific authority to take charge of local affairs, all of which have previously been referred to.

EMERGENCY FUND

In a number of states a fund is provided which is to be used only in an emergency. The theory is that it is to be employed only during an exceedingly severe or extensive outbreak, or when urgent measures are needed to prevent the introduction or spread of some exotic disease, as plague, cholera or yellow fever. Thus in Connecticut it is specified that it is to be used only against cholera and yellow fever. California and New York each have a fund of $100,000. Indiana and Pennsylvania $50,000; Alabama, Kentucky, Maryland, Mississippi and Tennessee, $10,000; Rhode Island and South Carolina, $7,000; Colorado, Connecticut, Kansas, Louisiana, Nebraska, New Hampshire, North Carolina and Oregon, $5,000; Illinois, $3,000; Maine, $2,000; and Ohio, $1,000. In Connecticut more money is available on unanimous approval of the State Board of Health and the governor, and in Ohio on approval of the governor, attorney general, auditor and chairman of the finance committee of the house and senate. In New Jersey no sum is named, but funds are available if action is approved by the governor, the comptroller and the treasurer of the state. It sometimes happens, as in Kansas, that this fund has been employed for what might be considered ordinary uses, as supplying antitoxin. Usually, however, these amounts are not drawn on except in great emergencies.

STATE REGULATIONS FOR MANAGEMENT OF COMMUNICABLE DISEASES

The authority to make administrative rules in regard to the communicable diseases is one of the prerogatives of the state health department. As is shown in Table 4, nearly every department possesses such power. Most of them have made use of it and have made sets of rules governing the health officer, the physician and the public. It is quite desirable that this should be so, for it is only in this way that elasticity can be secured and administration kept abreast of the progress of sanitary science. Many of the rules, as we find them, are antiquated or illogical, but statutes would be worse, rather than better, and more difficult to change. A careful compilation, analysis and discussion of existing regulations in the different states would be exceedingly useful, but is, of course, far outside the scope of this report. Such a discussion may be found in Public Health Bulletin 62 of the U. S. Public Health Service.

SPECIFIC ACTIVITIES

While a consideration of the varying details of the routine measures for the control of the common contagious diseases, as diphtheria and scarlet fever, is not here attempted, reference is made to a number of diseases in which unusual methods are employed, or of which states are only beginning to take cognizance, or to which, for other reasons, it was thought that it might be interesting to refer.

Typhoid Fever

Typhoid is the most serious of our acute infectious diseases, attacking as it so often does, young adults, and disqualifying for work for so long a time. In the northeastern part of the country it is not so prevalent as formerly, and indeed it is probably decreasing generally, but it is still very prevalent over most of the South and in certain parts of the Middle and Far West.

There are many ways in which the state health department can, and does, attempt to lessen this disease. Until quite recently the chief means was by improvement of public water supplies. The gross pollution of a large proportion of our water supplies forcefully, and at times, dramatically, called attention to this cause, and a number of states, of which Massachusetts was the leader, have, usually through the state department of health, brought about a vast improvement in the purity of municipal water supplies and a corresponding decrease in the typhoid death rate. In 1908, Whipple estimated that 40 per cent. of the typhoid fever in our cities was due to polluted water. At the present time, although there are too many polluted supplies, these play relatively a smaller part than formerly in the causation of the disease. Outside of water-borne infection and occasional milk outbreaks, contact and fly-borne infection are now considered the chief factors. These factors, however, are not operative except in the presence of defective excreta disposal. The privy vault, or what is worse, no method of disposal at all, is the real underlying cause of typhoid fever at the present time. Hence the people of the rural South are perhaps the worst sufferers.

Probably the Virginia health department has done more than any other state department to combat typhoid fever. The assistant commissioner, independently and in conjunction with the Richmond health department, and with the United States Public Health Service, has been of the greatest service in working out the causes and modes of prevention of typhoid fever in the South. Besides doing much to determine the modes in which the disease is commonly spread in the state, the department has for several years carried on an active campaign. In connection with hookworm work, excreta disposal has been constantly preached, reasonable methods have been advised, outbreaks are systematically investigated, intensive investigations have been carried on in connection with the federal government. The excellent educational work of the department has given due attention to this disease. Whenever a local increase is noted an inspector is sent to investigate, lecture, talk against foul privies and flies, distribute literature and advocate vaccination. In the other southern states the men engaged in hookworm work give more or less instruction in regard to typhoid fever, though it is likely to be less than more. However, the hookworm campaign, even if typhoid fever is not mentioned, cannot help but be a factor in its elimination. In Minnesota, too, active epidemiologic work by means of investigations, direct control of cases, education and water supervision has been carried on for several years with excellent results. Washington has carried on a good deal of active educational and epidemiologic work. The spectacular freeing of Yakima was largely brought about through the efforts of the State Board of Health. The board had made a careful study of conditions and, in order to bring home the facts to the people and arouse their interest, the United States Public Health Service was invited to cooperate. The sanitary awakening which followed this joint survey is well known. The Public Health Service has conducted similar intensive campaigns in Alabama, Indiana, Iowa, Kansas, Maryland, Mississippi, North Carolina and West Virginia, always in cooperation with the state health department and with its active assistance in Indiana, Maryland, Mississippi and North Carolina.

In Pennsylvania, too, the state department of health not only seeks to direct the control of each case, but makes special effort to see that those living on water-sheds used for public supplies do no harm. Besides Pennsylvania, daily reports of the disease are received in several other states by the state department, and in Maryland, Massachusetts and Utah literature is sent to the patient, and in Maryland disinfectants are furnished on request by the physician.

Leprosy

Most state, as well as municipal, health officials, seem ready to evade responsibility for this disease. Only two states have provided hospitals for isolation, namely Louisiana and Massachusetts. Neither institution is under the control of the department of health, though in Massachusetts there is talk of transferring it to that department. Another state, Minnesota, investigates and keeps run of the few cases in a way, but has provided no place for isolation. In California the law requires isolation in a separate building, and the state health department sees that it is enforced. In most states isolation is urged, but, of course, state health officials do what they can to render the conditions as little onerous as possible. In some places cases are kept in an ordinary isolation hospital. In New York, South Carolina and Texas, apparently no effort is made to isolate.

Hookworm Infection

The state health department of Florida was the first to take action against hookworm infection. The publications of Stiles and the results of the work of Ashford in Porto Rico called to this subject the attention of health officers in the South and the health department of Florida began an investigation of the prevalence of the disease in that state and a report was published in 1906. In 1908 an article on the. subject by Dr. Byrd of the department was sent to every teacher in the state. In 1909 an aggressive campaign was begun by sending men into the different counties to teach by means of lectures, demonstrations and treatment, the facts about the disease. It was intended to reach every community in the county in this way. The state also offered to pay the family physician for treating indigent cases if done according to directions. This latter plan was followed only a short time, but dispensaries were opened instead. The laboratory of the board was utilized to make the fecal examinations and still does a large amount of this work. From October 12, 1909, to December 31, 1910, $8,737.45 was expended. The campaign was carried on more or less extensively until 1913, when it was abandoned, the laboratory, however, continuing to make large numbers of examinations for physicians. Mississippi also made an appropriation of $8,000 in 1910 to undertake "rural sanitation," but before the work was fairly started arrangements were made to work with the Rockefeller Commission as was done in other states.

The Rockefeller Sanitary Commission was organized October 26, 1909, and following, to a considerable extent, the work of the Florida State Board of Health, began active operations against hookworm infection in January, 1910.

It was the intention of the commission to work at the invitation of, and in cooperation with, state departments of health. Hookworm infection is found widely spread in twelve states in the South and in eleven of these, all except Florida, the commission has been actively engaged. Infection has been demonstrated occasionally in other states, but except in those mentioned it seems to be of little importance. In all the twelve states named it is considered by nearly all health officials to be a very great injury to health and a handicap to human endeavor.

The purpose of the commission was:

1. To demonstrate infection.
2. To determine the degree of infection by counties.
3. To determine the amount of soil pollution by counties.
4. To carry on an educational campaign in each county.
5. To help physicians to recognize and cure the disease.
6. To induce medical schools to teach intestinal parasitology.
7. To enlist the services of the press.

8. To have the principles of prevention taught in the schools.

9. By intensive work to make at least one community serve as an example of successful control..

10. To lay the foundations for an efficient state and local organization.

The commission is supposed to work through the state board of health. The "director of rural sanitation," or some like named officer, is nominated by the state board of health, but is appointed by the commission and is an officer of the state department. Under him are a number of field workers, who do the lecturing and investigating, and operate the dispensaries and are assisted by several microscopists for making diagnoses. There are, of course, one or more stenographers or clerks. All these are theoretically employees of the state health department, but are practically appointees of the commission. Their salaries are paid by the state department, but most of the funds are supplied by the commission which makes quarterly remittances to the state health department. The state usually pays office expenses and in some states a part of the salaries of the director. The counties make an appropriation averaging from $100 to $300.

Since the above was written the International Health Commission, the successor of the Rockefeller Sanitary Commission, has withdrawn from this undertaking in most of the states. It completed its work as planned, in the other states, in June, 1915. In several of the states a new type of intensive work is now being undertaken in one or more small communities by which it is proposed to attempt by individual effort to better the sanitary conditions of each family and develop an appreciation of the value of public health work.

In this newer phase of the undertaking the "unit," or working force, consists of a field director' and three lay assistants, one of whom is a microscopist. This unit works in some rural community for three or four months until every dwelling is visited and the inhabitants examined. Personal effort is made in every case to cure infected persons, and what is more important to secure, if possible, a proper disposal of human excreta. Personal instruction is given in health matters, most of the emphasis being laid on the feces-borne diseases. Local appropriations are asked for and also state aid. At present, September, 1915, three units are operating in Virginia, two in South Carolina, two in Mississippi, one in Louisiana and Kentucky, and three in Tennessee. In Kentucky and Mississippi the expense is borne entirely by the commission. In Virginia the state appropriates $3,800. In South Carolina the state pays half the cost of one unit. In Louisiana the state and the commission share the expense not assumed by the county. In Tennessee the state appropriates $1,800 for each of the three units. The cost of a unit for a year is about $4,800.

It appears to an outsider that while the Commission nominally acts through the state health department it really carries on its work as an independent organization. Indeed it could scarcely be otherwise. It is difficult for an employee to serve two masters. Even when there is, in the main, an excellent understanding, there are likely to be differences on minor matters. Moreover it is scarcely conceivable that a successful campaign, along definite lines, for definite purposes, could be carried on under eleven different authorities. That definite and fairly uniform results have been attained in different states seems to be due to centralized organization and direction.

The last report of the Rockefeller Sanitary Commission states that a survey was made in 596 counties in eleven states. 548,992 children were examined of whom 39 per cent. were infected. 250,680 farms were inspected and on 125,584 no privies were found. Educational work was carried on in 579 counties, around the dispensary as a center, where 1,273,850 persons were examined and 440,390 were treated.

The Commission through its workers has brought health to thousands, has demonstrated an important preventable disease, has shown how its cause can be removed and has brought about a marked sanitary improvement in countless dwellings and schools, things certainly worth while. Nevertheless the incidental and indirect results of the campaign will probably prove to be of far greater consequence. The great results of the work would appear to be the demonstration to the press and to the leaders of public opinion, and also to the masses of the people of the South, that great and immediate results can be obtained by the application of the principles of scientific medicine through the medium of an organized public health service made possible by adequate appropriations.

Great as these benefits are there are many who feel that it is dangerous to have outside agencies initiate and direct the activities of state and municipal officials. There is scarcely a health officer who has not had assistance from one private organization or another. Yet there is probably not a health officer who is not in constant fear that some group of over-enthusiastic, and perhaps ill-advised, reformers, may not, by outside pressure, bring about a onesided diversion of the funds of his department, perhaps to lines of work of problematical value. While officials, owing sometimes to failure to keep abreast of scientific progress, are partly responsible for these suggestions from without, there is no degree of efficiency which will surely protect against the danger of earnest reformers who have not stopped to determine the scientific basis of their reforms.

Malaria

While there is probably no state in the country in which cases of malaria do not sometimes occur, it is only in the warmer and moister portions that the disease becomes a serious burden. The recent surveys made by the Public Health Service show that in many states it is an extremely prevalent disease, causing thousands and tens of thousands of cases. In a small manufacturing village in the South it was stated by the health officer that during the preceding summer 45 per cent. of the population had chills and fever. Of 1,666 blood smears collected indiscriminately at a locality in another southern state, 40 per cent. were positive for malaria. There is no community which cannot afford to spend the money needed to check this disease. Nevertheless little systematic work seems to have been done by the states thus far. The disease is notifiable in California, Florida, Kansas, Mississippi, New Jersey, Ohio, Pennsylvania and South Carolina. In Pennsylvania it is placarded, but probably to prevent the notification of typhoid fever as malaria so as to avoid the placard. Mississippi appears to be the only state in which the notification law is much more than a dead letter. Our knowledge of the prevalence of the disease is largely due to the survey carried on by Dr. von Ezdorf of the Public Health Service. Surveys have been carried on by the service in Alabama, Arkansas, Georgia, Mississippi, North Carolina, South Carolina and Virginia, which included taking indices in all the states except Georgia. Morbidity reports have also been collected in Alabama, Arkansas, Florida, Kentucky, Louisiana, Mississippi, North Carolina, South Carolina and Tennessee. During these investigations Dr. von Ezdorf has also done more or less educational work.

All of the states badly infected, as well as some of those where it is of less consequence, take cognizance of malaria in the educational work of the health department. Special bulletins on the disease are frequently issued and in Virginia a "Catechism on Malaria" has been prepared for use in the schools. The disease also receives attention in the monthly bulletins, in the press service and in the exhibits. In some states the field workers in the hookworm campaign have given considerable attention to this disease especially in Arkansas, Mississippi, North Carolina and Virginia. In the latter state the engineer has advised in regard to drainage operations. Little or no really effective intensive work appears to have been done.

Malaria certainly places a tremendous burden on the people where it prevails extensively and it is surprising that so little has been accomplished by state officials for its control. The means for controlling the disease are well known, and their efficiency and practicability have been demonstrated all over the world, but still the officials of this country are doing little or nothing. Some of the means of control are applicable in every community and all are possible in many communities. To determine just where malaria prevails is the first step and this the United States Public Health Service is doing, usually with the assistance and support of state and local health officials. Drainage and oiling, the screening of houses, the location of houses at a distance from breeding places and the prophylactic and curative use of quinine, are the chief prophylactic measures. Certainly every state should see that these facts are forcibly impressed on every individual living in a malarial region. Usually more than general education is needed. Intensive work is required such as has been carried on for typhoid fever in Washington and Virginia, and for hookworm infection by the Rockefeller Commission. The disease should be made reportable and abundant opportunity offered for laboratory diagnosis. North Carolina and Virginia and perhaps some other states are planning for just such work.

Rocky Mountain Fever

Cases of Rocky Mountain Spotted Fever have been reported from practically all of the Rocky Mountain States, including Arizona, California, Colorado, Idaho, Montana, Nevada, Oregon, Utah, Washington and Wyoming.

In Montana it is found in two valleys, namely the Bitter Root Valley and the Clarke's Fork Valley. In the Clarke's Fork Valley the type is very mild, but in the Bitter Root Valley assumes a malignant form.

The Montana State Board of Health began a series of investigations in 1902, employing skilled observers from various parts of the country and culminating in the demonstration of the mode of transmission of this disease by Ricketts in 1907. The United States Public Health Service has greatly assisted in these investigations and has had several workers in the field. Montana at present has a Board of Entomology consisting of the Secretary of the State Board of Health, the State Entomologist and the State Veterinarian, which is carrying on this work. In 1913 the sum of about $5,000 was expended. The board above referred to can make rules in regard to insects, subject to approval by the State Board of Health, and has made rules in regard to the dipping of animals to free them from the ticks which transmit the disease. The State Board of Health has distributed a good deal of literature in regard to the fever and the means of preventing it.

The other mountain states are less infected and the disease is generally milder and the health officials appear to be taking little if any action other than to record cases.

Cerebrospinal Meningitis

The State Board of Health of Massachusetts made a valuable contribution to our knowledge of this disease in 1898, based on epidemiological and pathological studies. During outbreaks most state health officers assist in diagnosis and control and a number of states, namely, Georgia, Kansas, Massachusetts, Oklahoma, Rhode Island, South Carolina and Texas, distribute sera, and Alabama, Arkansas, California, Connecticut, Iowa, Kansas, Louisiana, Minnesota, Oklahoma, South Carolina, South Dakota, Tennessee, Texas, Utah and Washington provide laboratory diagnosis.

During the severe outbreak in the Southwest in 1911-1912, several states took an active part in control. In Texas the bacteriologist was sent out to demonstrate diagnostic methods and he made large numbers of examinations of spinal fluid and vaccinated 800 to 900 persons. Most of the work in combating the outbreak was done by Dr. von Ezdorf of the Public Health Service and Dr. Sophian of the Rockefeller Institute.

The Commissioner of Health in Oklahoma, fearing the invasion of that state, sent representatives to Texas to study methods and later, a school of instruction for health officers was held, and literature was distributed to the laity and physicians. Serum obtained from the state department was distributed at the expense of the counties.

When the disease invaded Kansas the Health Department of that state distributed serum freely at its own expense, using its emergency fund for that purpose.

Poliomyelitis

Health officials have as yet been able to accomplish little or nothing in the prevention of this disease, as at present we know nothing definitely, but have only theories, as to its mode of transmission under natural conditions. Nevertheless ordinary methods of isolation and disinfection have been very generally insisted on in recent years and have been advised by state health officials. Meanwhile various agencies, the Public Health Service, state health departments, local health officials, and institutions, like the Rockefeller Institute, have done much in the study of the nature and mode of transmission of the disease. In these researches the states have taken a prominent part. An account of the outbreak in Vermont was published by the State Board of Health in 1904. In 1910 Massachusetts appropriated $5,000, $10,000 in 1911, and $5,000 in 1912 for the study of the disease. Under these grants extensive epidemiological studies were made and much experimental work was done. Valuable studies were also early made and published by Dr. Hill of the State Health Department of Minnesota, and later by the health department in Washington. Good experimental work was done in the State Laboratory in California. The Indiana State Board of Health in 1912 spent a considerable sum in following up and studying cases. The Rhode Island legislature appropriated $2,000 in 1911 for studying the disease, but there have been few cases since. In Minnesota every case is seen by an officer of the State Board. In Kansas, too, cases are investigated and followed up. Recently $25,000 from an unpublished source has been placed in the hands of the health department of Vermont for this purpose.

Mediterranean Fever

This disease has been imported and is found among the goats in the southwestern part of the United States and some cases have occurred among human beings. It has been studied by Major Russell, U. S. A., in conjunction with the State Health Department of Arizona. This board has also issued a circular on the subject.

Smallpox

Nearly every state health department is obliged to devote a great deal of time to this disease. Though generally of an exceedingly mild type, it has been very prevalent during the past eighteen years and state health officials are continually called on to assist in diagnosis or settle disputes between local health officers and physicians. The mildness of the type has caused a great deal of trouble in this respect. Some state executives have found their time so taken up in this way that they have been obliged to refuse these calls upon them.

Every state officer, of course knows full well, that all this trouble with smallpox is absolutely unnecessary and that with the proper vaccination of the people the disease would become a negligible quantity. In efforts at education these officials have not been remiss. The amount of vaccination literature which has been put out is very large and probably every state has taken a share in its distribution.

Some officials have become discouraged, both by the failure to secure general vaccination, and by the very common failure of isolation. A very considerable number, perhaps a considerable majority, have confessed the belief that the only solution is for the authorities to give up isolation and let the people make their choice between vaccination and smallpox, hoping in this way to induce them to accept the former. Moreover, it is argued that it is very unjust that the vaccinated, who do not have the disease, should bear the expense of caring for the unvaccinated when they contract it. Few state health officers have, however, had the courage to put these views into practice, even partially. In North and

South Carolina the State Board of Health advises against isolation, but in the larger communities it is generally insisted on by the public, though in the county it frequently is not. In North Carolina, it is said that in some instances non-isolation has resulted in the prompt vaccination of most of the inhabitants. In South Carolina, the State Board of Health has complete executive authority in unincorporated territory and does not isolate, but does vaccinate, as it has authority to do. In Minnesota, Montana and South Dakota strict quarantine is not approved of by the state health department but the houses are placarded, though vaccinated members of the family may come and go.

The importance of vaccination is so great that health officials have generally tried to secure it by legislation. Vaccination laws are on the statute books of nearly every state. An excellent summary and discussion may be found in a bulletin (No. 52) of the United States Public Health Service. It is stated that Kentucky and New Mexico are the only states which have laws requiring the vaccination of the inhabitants. In New Mexico nothing is done by the state to enforce the law, and how unsuccessful it has been in Kentucky is shown by the fact that the secretary of the State Board of Health estimated, in 1911, that from 50 to 90 per cent. of the people in the different counties had never been vaccinated, and that in the preceding thirteen years there had been over 21,000 cases of smallpox. Vaccination of schoolchildren is required by the statutes of twenty-two states and by the rules of the state health department of five others. These laws are rarely enforced except in the larger cities, and by no means always then. In very many states the laws provide for compulsory vaccination in the presence of outbreaks.

A number of states have provided for the distribution of smallpox vaccine. This is the case in Connecticut, Florida, Georgia, Iowa, Kentucky, Massachusetts, Oklahoma, Oregon, Pennsylvania, South Carolina, Virginia, West Virginia and Wisconsin. It is not free in all of these, though it is in Florida, Georgia, Massachusetts, South Carolina and West Virginia. Usually the amount distributed is small, not nearly enough to vaccinate all the children born, but in Massachusetts, in 1913, there were given out 112,039 tubes; in Virginia, 42,843, and in South Carolina, in 1913, 97,021. In Massachusetts the vaccine is made by the state health department.

Plague

For some time the State Board of Health of California spent large sums and did much to combat plague, especially to eradicate it from ground squirrels. Of late the actual work of control has been turned over to the United States Public Health Service, which also appropriates $15,000 annually. The expenditures of the state board of health for this purpose during the year ending June 30, 1914, were $39,256.52. The city of San Francisco, as well as many other communities, are also spending large sums. The state has enacted stringent laws for the extermination of rodents, making it incumbent on owners of property to do this, authorizing local governments to do it, and also the State Board of Health, and making the cost a lien on the property.

In Washington the health department has, in the past, furnished some inspectors, but done little plague work. As in California, the execution

of antiplague measures is with the Public Health Service. The city of
Seattle, however, bears most of the expense of rat proofing, which is
done under the direction of the federal officers. To prevent the spread of
the infection of other ports within the state, for which the Public Health
Service has no authority, the State Board of Health appoints the federal
officers as state inspectors.

In Louisiana, as on the Pacific Coast, the Public Health Service is
actually doing the work of plague eradication though the State Board
of Health appropriated $3,000 and loaned $20,000.

In Texas in February, 1915, the sum of $25,000 was appropriated for
the study and eradication of plague, but no information is available as to
its expenditure.

On the appearance of the plague in Porto Rico and Cuba, the Public
Health Service advised that a rat survey should be made all along the
Atlantic and Gulf coasts. This was done in a number of cities, and also
by the state departments of health in Florida, Louisiana and Texas.

Trachoma

A report by Dr. Swarts, at the last Conference of State and Provincial
Boards of Health, brings up-to-date information in regard to the acivities
of the states concerning this disease. At the present time it is reportable
in Arizona, Arkansas, California, Delaware, Illinois, Indiana, Kansas,
Kentucky, Louisiana, Maine, Massachusetts, Michigan, Minnesota, Montana, North Dakota, Ohio, Oregon, Pennsylvania, Rhode Island, South
Carolina, South Dakota, Texas, Utah, Vermont and Wisconsin. However,
the disease is not well reported, owing in a large part, at least, to the
difficulty of its recognition except by those who have had considerable
experience in its diagnosis. No idea of the prevalence of the disease
can be obtained from published reports of notified cases. The surveys
which have been undertaken by the United States Public Health Service,
often at the request of the state health officials, in Georgia, Kentucky,
Minnesota, South Carolina, Virginia and West Virginia, as well as on
several Indian reservations, usually demonstrate more of the disease
than was suspected.

Very little is done by any state health department to control the
disease. In a few states, circulars on the subject have been issued. In
Indiana, when cases are reported to the State Board of Health, letters
of advice are sent to the family, and the county health officer is directed
to follow up the patients and see that they are treated. Isolation is
required unless the case is under treatment. In Kentucky the state has
cooperated in the survey by the public health officials and local effort,
under the auspices of the Women's Christian Temperance Union Settlement School, has shown how much effective work can be done by a
traveling clinic, after the manner of the hookworm clinics. The Ohio
State Board of Health cooperated with the state commissioner for the
blind in the installation of special eye nurses in certain infected localities.
In other places, certain large corporations have carried on curative
and preventive work among their employees. In Pennsylvania, in some
instances of local prevalence, the state health department has succeeded
in having a trained oculist placed in charge. In Virginia a trachoma

hospital is maintained at Coeburn, for which the town furnishes the building, the state appropriates $100 per month, and the Public Health Service does the rest.

Venereal Diseases

Very little that is effective is being done by the states in the prevention of venereal diseases. The notification of these diseases has not met with much favor. They are notifiable in California, Indiana, Iowa, Kansas, Louisiana, Michigan, Utah, Vermont and Wisconsin, and perhaps in a few other states, but very few cases are reported. The best way of getting reports at present is probably by means of laboratory diagnosis. At least twenty-three states, as shown in Table 5, offer to make examinations for the gonococcus, and fourteen offer the Wassermann test for syphilis.

Quite a number of states forbid the employment of persons with venereal diseases in places where food is handled, but little can be done, under present conditions, in the way of enforcement.

A most drastic law, enacted in Vermont last winter, not only forbids the marriage of persons having gonorrhea or syphilis, but also forbids sexual intercourse for any one who has either disease. The State Board of Health must make and enforce rules for the quarantine and treatment of cases. A previous act provided that the department should furnish free salvarsan.

Tuberculosis

The campaign against tuberculosis, though begun by physicians, has been, to a large extent, carried on by laymen. Much has been done by voluntary organizations composed largely of laymen, with lay executives, though these organizations have often been the results of the efforts of physicians. ·Health departments, both state and municipal, have often followed rather than led. It seems, however, to be clear that the medical profession must continue to show an active interest and initiative, if the steps taken are to be wisely planned from the standpoint of medical science as applied to public health.

For many of the following facts, thanks are due the National Association for the Study and Prevention of Tuberculosis, for allowing examination of their material.

NOTIFICATION

The first step in the control of nearly every communicable disease is its notification. New York City was the pioneer in making tuberculosis a reportable disease, but now this requirement is embodied in the laws, or regulations, of a majority of the states. Special acts requiring reports are found in Colorado, Connecticut, Kansas, Maine, Maryland, Minnesota, Mississippi, Michigan, New Hampshire, New Jersey, New York, North Carolina, Rhode Island, Vermont, and Utah. The disease is specified in the general notification law of Alabama, California, Pennsylvania, Texas, West Virginia and Wisconsin, and in the state department of health regulations of Arizona, Indiana, Illinois, Louisiana, Massachusetts, Montana, Nebraska, Oklahoma, Oregon, South Carolina, Tennessee, Virginia and Washington. Reports are, however, in nearly every state very incomplete, the cases in many states being far below the number of deaths, and in only three or four are they double the deaths or even anywhere near it.

Mere notification accomplishes little unless the cases are really looked after and in some way kept under supervision. In quite a number of states the health department sends out literature to the reported cases, or at least does so when it is not done by the local health officials, but it is doubtful how much good this accomplishes. Some attempt to do more. In Maryland and Rhode Island an effort is made to get histories from the patients, and to keep them supplied with sputum cups and paper napkins, but half the cases are lost sight of. In North Carolina the department is making a vigorous effort to keep in touch with all cases by a system of correspondence. The Pennsylvania health department, of course, keeps the cases under supervision through its system of dispensaries and nurses. Pay patients are not carried. Patients are supplied with cups and napkins, and about 35 per cent. with milk and cotton-seed oil. Milk patients are seen twice a month.

SANATORIA

Historically, the first step taken by the states to control the disease, was the erection of sanatoria for curable cases. The first of these was erected in Massachusetts in 1898. Other states quickly followed until at present only the following are not so provided: Alabama, Arizona, California, Colorado, Florida, Idaho, Illinois, Mississippi, Nevada, New Mexico, Oklahoma, Tennessee, Utah, Washington and Wyoming. Laws providing for sanatoria in Alabama and Florida were passed but none have been erected. In Vermont, though there is no state sanatorium, provision is made, by means of an annual appropriation of $5,000, for the board of indigent patients at a private institution. In some of the states the sanatoria are quite small, occasionally mere camps. While so many states have erected sanatoria, in only three has their management been given to the State Board of Health. Usually a special board is created for this purpose, though in some states, as Alabama, Kansas and Texas, the board of health is represented on the board. In other states, as Iowa and New Hampshire, the management is under a board of control which looks after other state institutions. In North Carolina, Pennsylvania, South Carolina and Virginia, the state health department has full charge of the sanatoria. In Pennsylvania this involved an expenditure of nearly $600,000 in 1914. There are some who do not think that it is advisable for a state health department to be burdened with the care connected with hospital administration, and much prefer that the department should be relieved of all hospital management. There are others, and among them the executives of the departments in North Carolina and Pennsylvania, who feel very strongly the other way. They claim that sanatoria are only one feature in a general scheme for the control of tuberculosis, and that the state department should have control of the entire scheme and hence of the sanatoria. The educating influence of the sanatorium is, by many, considered of more importance than its curative value, and it is claimed that its usefulness, as a means of education, cannot be fully utilized unless it is in the hands of those who are carrying on the educational work, and the state department of health is the proper agency for this. This view is especially insisted on in North Carolina. Perhaps a compromise plan, which has worked well in some municipalities, and may also be found in some states, by which the executive of the health department is a member of the sanatorium board, will ultimately be found to be the best in practice.

HOSPITALS

The large central sanatorium for early cases is now, by many, believed to be not the most important means of controlling the disease. It is thought that it has not produced the anticipated results, either as a curative agent, or in preventive value. The isolation of the more advanced cases, which are more freely discharging bacilli, is more necessary. It is undesirable to isolate these in large institutions, at long distance from their homes, and local hospitals are now urged. The county is suggested as a proper unit, though very often it is better, and more economical, for two or more adjoining counties to combine. Local hospitals may also be utilized for all classes of cases, as well as the more advanced. It may be that without special legislation the counties in some states have authority to erect such hospitals, but this was not learned. In most states they certainly do not have it, and permissive legislation has been secured in California, Illinois, Indiana, Iowa, Kansas, Kentucky, Massachusetts, Michigan, Minnesota, Mississippi, Missouri, New Jersey, New York, Ohio, Texas, Washington and Wisconsin. In Illinois there is a permissive law for cities, and in Massachusetts it is mandatory on cities to establish hospitals for "diseases dangerous to the public health," and tuberculosis has been designated such by the State Board of Health. The state health department is to enforce this law, and plans for hospitals must be approved by it. Not very much has as yet been accomplished in most states, but the state health department in Minnesota hopes, through its authority to compel townships to care for infective cases, to induce the counties generally to undertake the erection of hospitals. At present, August, 1915, according to a note in *The Journal of the American Medical Association,* thirty-one counties have taken advantage of the law. The New Jersey State Board of Health has done much to encourage the establishment of county hospitals, and they have been built in fourteen of the twenty-one counties, and others will soon follow. The New York health department has carried on vigorous campaigns in counties where the question of erecting a hospital has been referred to popular vote as is provided by law. In thirty-one out of fifty-seven counties they have already been provided for. The Ohio State Board of Health is strongly urging county hospitals, but as yet only three have been established. In Washington, two or three county hospitals are under way, and here, as in Massachusetts, the plans must be approved by the state health department.

DISPENSARIES

Another essential for the discovery and management of cases of tuberculosis is the dispensary. Its chief function is the diagnosis of the disease, the distribution of patients suitable for sanatoria and hospitals, and, most important, the entrance into the homes by its instructive visiting nurses. There should be enough of these so that they will be easily accessible to every one. As yet the states have done little toward their establishment. The Pennsylvania State Department of Health maintains a dispensary in every county, 114 in all.. About 120 nurses are employed in these dispensaries, in addition to the physicians in attendance. In California, Massachusetts and New York, the state health department is to supervise dispensaries, but until recently little was done. In Massachusetts the law requires dispensaries in every city or township of 10,000 inhabitants, and a recent act places their supervision under the state health department. All of the cities and towns are now so provided. The New York department desires a dispensary with a nurse in every town, all under local management. At present there are about 150 in the state, but is impossible to find physicians capable of conducting them properly. They are rarely supplied with nurses.

NURSES

The visiting nurse is one of the most important factors in the fight against tuberculosis. She not only goes into the family and shows the patient how to live, but she finds other cases not before recognized, and, what is better, finds the children in tuberculous families and helps to save them. She also inspects and records the housing, sanitation, family dietary, etc., and advises how to correct evils that lie at the root of the family ill health. Such nurses are very generally found in our cities, but are rare indeed in the country. With the exception of Pennsylvania, few states have made any attempt to see that they are provided. The Florida state health officer has recently undertaken to substitute for nurses other women visitors, who shall do what nurses do in our northern states. Three have been engaged at $100 per month and twenty are proposed. It is difficult to see in what way such untrained women are superior to the graduate nurse. On the contrary, it would appear that a nursing training renders such a visitor more welcome and more efficient. New York has used nurses for its county hospital campaigns to discover cases and work up public interest. It is proposed in the future to employ them to supervise and standardize the work of the local dispensary nurses. The Ohio health department maintains a supervising nurse to supervise the eighty-nine local nurses engaged in tuberculosis work in the state. In Virginia one nurse is employed.

EDUCATION

Education of the people as to the nature, prevention and cure of tuberculosis, it is believed, must in most states be pushed before it is possible to secure the necessary laws and funds to do effective work. The distribution of literature is one way of doing this. An immense volume of such material is being distributed by state departments of health and by local health officials, private associations and many other agencies. The traveling exhibit, with its illustrations and lectures, is still considered the most effective means of statewide education. The feeling is growing with many that a general health exhibit is more successful than one devoted to a special subject. Still many others believe in specialized campaigns. Tuberculosis exhibits are now shown in Iowa, Maryland, New Jersey, Pennsylvania, Rhode Island, Vermont, West Virginia and

Wisconsin, and were formerly in California, Kansas, Washington and other states. Formerly, a great deal of this educational work was done by voluntary associations and special commissions, but there is a marked tendency for it to be taken over by state health departments.

The present tendency, too, seems to be to shift from the state to the cities, townships and counties, as far as possible, the management and financial burden of tuberculosis prevention. The state has still many things to do, and one of these is to stimulate the local authorities to activity. It must be confessed that in this most state health departments have been negligent. The voluntary tuberculosis associations have been more active in many states than have the officials. In all such movements it is the function of voluntary associations to pave the way only. The government must take up the work. Some states are doing this and striving to develop local interest, stimulate local health officers, and secure local dispensaries, nurses and hospitals. Among states which are making such an effort are California, Indiana, Kansas, Massachusetts, Michigan, Minnesota, New Jersey, New York, North Carolina, Ohio, Vermont and West Virginia.

STATE BOARD OF HEALTH WORK

Tuberculosis is one of the communicable diseases and, though the most important one, there seems to be no good reason why its supervision should require a separate bureau in the state health department. Indeed, in order that the activities of the department may be distributed properly among all diseases, and undue prominence be given to none, it is better not to have a separate tuberculosis bureau. This is the more important in that popular education as present plays such an important part in the work, and popular education should not be onesided. There is a tendency, on account of the importance of the subject, to establish a separate division in the state health department for the control of tuberculosis. Thus, in California, there is such a division with a chief at $3,000 and a $75,000 appropriation for the biennial period. It is occupied with the supervision of hospitals, sanatoria, dispensaries, and the care of tuberculosis in other institutions, and with the collection of morbidity and mortality statistics. In Massachusetts the work is done chiefly by the district inspectors of the department. They are to inspect hospitals and dispensaries, and formerly, when they had charge of the sanitation of factories, they did much in searching for cases of the disease, as well as in improving the sanitary condition of the establishments. They also investigate a large number of cases that are reported to them as endangering the public health. Tuberculosis surveys have been made in several communities. In Minnesota the epidemiologic division is developing a system of following up and searching out cases, using local health officers as well as it can, just as it does in the acute contagious diseases. The valuable and well-known county surveys by Lampson and Burns were among the activities of this department. The new organization of the state health department in New York provided a division of tuberculosis, but owing to lack of funds, it has not been established as yet, though much tuberculosis work has been done by other divisions. The North Carolina State Board of Health has a tuberculosis division, which has charge of the sanatorium as well as of the "correspondence," with reported cases all over the state. The Ohio department has a division of education and tuberculosis with a salary roll aggregating over $12,000 and an appropriation of $22,000. The Pennsylvania health department, spending as it does such large sums on tuberculosis, of necessity has a division for this disease which has charge of the sanatorium and dispensary work, and manages the exhibit.

In Michigan $100,000 has been set aside for tuberculosis for the biennial period. It is being used for intensive work in the counties.

Some states have indicated that the board having charge of the sanatoria should do all the supervisory and other work. This is the case in Connecticut, where the sanatoria board supervises all hospitalization of tuberculosis and distributes literature, but does not conduct a systematic campaign. In Iowa the board of control, besides managing the sanatorium, has an appropriation of $5,000 for educational purposes.

EPIDEMIOLOGY IN THE STATE HEALTH DEPARTMENT

The control of communicable diseases is of such supreme importance, so many problems remain unsolved, so much detail in supervision is necessary, so many outbreaks need investigation, and so often local officials call on the state for advice and assistance that one might expect that even if a state department of health did nothing else, it would employ at least one trained epidemiologist. There is certainly work enough in all but a few of the smallest states to occupy the whole of one man's time, and in most states the time of several men, nevertheless in the majority no such provision is made.

In most of the states all the epidemiologic work that is done, is done by the executive officer as a part of his multifarious duties, and is chiefly confined to a few outbreaks of smallpox. No attempt is made to thoroughly study the numerous outbreaks of typhoid fever that are constantly occurring, or to see that local health officials are properly carrying out routine measures of control.

The Illinois State Board of Health has recently engaged an epidemiologist at $2,400.

In Iowa money was appropriated for an epidemiologist, but for a while no agreement could be reached by the university and the health department as to how it should be expended. Recently an epidemiologist has been engaged by the university. In California the director of the laboratory, as is well known, does some excellent epidemiologic work. In Indiana the assistant secretary devotes some time to communicable diseases, and the general inspectors in Nebraska and Vermont do the same.

In Kansas there has recently been established an epidemiologic division with a director at $2,400, and a stenographer and clerk. Attention is at first being directed to securing improvement in morbidity returns. The division will also carry on "sanitary surveys" by counties, employing four field workers for this.

In Maryland the division of communicable diseases was organized in 1911. The acting chief receives $1,800, and there is an inspector, a stenographer and three clerks, the salary roll amounting to $4,720. A large part of the work has been the collection and compilation of morbidity statistics and the issuing of a monthly bulletin and the distribution of vaccines, disinfectants and prophylactic material for tuberculous patients. Three or four outbreaks a month are investigated. The recent provision for ten deputy state health officers and four deputy engineers will give an excellent opportunity for developing the work of this division.

The state department of health in Michigan for some time has had twenty-five district medical inspectors scattered about the state who are to assist in the suppression of outbreaks of communicable diseases. They receive $10 a day and their expenses, and the small amount of work done is indicated by the fact that only $1,212.90 was expended during the year ending June 30, 1914. There are five clerks in the epidemiologic division of the office force, of whom one is occupied with tuberculosis. Their attention is chiefly taken up with morbidity statistics.

Minnesota has the best organized and most effective epidemiologic division of any state, called the "Division of Preventable Diseases." The director receives $3,500, and the three epidemiologists $2,400 each. There are four stenographers and a clerk. The total expenses for the year ending July 31, 1914, were $14,316.16, but the entire staff was not employed during the whole of this period. The diagnostic laboratories and the Pasteur Institute are a part of this division, but their expenses are not included in the above. The division also has charge of the distribution of typhoid vaccine and diphtheria antitoxin. The division has done a large amount of very thorough and effective work in the investigation and suppression of outbreaks, accounts of which may be found in the reports of the department. Lately special attention has been given to "follow up work," which has been referred to on another page. At first the local health officials looked askance at the work, but they have come to consider it a support and aid, and not as an interference. In 1914 there were received from local health officers 126 requests for assistance.

The newly organized Massachusetts division of communicable diseases consists of a director at $4,000, an acting epidemiologist at $2,000, and five clerks.

The New Jersey department has a bureau of communicable diseases with a chief at $2,750, who is also assistant secretary of the department, and an inspector at $2,120, and three clerks. There are also two sanitary inspectors, so that the work of the bureau is not wholly epidemiologic, though a large part of it is.

In New York the division of communicable diseases has a director at $4,000. He has an assistant who is a physician, two clerks, and two stenographers. It is the intention that the epidemiologic work throughout the state shall be done chiefly by the sanitary supervisors, and the director of this division is in immediate charge of them. In typhoid outbreaks, an engineer is frequently sent with the supervisor. This division receives and tabulates morbidity reports.

The Ohio department of health has a division of communicable diseases, with an epidemiologist at $2,250, an assistant at $1,200, and one stenographer. There are eight medical inspectors living in different parts of the state, as in Michigan, and they are called on somewhat for local work, such as simple diagnoses, etc., but only about $500 a year is used for their fees and travel, so their activities are of small account.

In Pennsylvania the state department of health does a good deal of epidemiologic work, though it has no division expressly for this purpose. The general medical division supervises the local health officers in all their activities, as well as in their routine control of communicable diseases. This is a very large task. The division also supervises the work of the small municipalities, and has charge of school inspection and carries on campaigns for infant mortality. A large part of the communicable disease work of the division is supervising the control of cases by the local health officers, which has already been referred to. Besides this the division investigates numerous outbreaks in different parts of the state. In the investigation of typhoid fever this division and that of engineering are constantly acting together, and a great deal is done by the engineering division itself, often discovering cases through its numerous inspectors on the watersheds of municipal supplies.

In West Virginia the department of health has just engaged an epidemiologist at $2,000.

In Wisconsin there is a bureau of tuberculosis and communicable diseases, with one clerk at present, in the central office, engaged chiefly in collecting morbidity statistics. The field work is done by the five deputy state health officers who, however, probably do not devote more than half their time to this part of their work. There appears to be no real central supervision.

DIAGNOSTIC LABORATORY

The diagnostic laboratory is the most essential part of the machinery for the control of communicable diseases. Without it municipality and state can do nothing. It has been well said that "the laboratory is the handmaid of epidemiology." The laboratory has a three-fold function.

1. It discovers cases of communicable diseases.
2. It keeps the physician acquainted with scientific methods of diagnosis.
3. It teaches that the mild, atypical case is more common than the typical case of the textbooks. This is probably its most important function.

The municipal laboratory preceded the state laboratory, but only by a little. The first state laboratory was established in Rhode Island, Sept. 1, 1894. Now all the states but New Mexico and Wyoming have a laboratory, and in most it is well manned and capable of doing a large amount of work.

It is very desirable that a diagnostic laboratory be as close as possible to the physicians who use it. To accomplish the most in the suppression of disease and to keep the interest of physician and patients, specimens should reach the laboratory promptly, and what is of more importance, reports of results should reach the physician promptly. This is especially important in diphtheria, and though speed is not so essential in the diagnosis of typhoid fever and tuberculosis, it is very annoying to the physician and patient to wait long for a laboratory report. Every considerable city should have its own laboratory, operated by its own health department, but small cities and towns, and the county, must look for outside assistance. With one or two exceptions, state health departments wisely do everything they can to encourage the establishment of local laboratories, but in Vermont, for instance, the state health department does not want local laboratories, for the reason that the department, through its appointed health officers, exercises a quite direct control over communicable diseases, and prefers to control the laboratory work also. It certainly is desirable that the officers who attempt to control communicable diseases should control the laboratory where diagnoses are made. Hence, most state laboratories discourage the sending in of specimens by the physicians of the city where the laboratory is situated and even forbid it, as in Tennessee and Wisconsin. In a few instances counties, or a group of communities, have established their own laboratory. Such cooperative laboratories have been established at two or three points in Massachusetts and in Illinois. Usually, however, it has been the state health department which takes the initiative and attempts to do what it can to give diagnostic facilities to the physicians of the state outside of the great centers of population.

A state laboratory should be as centrally located as possible in relation to railroad traffic. Indeed, the whole health department should be so located. This does not necessarily mean that it should be in the geographic center, though that would usually be the case. In a number of states the laboratory is not well situated, at least as regards mail service. Thus Middletown, Conn., and Morgantown, W. Va., are off the main lines of railroad. In Idaho and Michigan the configuration of land and water is such that a branch laboratory is a necessity. In Nevada transportation is very poor between many parts of the state. Even in a state as well supplied with trunk lines as is Illinois, the laboratory at Springfield, though near the center of the state, is found to be too far removed from either end to offer adequate facilities. Even in a small state like Massachusetts, communication between the western portion and Boston is such that the communities in the west part have found it impossible to depend on the state laboratory at Boston, and have established a sort of cooperative laboratory at Pittsfield. Hence almost all who have had anything to do with state diagnostic laboratories feel that every effort should be made to secure the establishment of as many local municipal laboratories as possible, or that the state should have branch laboratories, or that there should be both.

In California, cities of over 20,000 inhabitants are not allowed to send to the state laboratory specimens for diagnosis. Eight of the nine cities in this class have laboratories, and the other is about to establish one. In addition, the State Board of Health has found it necessary, on account of the size of the state, to establish three branch laboratories of its own, at Sacramento, Fresno and Los Angeles. These, however, are only for the diagnosis of typhoid fever, tuberculosis, diphtheria and malaria. During the year 1914, 6,024 specimens were examined in the central laboratory, and 2,441 in the branch laboratories. Part time men are employed in the branch laboratories at $50 per month. They also administer free antirabic treatment.

In Florida there are no local laboratories, but besides the central laboratory of the State Board of Health at Jacksonville, the department maintains branch laboratories at Tampa, Key West, Miami, Pensacola and Tallahassee. The laboratory buildings at Tampa and Pensacola were built by the State Board of Health at a cost of from $18,000 to $20,000 each. In the other cities the municipalities furnish the rooms. There is a full time bacteriologist, with helpers, in each laboratory. The total expense of operating the laboratories in 1914 was $30,324.46.

In Idaho there is a branch laboratory at the university at Moscow, but, owing to lack of laboratory assistance, very little is done there.

In Illinois, during the summer of 1915, two branch laboratories were established, at Chicago and Mount Vernon.

In Iowa there are seven "auxiliary" laboratories which partake more of the character of municipal laboratories than they do of state laboratories. The rooms and the bacteriologist are supplied by the city, but the bacteriologist must be approved by the State Board of Health, and the central laboratory merely furnishes media and stains. Specimens are received from the city only, none from the surrounding territory. During the two years ending July 1, 1915, 15,716 examinations were made at the central laboratory, and 1,364 at the auxiliary laboratories.

In Michigan a branch laboratory has been established at Houghton in the Upper Peninsula.

In Minnesota there are branch laboratories at Duluth and Mankato. Both are equipped by, and supervised by, the State Board of Health and operated at the expense of the state, but at Duluth the city contributes $300, the water company $300, and the county $600.

In New York, besides the central laboratory in Albany, the department has arranged to have a laboratory in New York City act as its branch laboratory for the southern part of the state. There are ten county laboratories, and twenty-three municipal laboratories outside of New York City, all subject to supervision by the state.

Table 5 shows the states which have established laboratories, how they are controlled, the number of employees, and kinds and amount of work done. As will be seen from Table 10, the cost of operating the laboratory is available in comparatively few states. As will be referred to, the financial statement of most state health departments is very unsatisfactory and little attempt is made to segregate expenditures according to function. As regards the laboratory, a practical difficulty in determining the cost of diagnostic work arises because many bacteriologic laboratories do other work than that of diagnosis, such as chemical work of various kinds, bacteriologic examinations of sewage and milk, the administration of antirabic virus or typhoid vaccine, and the study of outbreaks of communicable diseases, and in some instances there is a division of expense with the university or some municipality.

In quite a number of states the laboratory is not exclusively controlled and operated by the state department of health, and in a few the department of health has little or nothing to do with it.

In Colorado, Louisiana and Maryland the department has some cooperative arrangement with the municipal health department of the city where it is situated. In Colorado the state merely employs a man in the Denver laboratory to make its examinations. In Louisiana, where both the city and the state do a great deal of work, the laboratory is in the municipal building, but the salaries and other expenses are divided between the two departments, in what appears, however, to be a rather complicated manner. The arrangement does not seem to work especially well, as it does not permit of the freedom of planning work which there would be if the departments were separate. In Maryland the state and the city of Baltimore also maintain a cooperative laboratory with apparent success, but it is easy to see how differences of opinion might arise, and different uses for the laboratory might develop, which would interfere with its efficiency. While some economies may be en such a plan of cooperation it would seem that laboratory development would be favored and chance of trouble avoided, if each state would maintain laboratories entirely independent of any municipal connections. The state laboratory ought to occupy a broader field than the city laboratory and especially should be free to take up research, which certainly is not favored by municipal routine.

THE LABORATORY AND THE UNIVERSITY

While there are theoretical and practical objections to the union of state and municipal laboratories, there are certainly very strong reasons for a state laboratory having university connections. The university is the center of scientific knowledge and of the scientific spirit of the territory which it serves. What health officials need more than anything else at the present time (except freedom from politics) is more scientific knowledge and inspiration. It would seem that such ought to be obtained from the university and that it would be worth while to get it, even at considerable cost. But besides a broad scientific outlook, the health department, especially the state health department, needs to do much routine scientific work, and it would seem to be economy to seek its workers at the university. An example of the advantage of such a connection is shown by the relation between the health department of Providence and Brown University. For over fifteen years the department has been allowed to use the services of professors and graduate students, making individual arrangements with them for compensation, for much of its scientific and semiscientific work. This connection, on the one hand, has enabled the department to secure a high class of assistance in an economical manner, and has served to keep it in touch with scientific progress, while it has enabled the university to obtain for its students laboratory material and, what is still more important, practical experience in public health work.

The advantages of a connection between the state health department and the university is so apparent that it has appealed alike to health officials and legislators. Where there is a state university such relationship, at first thought, seems especially natural and easy, though it probably really is less easy. All sorts of arrangements have been made, but it must be confessed that they have not been particularly successful. Every sort of combination is found from one in which there is only the loosest sort of connection, to one to which the university is altogether the dominating partner.

In some states the university does little more than give the state health department house room, while the laboratory staff is appointed and paid by the health department, and the running expenses are borne by the latter. Such an arrangement may be of very great value to each, for being housed in the university gives the staff an opportunity for intercourse with scientific men and permits the university to get material. This is the plan in Arkansas, California, Delaware and Minnesota. In Arkansas the State Board of Health was authorized to establish a hygienic laboratory in connection with the department of chemistry and bacteriology of the medical department of the university. It is to be under the control of the secretary of the State Board of Health. As a matter of fact no funds were provided, so the secretary acts as director and the work is done by medical students for their tuition. In California the director of the laboratory was at first appointed by the university, it is said, for the purpose of keeping the position out of politics, but later the appointment was transferred to the State Board of Health. There is no medical school at Berkeley, where the laboratory is, and the university makes little or no use of the laboratory, though it might easily do so with great advantage to its students. With the demand that there is at the present time for men with a bacteriologic training, there is a splendid opportunity for this university, with its fine situation and the high character of its laboratory staff, to do much needed educational work of this kind for the Pacific Coast and Mountain region.

In Minnesota, at first, the attempt was made by the Board of Health to establish relations with the university by appointing as director the professor of pathology and bacteriology of the university. Friction arose, however, owing as far as can be learned, from a desire on the part of the director that the laboratory should take over administrative duties in regard to communicable diseases, and now the only connection of the laboratory with the university is that the former is housed on the campus.

In some other states, while the state health department bears more or less of the expenses of the laboratory, the university, besides bearing a part of the expense, exercises more or less control by the appointment of the staff or otherwise.

In Arizona the state laboratory is established in connection with the university and is maintained by a special appropriation of $4,500, together with $400 appropriated by the State Board of Health. The work of the laboratory is almost wholly chemical and is chiefly occupied with food control. The diagnostic work, which is done by an assistant, is insignificant. The management of the laboratory is by the regents of the university and the state superintendent of health. As almost nothing is done in connection with disease prevention a fertile source of trouble is removed, and also the chief value of the laboratory is lost.

In Iowa the laboratory is located with the medical department of the university. The professor of bacteriology in the university is by statute made the director of the laboratory. Most of his time is given to the university, and his salary is paid by the university. The assistants are nominated by the director, but appointed by the State Board of Health. The expenses are covered by a special appropriation, but the bills are audited by the executive council, which is a committee of the State Board of Health, composed of four ex officio members of that board. The laboratory is to make such analyses, tests and "other scientific investigations" as are required by the State Board of Health. Serious friction has arisen between the State Board of Health and the university, chiefly because of certain epidemiologic work done by the latter, and especially in connection with the appointment and work of an epidemiologist to be appointed by, and to work under, the direction of the university. The whole trouble here seems to have arisen because of the investigations of outbreaks made by university men or because of advice given on public health matters.

In South Dakota the state health laboratory was established at the university on the same lines as in Iowa, except that the State Board of Health pays one half of the salary of the director, and the appointments and finances are wholly in the hands of the regents of education. The plan seems to have worked well thus far, perhaps because the State Board of Health, because of its meager appropriation, does very little public health work of any kind, and where there is no motion there is no friction.

Another and different arrangement exists in Oklahoma. It is rather difficult to determine just how the control is provided for. The statute reads "the board of health shall establish and maintain a laboratory," and that "it shall be maintained at the university in connection with the department of chemistry and the department of bacteriology." Again, "the board of health shall have supervision by rules and regulations over the work," and then, further, "such work shall be done under the supervision of the professor of chemistry and the professor of bacteriology." The cost is borne by the university.

In other states the laboratory is exclusively a department of the university. This is so in Nevada, where the state hygienic laboratory is established at the university under the management of the board of regents. The professor of bacteriology is the actual director, and the work is done in the university laboratories. A special appropriation of $5,000 has been made each year for the laboratory. There is no organic connection with the State Board of Health.

In North Dakota the management is vested in the trustees of the state university, and the professor of bacteriology and pathology is director and state bacteriologist. There is a special appropriation of $8,000, but the university pays a part of the salaries. There is no control by the State Board of Health, neither does the latter furnish any funds. The laboratory is no more required to do work for the State Board of Health than it is for county superintendents of health or for physicians. Moreover, the trustees are required to collect "sanitary statistics," to do research work, to improve sanitation, and the director is to publish bulletins. Thus the laboratory has much given to it to do which is usually given to the State Board of Health. The State Board of Health is poorly supported and seems perfectly willing to let the university perform functions which properly belong to the health department.

In Utah, also, the laboratory seems to be exclusively a department of the university. The professor of bacteriology and pathology is director. The appointments are made, and the expenses are borne, by the university, though the State Board of Health expends a few hundred dollars for printing, etc.

Another plan, one of cooperative control, has recently been inaugurated in Wisconsin, where the relations of the laboratory, the university and the state department of health have previously been quite strained. The laboratory is now controlled by a board of four, consisting of the director, who is dean of the medical department, the president of the university, the president and the secretary of the State Board of Health. The expenses are borne by the university, and the men are appointed by the university but they are not on the university staff.

In Missouri the State Board of Health maintains a diagnostic laboratory which does the usual work. It seems to be doing it well, though the volume is small, owing to the fact that the department is doing little in the way of communicable diseases control. At the state university there is a department of preventive medicine, with a course required for some students and optional for others. In connection with it is a laboratory. In this laboratory is done the usual diagnostic work, and vaccines are made and sent out. The department publishes bulletins, gives lectures, and attends to a considerable correspondence on public health matters. In a word, the department is doing the same sort of educational work that the State Board of Health is supposed to do. Two departments of the state government are occupying the same field, a condition which affords ample opportunity for the development of future trouble.

Another kind of connection between the State Board of Health and the university is found in Connecticut, Tennessee and West Virginia. In these states there is no statutory provision for a union between laboratory and university. Any arrangement that is made is purely voluntary. In Connecticut, the State Board of Health, with the approval of Wesleyan University, has arranged with Professor Conn to direct its laboratory work, both in bacteriology and chemistry. Graduate students in the department of arts are largely employed as assistants. The board of health considers itself fortunate in having university men of high standing do its work and, on the other hand, the university fully appreciates the advantage in having its students gain practical experience in the relation of the laboratory to the community and in securing such laboratory material as it needs.

The Tennessee Board of Health has made a similar arrangement with the medical department of the university, as has, also, that of West Virginia with the state university at Morgantown. In neither of these states has the arrangement been long enough in operation to permit of any deductions, but in Connecticut, certainly, the results are very satisfactory, as they have been in Providence from the connection between the municipal health department and Brown University.

One reason for the frequent lack of success in cooperation between the health department and the university is doubtless the attempt to provide for it by statute. It is not easy for a legislature to make any such arrangement for dual management. Successful cooperation must grow up naturally, preferably voluntarily, and not be forced from without and arranged by other parties beforehand. Another reason is the temptation to which universities, especially state universities, seem inclined to yield, to take on administrative and executive functions. The university is not content to teach its students and carry on the work of the laboratory, but wants to carry on publicity work of its own throughout the state, to carry on investigations of its own and to give advice on sanitary matters. Such activities cannot fail to bring about more or less of a conflict with the department of health, which also, and more properly, is charged with these same duties. It is confusing to have two agencies engaged in teaching the same things, for they can never do it in exactly the same way. It is bad enough to have private organizations doing public health work which the State Board of Health ought to do, but it is especially likely to make trouble to have a coordinate branch of the government doing it. Another source of difficulty is that in several states, the university, owing to the comparative freedom of the professors from political dictation, their permanency in office and their scientific training, is far more competent to do public health work than is the state board of health. The university men know this and so do the public, and it must even be suspected by the rapidly changing political members of the health department. Successful cooperation, voluntary or involuntary, under such circumstances is very unlikely. The remedy is for the people to wake up and demand that only men of the character and attainments of university men be placed in responsible public health positions. They will then certainly arrange in one way or another to secure university connections. Lastly, successful cooperation is less likely to develop between the medical department, than between the department of arts, and the board of health. In the medical department the students are extremely busy and have no time to assist in the health department laboratory. In the department of arts graduate students in chemistry and bacteriology are often found who are glad to do this, and who do it with profit to themselves and to the health department. In some of the western universities, however, where such a union has more often been attempted, graduate students are not as numerous as in eastern institutions. If the pitfalls are seen they can be avoided, and if the advantages are appreciated, doubtless in the future closer relations will be established between our state health departments and our universities.

The diagnostic laboratory was originally for the purpose of assisting in the diagnosis of diphtheria. Tuberculosis and typhoid fever were soon added and their diagnosis is now provided for in every laboratory. Probably malaria furnishes the next largest number of specimens. The inception of antihookworm work made necessary the examination of feces for intestinal parasites. The diagnosis of cerebrospinal meningitis has, during outbreaks, been of importance. Search for Negri bodies is made in nearly every laboratory. Later more attention was paid to the venereal diseases, of which gonorrhea first received attention. During the last year a considerable number of states have taken up the Wassermann reaction for syphilis. The well equipped laboratory prides itself on being ready to assist in the diagnosis of any disease where laboratory methods can be used.

The diagnostic laboratory, being of necessity a bacteriologic laboratory, has undertaken much besides the recognition of disease for the assistance of the physician. The plant was soon used for the examination of potable water and of sewage, making the tests sometimes for individuals, sometimes for local health officers, or more often for the executive of the department, the engineer, or the epidemiologist. So, too, the bacteriologist has in many states made tests of milk.

The preparation of antitoxins and vaccines, essentially bacteriologic work, has been undertaken in a number of laboratories, and is considered on another page. Closely allied to this is the administration of antirabic treatment.

What is more properly called pathologic work, such as the examination of urine and other fluids, and section cutting and the study of tissues, has occasionally, but not usually, been done. Some laboratories do a little, but do not advertise it. Others, as in South Dakota, make a charge for it. It has usually been taken up by those laboratories where the other work is not excessive and where other facilities for pathologic work in the state are scanty.

The success of a diagnostic laboratory depends on a number of factors, first of which, of course, is the character of the staff. They must not only be men of ability and industry, but they must have tact and good manners. A laboratory must be looking for business and must, in many ways, do as retail merchants do to secure it. Agreeable manners and an earnest effort to accommodate count for much. The laboratory ought, if possible, to be in the railroad center of the state. Arrangements should be made to utilize all mails. If late mails are not delivered they should be sent for, as in Florida, Maine, Minnesota, New Hampshire and North Carolina. Results should be secured as promptly as possible. In some states diphtheria cultures are examined only once a day and, moreover, so late that they cannot be utilized till afternoon. In other states they are incubated at once and examined as soon as possible, and sometimes, as in Indiana, North Carolina and Vermont, smears are made from the swabs. In nearly every state diagnostic work is done on Sundays and holidays, but usually is confined to diphteria cultures and, perhaps, Widal tests. In almost every state it is the custom to send the results by mail except when, on request, they are telegraphed or telephoned. In some states it is said that ten per cent. of the physicians desire this. In North Carolina the results of diphtheria cultures are telegraphed unless the physician requests that it be not done. About one half so request. In New York and Texas, in what seem to be urgent cases, the department pays the cost of the telegram. Positive reports of rabies are paid for by the state in Missouri, and of diphtheria in Oregon. In Vermont the state pays for the telegrams to certain places. Whenever the question of treatment of persons is involved, reports of rabies examinations and special advice are telegraphed, or telephoned, in Minnesota, to the parties concerned.

It is quite important, too, that mailing outfits be of a convenient sort and be easily accessible to every physician in the state. In some states they are mailed to physicians only on request. This is the case in Florida, Minnesota, North Carolina, South Carolina, South Dakota, Wisconsin and Virginia. In most states stations are established, often the same as antitoxin stations, where they can readily be obtained. In New York there are over 1,300 stations.

ANTITOXINS AND VACCINES

The immense value of antitoxin in reducing the mortality from diphtheria was at once appreciated by health officers. Its cost, however, was so great that it was seen that, without official action, only the rich would be likely to receive it promptly and in sufficient quantities. Municipalities at once began to distribute it free to the poor, and the states soon followed. Rhode Island was the first of these, beginning to do so in December, 1894. Owing to the great demand, it was exceedingly difficult to obtain it at any price, and its manufacture was undertaken by a number of cities and by the state of Massachusetts. In fact, that state began to manufacture in a tentative way in the autumn of 1894, but its distribution was not possible until early in the spring of 1895.

Diphtheria antitoxin was not only the first to be distributed, but it has, so far, held the place of first importance among the curative sera, for not only is its curative value thoroughly established, but diphtheria is the most prevalent disease for which an effective antitoxin has been discovered. Tetanus antitoxin and cerebrospinal meningitis serum seem to appeal to state health officials as of next importance.

The fundamental value of smallpox vaccine in the control of that disease has, of course, been well recognized by health officials ever since the time of Jenner, but its distribution has not generally been undertaken by health departments. The fact that for more than half a century after its discovery the "humanized virus" was chiefly used, and that this only gradually gave place to the commercial "bovine virus," prevented health officials from seeing any need of undertaking its distribution, though an old statute in Maryland provides a special vaccine agent, who, however, has nothing to do with the state department of health, to distribute the virus. The low price of smallpox vaccine, and the fact that local health officials commonly vaccinated the poorer people without charge, made free distribution less necessary. The vaccines which have come into use in recent years are, at present, as obtained from commercial houses, more costly than smallpox vaccine, but, unlike the curative sera, can, or at least some of them can, easily be made in the bacteriologic laboratory with which every important health department is equipped. Hence several of these vaccines, especially typhoid vaccine, are now made and distributed by state health officials.

According to the best statistics available the case fatality of diphtheria was formerly 40 per cent., or more, but it has been reduced in many places to below 10 per cent., it is generally believed, chiefly by the use of antitoxin. But it is the experience of everyone that it is difficult to bring about the adequate use of a remedy, even though it yields such astounding results, without a good deal of effort. Not only must the agent be brought forcibly to the attention of the medical profession, and often to the laity as well, but it must be made accessible, and reasonable in price, and free for the really poor. To get the full value of such a remedy, at least in cities, it may be even necessary to administer it as well as provide it. Thus in New York City in 1909 the case fatality among the 566 cases treated by private practitioners was 12.2 per cent., while of 1,749 treated by health department physicians only 3.3 per cent. died. This is not given to show that the state should administer antitoxin, but as an example of the need of official action to secure the best results even with such a well-known agent as antitoxin.

There are quite a number of ways and conditions in and under which diphtheria antitoxin is distributed.

In Georgia, Illinois, Massachusetts, Minnesota, South Carolina, New York and Vermont, it is furnished by the state department of health free to all persons within the state, and soon will be in New Hampshire.

In Alabama, Connecticut, Florida, Kansas, Oklahoma, Pennsylvania and Rhode Island the state pays for the antitoxin but it is given free only to the indigent, but in Rhode Island at least, owing to the small appropriation, it is not supplied to hospitals or other institutions. It seems to be the quite general practice to interpret the term indigent rather liberally, so that even the really well-to-do rarely pay for their antitoxin.

In other states, the state furnishes no antitoxin free, but municipalities, or counties, are required by law to furnish it free to the poor. This is so in Delaware, Indiana, Iowa, Maine, Michigan, Missouri, North Carolina, Ohio, Texas, West Virginia and Wisconsin, and in many other states local governments do furnish it free to the poor, though it is not required by law.

The most common modes of providing for the distribution of the remedy is for the state department of health to contract with some manufacturer to sell it at a figure very much below the regular retail price. The so-called "board of health antitoxin" is now generally sold by the makers at almost one quarter the retail price, and is usually not returnable after the expiration of the time limit marked on the package. In Iowa it may be returned by the payment of a small sum. The usual plan is for the state health department to make an arrangement with some one manufacturer to sell antitoxin at these prices, though, in Indiana, a number of makers entered into the agreement. In the simplest form of this arrangement the state department handles neither the virus nor the money, though it is supposed to receive a report from the physician for every dose used. This is the plan pursued in Alabama, Indiana, Kansas, Maine, Mississippi, Missouri, North Carolina and Oregon. The antitoxin is offered for sale usually in drug stores, but sometimes also, as in Maine, it is kept on hand by the local boards of health. Although the antitoxin is offered for sale at the discount prices at these stations, it is, as was stated on another page, furnished free to the really indigent, by the state in Alabama and Kansas, and by the local governments in Indiana, Maine, Missouri, North Carolina and Ohio.

A somewhat different plan is followed in Iowa, Texas, Virginia and Wisconsin. In these states the health department acts as the distributing agent for the antitoxin, the supply being sent to the department and forwarded by it to the distributing stations scattered over the state, where it is sold at the list price. The manufacturer, however, does not collect from the state but from the distributor, a druggist usually, or health official, who has collected from the ultimate purchaser. However, if the remedy is furnished to the indigent on order of town or county officials, the manufacturer collects from the town or county, but in Iowa and Wisconsin the local officials are required to furnish it free to the indigent.

In Delaware the state health department purchases the antitoxin and sends it to the depots and collects the sale money from them. In this state the counties furnish to the indigent. Practically the same plan is followed in Kentucky.

In Connecticut, Oklahoma, Pennsylvania and Rhode Island the state purchases the antitoxin and distributes to the depots, but no money is handled, for the state furnishes it free to the indigent. Provision has just been made for a similar distribution in New Hampshire.

In Florida, Illinois, South Carolina and Vermont, though the state supplies antitoxin free to all residents, none is handled by the health department. In these states a contract is made with the manufacturer, who keeps the depots supplied. Every order of the physician is made in triplicate and one copy is retained at the depot, one is sent by the depot to the state department of health, and one is sent to the manufacturer, who is thus enabled to keep run of the stock in the depots. The antitoxin used is paid for by the state on the triplicate copy of the orders.

In Louisiana diphtheria antitoxin as well as other sera and vaccines is kept on hand in small amounts at the central office for call in emergencies.

Usually the distributing stations for antitoxins and vaccines are drug stores, or more rarely offices of local health officials. Sometimes the druggist receives no compensation for his trouble in handling the remedy, being glad to do so for the sake of drawing customers to his establishment. In some states, however, the druggist receives about 10 per cent. on the value of his sales. In Iowa, and perhaps other states, this is added to the usual price for "health department" antitoxin, and so is paid by the ultimate purchaser. In Florida, North Carolina, South Carolina and Vermont the druggist, though selling at the "board of health" prices, receives a commission from the manufacturer. Though not noted, doubtless this practice obtains in other states.

At present three states are manufacturing diphtheria antitoxin, Georgia, Massachusetts and New York. Its manufacture was begun in Massachusetts in 1894, because at that time it was impossible to obtain it in sufficient quantity to accomplish the desired results. Several cities also began to make it at about the same time. Provision has been made by the present legislature for the manufacture of diphtheria antitoxin by the state health department in North Carolina and Ohio. The cost, under favorable conditions, of making the remedy is very, very small, only a fraction of the usual list retail price. The cost of putting it up in the proper packages and distributing is very considerable, even for a health department, and of course there are other large expenses connected with its sale which have to be borne by the manufacturers. Doubtless the fact that health departments can make antitoxin, and that some do, is what has caused the manufacturers to sell what is known as "board of health" antitoxin at a greatly reduced price.

When a state or city health official is told that antitoxin can be made at the cost of a few cents per 1,000 units he is tempted to go into the business, but there are several reasons why he should study the matter very carefully before doing so.

First, it must be remembered that a laboratory cannot be built and equipped for less than $15,000 to $20,000. Furthermore, the cost of running it is very considerable. The cost in Massachusetts .is about $20,000 a year. In New York the appropriation last year was $16,000, but as it is not entirely separate from other laboratories, overhead and other charges are saved. It is true, of course, that the laboratory once established, the expense attendant on a great increase in product would be very little, and this would doubtless encourage the very free use of the remedy.

A consideration of far more importance is the personnel of the laboratory. It is essential that only men of especial fitness, training and ability should be employed. It is not easy to get or keep such men. The slightest suspicion of politics would be fatal. A single mistake in such a laboratory might cause the loss of many lives and bring disgrace on the department, and discredit public health work throughout the county. Let no health department for an instant think of establishing such a laboratory if the governor would appoint a man on the board for political reasons, or if the executive officer would listen to a personal or political suggestion from anyone in the selection of his subordinates.

One might think it easy to determine the relative value of what the different states are doing to bring about a prompt use of diphtheria antitoxin, but it is by no means so. The apparent mortality from this disease depends on its prevalence and severity, as well as on the use of antitoxin, and also on the accuracy with which deaths are recorded. The apparent case fatality is dependent not only on the above factors, but on the completeness of notification, and this last in turn depends on accuracy in diagnosis, and this on the use of the laboratory. The accompanying table shows the mortality in several states for the year 1913, and also the case fatality where morbidity statistics were available. The apparent low fatality of the western states is believed to be due to a milder type and lesser prevalence of the disease. The high case fatality in several of these states is probably due to defective notification. If, however, we compare the eastern and middle western states, where notification is more complete, it is seen that there is a good deal of variation in the mortality, varying as it does from 9.7 in Vermont to 25.9 in Pennsylvania. There is less variation in the case fatality, the range being from 8 to 12 per cent., several states having the lower rate and several the higher. It does not appear that the states which distribute antitoxin free to all, or free to the indigent, have any marked superiority over those which do not.

States Which Distribute Free Antitoxin			States Which Do Not		
State	Mortality	Case Fatality	State	Mortality	Case Fatality
Connecticut	19.1	8	Indiana	18.6	12
Massachusetts	17.6	9	Maryland	15.3	8
New York	19.5	9	Michigan	23.	12
Pennsylvania	25.9	12	Minnesota	10.	6
Rhode Island	24.3	10	New Jersey	21.3	8
Vermont	9.7	9	Ohio	21.3	8
			Wisconsin	11.2	12

There is nothing in the above figures to indicate that it is necessary for the state, as distinguished from the local authorities, to furnish antitoxin. It is noticeable, too, that the amount distributed seems to bear little relation to the mortality or the case fatality. Thus in Massachusetts the number of million units distributed per million of inhabitants was 127, in Pennsylvania 18, in New York 17, in Connecticut 14, and in Rhode Island 14. (Allowance is made for the fact that in Pennsylvania antitoxin is not distributed by the state in Philadelphia and Pittsburgh, and in New York not in the city of New York.) This conclusion, which seems warranted by the facts, is quite different from the belief held by the writer before this investigation was begun. One would expect that the more antitoxin the state distributed, the lower would be the mortality and case fatality. It was believed that the effect of this free distribution would be so great that other factors could not hide it. It must not, however, be inferred that the free distribution of antitoxin is not necessary. It doubtless is very necessary, but, in the absence of free distribution by the state, free distribution will doubtless be made by towns and counties. If this method yields as low a mortality and as low a case fatality as where the state does it, is it not better to save the state's money for things which the local government cannot, or will not, do, and is it not better to place this duty on the local governments if, as appears, the results are the same? It is always well to develop local responsibility as much as possible. As was previously shown, several states provide by law that the local governments must provide antitoxin for the poor, and is it not best to provide for this in all states? Then if the state makes arrrangements so that the towns and counties and practicing physicians can get antitoxin easily, promptly and at a low price, is not the state accomplishing as much, and perhaps in a better way than if it made or purchased antitoxin and distributed it freely to all?

Next to diphtheria antitoxin, more states distribute typhoid vaccine than any other serum or vaccine. There is no doubt that this vaccine has a very important field of usefulness, though its universal application is by no means called for, as it is in the case of smallpox vaccine. Fully as important as distributing it, is educating the public and medical profession as to its proper use. The fact that it is cheaply and easily made has induced many state departments of health to manufacture it. This is the case in California, Georgia, Idaho, Indiana, Kentucky, Maryland, Massachusetts, Minnesota, Nebraska, New York, North Carolina, Ohio, Pennsylvania, South Carolina, Texas, Vermont, Washington and Wisconsin. Besides these the following purchase it for distribution: Florida, Illinois, Iowa, Kansas, Mississippi, Oklahoma and Rhode Island. In nearly every state its distribution is entirely free.

In quite a number of states, namely, Connecticut, Florida, Georgia, Iowa, Kentucky, Maryland, Massachusetts, Mississippi, Oklahoma, Oregon, Pennsylvania, South Carolina, Virginia, West Virginia and Wisconsin, provision is made for the distribution of smallpox vaccine. One might think that the great prevalence and importance of smallpox, and the unique effectiveness of this preventive, would have long ago induced state officials to provide for its distribution, but, for the reasons already given, this does not seem to have been the case. In Maryland the distribution is made by a vaccine agent, and comparatively little is accomplished. In the other states it is by the state board of health. In most instances it is free, but in Wisconsin the vaccine is sold. Few data were obtained as to the amount distributed, but in most instances it is not large, though in Massachusetts over 100,000 tubes are sent out yearly.

Cerebrospinal meningitis serum is distributed in Georgia, Kansas, Massachusetts, Oklahoma, Rhode Island, South Carolina and Texas. In Georgia it is manufactured by the State Board of Health. Its distribution in Kansas, Oklahoma and Texas was of great value during the severe outbreaks of a few years ago.

In Georgia and Pennsylvania two kinds of tuberculin are made and sent out. In the latter large quantities are used, but chiefly in the hospitals and dispensaries of the state department of health.

Scarlet fever vaccine is distributed in Kansas.

Whooping cough vaccine is distributed in Oklahoma.

Tetanus antitoxin is distributed in Connecticut, Florida, Illinois; Kansas, New York, Pennsylvania, Rhode Island, South Carolina and Wisconsin.

RABIES

The recrudescence of rabies during the last decade, or so, has called increased attention to the importance of this disease and its prevention. It has been reported from most of the states of the Union, but varies greatly in prevalence. Though the danger of infection from the bite of a rabid animal has been overestimated, it is serious enough, and a good many authentic deaths from rabies in human beings have been recorded. The value of preventive treatment by means of vaccine is well established and, owing to the properly great fear of this disease on the part of the public, a strong popular demand for the treatment has arisen. The great cost of treatment at private Pasteur institutes, the necessity of going long distances from home for it, as well as its unsatisfactory character in some instances, led many municipal and state health officials to undertake the treatment themselves.

The following states have provided for giving antirabic treatment: Alabama, Arkansas, California, Delaware, Georgia, Illinois, Indiana, Iowa, Kansas, Kentucky, Louisiana, Maryland, Massachusetts, Michigan, Minnesota, Missouri, New York, North Dakota, Oregon, South Carolina, Utah, Vermont, Washington and Wisconsin. In most of these the treatments are given in connection with the laboratory by some member of the regular laboratory force, or more rarely by some one employed especially for this. In California treatment is given at branch laboratories also. As may be seen from Table 6 the number of persons treated in some states is very considerable. The cost cannot usually be separated from other laboratory expenses, but when possible it is given (see Table 10). In a few states the treatment, though provided for and paid for by the health department, is given at a private Pasteur Institute. This is the case in Illinois and Maryland. In the latter state the institute is paid $60 per case, but if the amount of the annual appropriation, $2,500, is exceeded, the excess of cases are treated for nothing. In Illinois the board and other expenses of the patient are paid by the state. In Kansas and Michigan the treatments are given at the medical school in connection with the state university. In Louisiana they are provided for at the Charity Hospital, a general hospital at New Orleans supported by the state. In Texas they are given at the State Hospital for the Insane. In Massachusetts and New York treatment is given by the inspectors and supervisors of the state department of health.

In Connecticut, Ohio, Pennsylvania, Rhode Island, and doubtless in many other states, free treatment is furnished by the local political units. In Delaware, where treatment is furnished by the state, indigent cases are paid for by the towns.

In most of the states the virus is obtained from the United States Public Health Service, but in a few, as in Florida and Oklahoma, it is purchased, and in California, Georgia, Minnesota, South Carolina and Texas it is made in the department laboratory.

In Connecticut it was stated by the secretary of the State Board of Health that, on the recommendation of the attending physician, cases are treated at the expense of the township, which is reimbursed by the state from the fund resulting from the dog tax. In Indiana 5 per cent. of the dog tax is turned over to the State Board of Health as a fund for giving antirabic treatment to the indigent. Treatment is given by one of the laboratory staff, but not at the laboratory.

In Florida and Oklahoma treatment is not given by the state, but antirabic virus is furnished, being sent out to the physicians of the state, as is also done in Washington, where treatment is given as well. In South Carolina a few treatments are given, but most of the virus is distributed to physicians. In California virus is furnished the municipal laboratories and the distribution to physicians is being considered.

VITAL STATISTICS

Fortunately, the registration of vital statistics is as important for legal purposes as it is for the science of preventive medicine, so that many persons besides those interested in the latter subject can be counted on to support effective registration methods. Yet it is true that such registration is so essential for effective health work that the expense and effort involved in securing it are amply justified. Without registration, we must remain in ignorance of where the work of preventive medicine must be carried on and against what diseases. We cannot know whether our methods are successful. Vital statistics are the very foundation of sanitary science and without it we are but building castles in the air. While some sort of registration was provided for in the first settlement of the country, it never was even approximately complete until after the middle of the nineteenth century and then only in a few of the older states. During the last fifteen years there has been a wonderful development of public interest in this subject and remarkable progress has been made. The Federal Census Bureau reckons a state in the "registration area" for deaths when it is believed that at least 90 per cent. of the deaths are registered. At the present time, twenty-five states are included in this list, as shown in Table 7. In very many of them, the percentage of perfection is much more than 90, perhaps reaching 99 or even more in a few. If one should apply a similar test for the registration of births, it is believed that not more than fifteen states, namely, Connecticut, Indiana, Maine, Maryland, Massachusetts, Michigan, Minnesota, New Hampshire, New Jersey, New York, Pennsylvania, Rhode Island, Utah, Wisconsin and Vermont would exceed the minimum of 90 per cent. of completeness, and in none of them would the percentage be as high as has been attained for deaths, and several are just on the border line.

REGISTRATION IN STATE DEPARTMENT

In all the states where there is any registration, it is under the department of health, except in four, namely, Massachusetts, Michigan, Ohio and South Dakota. In the first three, it is in charge of the secretary of state, and in South Dakota of the state department of history.

That the registration of births and deaths should be in the department of health is believed by nearly all who have had much to do with this work. It is the opinion that the health department, more than any other, will feel the necessity not only of completeness of the record, but of accuracy in the statement of the causes of death and in promptness in the returning of births. It is of great importance, too, that deaths from certain causes should be, as promptly as possible, in the hands of health officials. The tabulation and analysis of causes is properly scientific work, and is best done by men trained in the science which is to utilize the results. The increase in the number of State Board of

Health inspectors, especially for supervisory and epidemiologic work, provides an inexpensive machinery for stimulating the work of local registrars as well as improving the returns of physicians. No reason at all can be advanced for having it in any other department. Even if some other department is equally competent in every way, it is a disadvantage to have registration separated from health work. When another has charge, it is impossible to criticize the mistakes of clerks, to put a stop to delays, to smooth out differences with local health officers, or to introduce new methods or tabulations, unless they happen to appeal to the registrar. All this the writer well knows from personal experience, though, in the instance referred to, the registrar was a man of exceptional ability and well disposed. As the health department is the one to use the returns, it should be the one to collect them.

When arguments are advanced in favor of registration by the health department it is usually the registration of deaths that is first in mind, because the health department has such a lively interest in the accuracy of the statement of causes and in the promptness of returns. It is almost equally important that health officials should control the registration of births, for the solution of many statistical problems depends on the accuracy and completeness of the returns, and the success of preventive measures on their promptness. With marriages, the case is different, as their registration has no immediate relations to the problems of the health officer. This is doubtless the reason why, while all the states but one are attempting some sort of registration of deaths and births, there are sixteen in which there is no state registration of marriages. Yet there is every reason why the registration of marriages should go with the registration of deaths and births. The study of many important social questions depends on correct marriage statistics and the same agency, both local and state, which collects one should collect the other. There is only loss by duplicating agencies for the collection of vital statistics. In local registration, the accuracy of registration is greatly helped by not only registering marriages, but by issuing licenses as well. The signatures of the parties, and other data obtained from applicants for a license, serve as basal facts for the verification of future births and deaths in the family. As a fee can well be charged for a marriage license, and usually is, the cost of registration can partly be defrayed in this way. Usually the fee goes entirely to the local official issuing the license or to the local treasury, but in Kansas, 50 cents was added to the fee to go to the state. This yields about $8,000 a year, which defrays most of the expenses of state registration except printing. In most of the states, the license fee is smaller than in Kansas and can well be increased for this purpose. It is said in Kansas that practically no objection is made to the payment of this fee. There is much to be said in favor of this plan for, as was mentioned, the correct statements on the marriage license, which can easily be obtained in the local office, are not only of great importance in themselves to the parties, but serve as a reference for the verification of all future returns relating to the family.

The registration of divorces in the same office as marriages is also desirable for social study, and eighteen states, as shown in Table 7, have provided for such registration by the state registrar.

In order to carry on registration successfully, sufficient clerical force must be provided and properly directed. In most states where registration is placed in the health department, the executive officer is made the registrar, though, of course, in most cases he cannot be, and is not, expected to do much else than direct. In Florida, Illinois, Kansas, Louisiana, Maryland, Mississippi, New Jersey, New York, Pennsylvania, Tennessee, Texas and Wisconsin, a man who is virtually a registrar is appointed by the executive, or by the board. In about half the states, namely, Alabama, California, Illinois, Indiana, Iowa, Kansas, Kentucky, Maine, Maryland, Massachusetts, Michigan, Minnesota, Mississippi, Missouri, New Jersey, New York, North Carolina, Ohio, Pennsylvania, Tennessee, Virginia and Wisconsin, what is really a bureau of vital statistics is created in the department. These are all among the larger states. The number of clerks varies. In most of these states from four to six are employed; in Minnesota and Wisconsin, eight; in Massachusetts, nine; Missouri, ten; Michigan, twelve; New York, thirteen; and Ohio and Pennsylvania, twenty-four each; but in the latter state they do a large amount of statistical work outside of births, marriages and deaths, as on morbidity statistics and the data of school inspection. In some of these states tabulating machines are used. In Pennsylvania there is one Hollerith machine and eight punches, and in New York a Powers machine and two punches. In Missouri, North Carolina and Ohio, machines are used. In New Hampshire, three clerks are employed; in Nebraska, Rhode Island, Utah and Washington, one; and in Delaware and North Dakota, only the part time of one clerk; while in Nevada, West Virginia and Wyoming, the details of registration fall on the executive officer.

LOCAL REGISTRATION

Besides the central organization, another essential of registration is local machinery. This is a matter of very great importance. The states must be divided into districts with a local registrar in each. To provide districts of convenient and workable size, with an efficient registrar, is no simple task. It is believed that one reason why registration was so early developed in the New England states was because the township was of a fairly good size for a primary registration district, and the town clerk usually possessed qualifications which made him a very good registrar. Outside of New England, New York, New Jersey and Michigan are examples of states with a well developed township organization, which enabled them to carry on registration for years before the country as a whole became interested in the subject. Under the modern system, which requires a burial permit and the payment of local registrars by fees, if the registration district is too large it is difficult for the undertaker to obtain the permits, and if the district is too small, the fees will be insufficient to excite the interest of the registrar. Unfortunately for registration, over most of the country the county is the political unit, and a county is too large to serve as a primary registration unit. The attempt to so use it has resulted in many failures. In the few instances in which county registrars have been retained, it has been necessary to supplement them with deputies, or subregistrars. The states which make the county the primary registration unit are Alabama, Arizona, Montana, Nevada, Oklahoma, South Dakota and West Virginia, only one of which, Montana, is a registration state. In this state, as also in Arizona, Nevada and South Dakota, deputies or subregistrars are appointed, though in Montana, the deputies are practically registrars, as they report direct to the state registrar. In Maryland county registrars were, for reasons of expediency, retained, but they are merely recording officers and have nothing to do with the essentials of registration.

Modern registration laws usually provide for smaller units than the counties. A natural unit is the incorporated municipality, whether it be city, borough, town or village. The only states in which municipalities are not made primary registration districts are Alabama, Delaware, Iowa, Kansas, Nevada, South Dakota and West Virginia, and in none of these but Kansas is registration sufficiently advanced to put the state in the registration area. In Kansas, the State Board of Health divides the state into registration districts, and the law provides that every municipality shall constitute the center of a registration district. In Delaware, the State Board of Health is to divide the state into districts and, as a matter of fact, makes the municipalities primary districts.

As before stated, the State Board of Health in Kansas is to divide the state into districts with a municipality as the center, but if the county has no municipality then it is to be a primary district. This law has been amended so that the state registrar may designate the territory over. which the city and township clerks shall serve as registrars. In Idaho, Kentucky, Louisiana, Missouri, Nebraska, Oregon, Washington and Wyoming, the unincorporated portion of counties is to be divided into districts by the state department of health.

In California, Colorado, Indiana and Texas, the unincorporated part of each county is a registration district. This is seen to be too large and in all, except Texas, numbers of subregistrars are appointed. Thus, in the ninety-two Indiana counties there are 334 deputy registrars for the unincorporated portions who are practically subregistrars. In Arkansas, Connecticut, Maine, Massachusetts, Michigan, Minnesota, New Jersey, New York, North Carolina, North Dakota, Pennsylvania, Rhode Island, Wisconsin and Vermont, the township forms a primary registration district, though, outside of New England, it is usually only the unincorporated portions of the townships, the incorporated portions being independent districts. In New England, municipalities within the townships are almost unknown. In Maryland and Mississippi, election districts constitute the primary registration districts; in Illinois, road districts in the few counties not under township organization; in South Carolina and Virginia, magisterial districts; in Tennessee, civil districts; and in Utah, precincts.

In many states, certain officers are ex officio registrars. Thus, in the New England states, township clerks are the registrars and this includes city clerks as well, except in the few cities where registrars are appointed by the city government. So, too, township clerks are registrars in Michigan, Minnesota and Wisconsin. In New Jersey, it is the township assessor. Municipal clerks are registrars also in California, Georgia,

Idaho, Illinois, Kansas, Kentucky, Missouri, Montana, New Jersey, North Dakota and Virginia; city health officers in Indiana, Maryland, Oklahoma, Oregon, South Carolina, Texas and Washington. In Oregon and New York, registrars are appointed by the municipal, or township, government, and in North Carolina by the county government. Justices of the peace are registrars of the magisterial districts of Georgia and Virginia and it was so provided in the South Carolina law, but this has been ruled against by the attorney-general. County health officers are registrars in Alabama, Arizona, Indiana, Nevada and Oklahoma, and county recorders in California and Maryland.

The state department of health appoints the registrars in Arkansas, Colorado, Delaware, Florida, Ohio, Kansas, Louisiana, Mississippi, Missouri, Nebraska, North Dakota, Oregon, Pennsylvania, Tennessee, Washington and Wyoming, except that sometimes in cities, existing registrars are recognized, or local appointments permitted. Of course, in most states, the officer who appoints the local registrar can remove an unsatisfactory official.

Subregistrars are provided for in very many states, but they are not of much importance except in states where the county, or a large unincorporated portion thereof, is the registration unit, where it becomes essential, as was before referred to, that there should be a considerable number appointed. Sometimes they are called deputy registrars, but the real deputy is the one who merely takes the place of the registrar during absence. Such, also, are provided for in most states.

In Indiana, Nevada, Vermont and Wyoming, there are no subregistrars known as such, but while actually subregistrars they are called deputy registrars. In Indiana, the undertaker in an unincorporated place may get his burial permit from the nearest town registrar, who transmits the certificate to the county registrar. The appointment of subregistrars is provided for in all the other states except Iowa, Kansas, Massachusetts, New Jersey, Oklahoma, Oregon, Rhode Island, Texas, Utah, Virginia, Washington and West Virginia. In about half of these there is no efficient registration. In Kansas and Utah, the districts seem to be sufficiently small without appointing subregistrars. In Massachusetts, New Jersey and Rhode Island, registration is under old laws which did not contain this provision and though sometimes their appointment is desirable, it has not been thought best to amend the law just for this small defect. In most states the subregistrars are appointed by the local registrars, usually subject to the state registrar, but the state registrar makes the appointments in Florida, Mississippi, Montana, Nebraska and Michigan. Where subregistrars have much to do there is sometimes trouble in regard to the division of the fees, as in Idaho and Utah.

All sorts of persons may be appointed registrars. Physicians are often so appointed, but they are away from home, or office, so large a part of the time that, unless some member of the family is deputy, much inconvenience may result. Undertakers are sometimes appointed, but as one purpose of the appointment of a registrar is to have a check on undertakers, this is not considered a good arrangement. Nevertheless, in Minnesota, embalmers are very generally appointed. Druggists and merchants, who may usually be found at their places of business, are frequently appointed, and men of high standing in the community have in many cases been willing to serve. Women have often made excellent registrars. Postmasters at times serve in this capacity. In Arizona, as only notaries public and justices of the peace can receive fees, the law provides that they alone may be appointed registrars.

DEATH REGISTRATION

The most essential requirement for a successful registration of deaths is, of course, the requirement of a permit from the local registrar before burial. Every state except Alabama, Iowa, New Jersey, New Mexico, Oklahoma, Texas and West Virginia, has this requirement, but in South Carolina and Virginia it is provided that in sparsely settled districts, or when it is impracticable to file a death certificate and obtain a permit, a body may be buried without a permit, but the certificate of death shall be filed with the registrar within ten days. In Wyoming, in sparsely settled districts, where it is impracticable to provide a registrar, the undertaker may make out two certificates of death and use one as a burial permit and send the other to the State Board of Health. In New Jersey, while the law does not require a permit for burial in the townships, it is said that in practice a permit is in almost all cases secured by the undertaker from the registrar before interment takes place.

A number of the more recent laws, as those of Arizona, Arkansas, California, Florida, Georgia, Idaho, Illinois, Louisiana, Michigan, Minnesota, Mississippi, New York, North Carolina, Oregon, South Carolina, Washington, Wisconsin and Wyoming, provide that a body shall not be kept more than seventy-two hours without a permit. In Texas, the limit is five days.

The object of requiring a permit from some authorized official is, of course, to secure a proper certificate or return of the death for record. Hence all the states mentioned which require a permit before burial, also require that a certificate of death must be filed before the permit is issued. In Maine, however, exception is made in cases where it is impracticable to obtain the certificate, but the latter must be filed as soon as possible. Similar provisions are found in Kentucky and Michigan. In Michigan, the provision only applies to townships and the certificate must be filed within ten days. In Kentucky, it must be filed within five days.

In Indiana, if a body is interred without a permit the coroner shall disinter the remains and hold an inquest, and this provision has been enforced on at least one occasion.

The primary object of a registration law is to secure a record of each birth, death and marriage which occurs in a community. It is, however, desirable that the death of persons who die outside of the state, but are brought in for burial, should be recorded, not only for legal purposes, but to render less likely neglect of the law by requiring that a permit shall be required for the disposal of every dead body, no matter where death occurs. About two thirds of the states, therefore, provide that transit permits accompanying bodies from another jurisdiction shall serve as a certificate on which the local registrar shall issue a burial permit. In California, the transit permit must be endorsed by the state registrar. In Connecticut and Vermont, if there is no transit permit, a burial permit may be obtained from the local registrar on information as to the identity of the remains.

Stillbirths are to be registered both as births and deaths in Arizona, Arkansas, California, Colorado, Delaware, Florida, Georgia, Idaho, Indiana, Kansas, Kentucky, Louisiana, Maryland, Mississippi, Missouri, Minnesota, Montana, Nebraska, Nevada, New York, North Carolina, North Dakota, Ohio, Oregon, Pennsylvania, Rhode Island, South Carolina, Tennessee, Texas, Utah, Vermont, Virginia, Washington and Wisconsin. In Illinois, it is specified that they shall be registered merely as still-births. Wherever registered as deaths, burial permits, obtained only on presentation of a certificate, are required as in case of deaths of living persons. In Alabama, a special form of certificate for stillbirths is required.

The new form of the model law provides that a certificate and permit are not required for a child not advanced to the fifth month of utero-gestation. This provision is found in Arkansas, California, Florida, Georgia, Illinois, Minnesota, Mississippi, New York, North Carolina, and Oregon, but the period so fixed is the end of the seventh month in Indiana, Washington and Texas. In thirty states the law requires that the period of uterogestation shall, if known, be stated in months (in Nevada, as nearly as possible). In Illinois, midwives are allowed to sign certificates of stillbirths. It is unfortunate that the Federal Census Bureau has not made a ruling on what constitutes a stillbirth. Until some central authority has decided what a stillbirth is, that is, after what period of uterogestation they are to be reported, statistics will be hopelessly confused. This is a matter where uniformity is of great importance, but so far attempts to secure it have resulted in failure. The American Public Health Association has by resolution recommended that *all* stillbirths be registered, irrespective of the month of uterogesta-tion, but only those be tabulated which have completed the sixth month.

The ultimate purpose of all this machinery is to obtain a record of the death which may be used for various legal, social and medical purposes. As registration gradually developed, the different states and cities devised their own form of certificate which, of course, varied more or less. Over forty of the state laws make it incumbent on the state registration department to prepare the forms. In over thirty states the blanks, and the local record books as well, must be furnished by the state. In this way uniformity has been generally secured through-out any given state, but the forms in the different states naturally varied quite a little. It was not until the federal census bureau began to develop registration that the need for national uniformity was felt. In order to meet this demand, the "Standard" certificate was adopted by the census bureau, the American Medical Association and the American Public Health Association, and has taken the place of the older forms in all but a very few states. Naturally, all the newer registration laws provide for the standard form, and most of the older forms have been modified so as closely to approximate the standard. It is, perhaps, rather difficult to say how much deviation is permissible without throwing a certificate out of the standard class. The census office considers that the only states in the registration area not using the standard death certificate are Connecticut, Maine, New Hampshire, New Jersey and Rhode Island. Among nonregistration states which use other than the standard forms are Alabama, Delaware, Oklahoma and West Virginia. Some of the older registration states, as Connecticut, Maine, New Hampshire and Rhode Island, have hesitated to adopt the standard form, as it would necessitate an entire change in filing cabinets, record books and forms for certified copies. Some of the undertakers in these states also object to a change.

A few certificates have information not called for on the standard. Thus, the name of husband or wife is asked for on the California, Rhode Island and Vermont certificate; in Massachusetts, the husband's name; in Michigan, in the case of a married woman, the age at first marriage is to be given, the number of children borne and the number of living children. In North Carolina, educational attainments must be given, or, if the deceased was under 15 years, the educational attainments of father, mother or guardian. Delaware requires the time of residence in the United States of foreigners. Connecticut requires a statement as to whether the body was embalmed and if so by whom, also the number of families in the house where the person died. In Alabama, length of residence is asked for in all cases, as well as whether the deceased had had a surgical operation. The Rhode Island form requires the relationship of the informant to the deceased.

The model law prescribes that the personal data shall be attested by some competent person acquainted with the facts, the medical data by the physician last in attendance, and the facts relating to the disposition of the body by the undertaker, and the latter is made responsible for obtaining the certificate and filing it with the registrar. In some of the older laws, these points were not so clearly brought out, though it has come about, through custom, that this is actually what is done. In New Hampshire, New Jersey and Vermont, the physician is to make the certificate and deliver it, to the family in Vermont and to the undertaker in New Hampshire and New Jersey. In Vermont, there is a time limit of thirty-six hours and the physician receives a fee of 25 cents. In South Dakota, the law requires that the physician shall make the certificate to the clerk of court. The provisions of the model law are by far the best, and to a large extent are followed even when not prescribed.

From the standpoint of preventive medicine, the most important part of the death certificate is the statement of the cause of death. For this the medical attendant is responsible, but there are many instances where there is no medical attendant. Provision is made for these in the model law by requiring reference to the registrar for investigation and certification, but if there is a health officer, who is a physician, the registrar is to refer the case to him. If the death is probably "caused by unlawful or suspicious means," it must be referred to the coroner. Most of the states follow substantially this provision. In Vermont, the health officer is authorized to make an autopsy if deemed necessary. In Kansas and South Carolina, however, there is no reference by the registrar to the health officer, and in Maine and New Hampshire, the town clerk is authorized to make the certificate, and in Vermont, the local registrar is authorized to do so, if the county board of health does not make the certificate within twenty-four hours after reference. In California, Florida and Washington, all deaths without a medical attendant are to be referred to the coroner when the local registrar is not a physician; in Florida and Oregon, to the health officer; and in Louisiana, to the coroner if the latter is a physician. In South Dakota such cases are referred to the justice of the peace. In Rhode Island, deaths without medical attendance are to be referred by the registrar to a physician who receives $2 for making the certificate. In Minnesota, the registrar may refer the case to a physician, and in Wisconsin the registrar may request any physician employed for the purpose to sign the certificate.

While the requirement that a burial permit shall be obtained is the most important means of securing complete registration, other checks may be added. Thus, the model law provides that the undertaker shall deliver the permit to the sexton or other person in charge of the burial place. This provision is found in all states except Alabama, Connecticut, Indiana, Iowa, Maryland, Massachusetts, New Hampshire, New Jersey, New Mexico, Oklahoma, South Dakota, Texas, Vermont, West Virginia and Wyoming. This is, however, not so important as it is to forbid the sexton to allow an interment until a permit has been presented. All the states require this but Alabama, Delaware, Iowa, Massachusetts, New Jersey, New Mexico, Oklahoma, South Carolina, Texas, West Virginia and Wyoming. While the New Jersey law does not require this in townships, in practice it is required generally throughout the state.

A still further safeguard is to require that the permits be returned by the cemetery authorities to some official who will check them up. All of the states, but the following, have this requirement: Alabama, Delaware, Indiana, Iowa, Massachusetts, Michigan, Minnesota, New Jersey, New Mexico, North Carolina, Oklahoma, South Dakota, West Virginia and Wyoming. In most, the model law is followed, which requires the return to be made within ten days, but it is to be immediately in Utah, within one day in Colorado, within three days in Illinois, within five days in Arizona, six days in Maine and New Hampshire, seven days in New York, and thirty days in Wisconsin. In Rhode Island, the permits are to be returned by the fifth of the next month, and in Vermont during the first week of each month. In Rhode Island, the permits are then to be transmitted to the state registrar. In Michigan, the permits are to be retained by the sexton. In Wisconsin, it is provided that, where there is no sexton or other person in charge of a cemetery, the undertaker shall note that fact on the burial permit and return it to the registrar, and this is done in other states.

Another method of checking returns is the so-called coffin law, which requires that every person or firm selling a casket shall keep a record and report to the state registrar. In the newer registration states this seems to have helped to perfect the records, but in some of the states at least, where death registration is good, it would seem to be unnecessary. In Alabama, it is said to have increased the number of death returns 5 per cent. Such a provision is found in Alabama, Arkansas, California, Georgia, Florida, Minnesota, Mississippi, Oregon, Tennessee, North Carolina and Washington. An additional requirement, found in

Arkansas, California, Georgia, Florida, Minnesota, Mississippi, Oregon, Tennessee, North Carolina and Washington, is that, if the person to whom the casket is sold does not have charge of the disposition of the body, the seller shall inclose in the casket a notice furnished by the state registrar and calling attention to the requirements of the law.

It would scarcely seem necessary to specify the form of burial permit, yet this is done in the model law which has been followed by about half the states.

While it is not really necessary for good registration that cemetery authorities should keep a record of all interments, it is desirable that they should do so, and in a general way conduces to accuracy. Over thirty states have a provision of the law which requires this. It is desirable, too, that the exact location of each interment should be recorded and, of course, this is frequently done.

BIRTH REGISTRATION

The registration of births is almost as important, for public health purposes, as the registration of deaths. The essential requirement is that the birth should be reported by some responsible person as soon as possible after its occurrence. The "model law" has been adopted by the majority of states. As there are all sorts of deviations from the model law, it is difficult to decide in all cases how specific statutory provisions should be classed. It will probably be agreed, however, that the following states have not adopted the model law: Alabama, Connecticut, Iowa, Massachusetts, Maine, New Hampshire, New Jersey, New Mexico, Oklahoma, Rhode Island, Texas, Vermont and West Virginia; nevertheless, it will be noted that among these are included several of the registration states.

The model law requires that all births shall be "immediately registered," and then in the next section states that returns shall be made to the local registrar within ten days from the date of birth. The majority of the states have adopted this provision, but among the others are many variations in the time limit. It would seem better to have a shorter limit than ten days, and the only objection that is urged is that the child is often not named before that time, but even at ten days the child frequently is not named and, in any event, provision must be made for securing the name in all cases where the naming is delayed. The earlier the time fixed for the return, the less likely it is to be forgotten by the physician, and the more useful it is to those health officials who are attempting to reduce infant mortality. In Missouri, Nevada and Idaho, the law provides that cities may fix an earlier date for reporting than the ten-day limit of the statute, In Illinois this may be done by the State Board of Health. In California and Indiana, all births must be reported within thirty-six hours. It is claimed that 90 per cent. are thus reported. In Massachusetts, the physician is required to give notice of each birth within forty-eight hours, and send in a complete return within fifteen days, or he may make the complete return within forty-eight hours if he prefers. In Delaware, a postal card report is to be sent in within twenty-four hours, and a complete report later. Three days is the time limit in Nebraska and North

Dakota, four days in Maryland, five days in Alabama, Arizona, New Jersey, New York, North Carolina, Texas and Wisconsin, and six days in Maine and New Hampshire. The time allowed is too long in several states, longer than in the model law. In West Virginia, it is thirty days; in Connecticut, it is within the first week of the next month; in Oklahoma, the first day and in Rhode Island on or before the fifth day of the next month.

Every state, except Iowa and New Mexico, has a requirement that physicians and midwives shall report to the local registrar all births attended by them. Usually no fee is paid, but in some a fee is paid by the county, township or municipality. It is 10 cents in Oklahoma, 15 cents in Montana, 25 cents in Connecticut, Maine, Massachusetts, New Hampshire, Rhode Island, South Dakota, Vermont, West Virginia, Wisconsin and Wyoming. Most of the states provide that when there is no physician or midwife in attendance, the father, mother, householder, or owner of the premises, or head of an institution, and in some states the masters of vessels, shall report births. The model law also provides that the registrar shall then secure the full return with signatures, and this has been incorporated in the newer acts. The later acts, as those of Arkansas, Florida, Georgia, New York and North Carolina, make it incumbent on all persons interrogated to answer correctly.

In Iowa, the physicians are not required to report births, but reliance is placed on an annual enumeration by the assessors. Such an enumeration is used as a supplementary means of completing the records in Massachusetts and Rhode Island.

As it so often happens that a birth is reported before the child is named, the model law, and that of more than thirty states, requires that the registrar shall send to the parent a blank for a supplemental report of the name which must be returned as soon as the child is named. In Vermont, it is to be returned in thirty days. The South Dakota law requires that the child must be named within sixty days.

The form and content of birth returns are not so important from a public health standpoint as are the details of death returns, yet uniformity is desirable. The model birth certificate is excellent, but some of the older states have hesitated to adopt it on account of the changes necessitated in record books and filing cases. It has been adopted in all states except Alabama, Connecticut, Maine, Massachusetts, New Hampshire, New Jersey, Oklahoma, Rhode Island, Vermont and West Virginia. The most common deviations are in form, and in the omission of the items relating to plural births, to number of children born and ·number of children living. Some of the returns have data not called for on the' standard form. Thus, in North Carolina, the educational attainments of parents is asked for; in Arizona, California, Indiana, Michigan, New Jersey, New York, North Dakota and Wisconsin, whether preventive treatment for ophthalmia has been applied; and in Alabama, the presentation, duration of labor, number of children of father, living and dead, and the number of marriages of father.

OTHER DETAILS OF REGISTRATION

It is an aid to the administration of a registration law to have a correct list of the physicians, midwives and undertakers. The model law provides that all such shall register name, address and occupation with the local registrar, and that the latter shall annually transmit the list to the state registrar. The following states have this provision: Alabama, Arizona, Arkansas, California (not midwife), Colorado, Delaware, Georgia, Kansas, Kentucky, Idaho, Louisiana, Maryland, Mississippi (also retail dealers in caskets), Missouri, Montana, Nevada, New York, North Dakota, Ohio, Oregon, Pennsylvania, Rhode Island (not midwives), Utah, Washington, West Virginia and Wisconsin. In Illinois, sextons are required to register.

The model law, as also the acts in Alabama, Arizona, Arkansas, California, Colorado, Delaware, Florida, Georgia, Idaho, Indiana, Kentucky, Maryland, Michigan, Mississippi, New York, North Carolina, North Dakota, Ohio, Oregon, Pennsylvania, Rhode Island, South Carolina, Utah and Virginia, require that certificates shall be written legibly in unfading black ink, but in Indiana an indelible pencil is permitted. This provision seems to be very generally enforced so far as the use of black ink is concerned, though occasionally pencil returns are seen. Most persons, however, use whatever ink they are accustomed to, and most of it is far from unfading. There is little doubt that in the course of time, many of these returns will become illegible. The typewriter is used somewhat in making returns, and unless a black record ribbon is insisted on, such returns, too, will fade away.

The most defective returns of births and deaths come from hospitals and other institutions. Persons in institutions are often without friends or relatives, or at least if they have such, they are in distant places and not accessible. The details of personal and family history are, therefore, often unattainable after the death or removal of the person. In order to ensure correct returns all data necessary must be secured from the individual himself on admission. Hence, the model law makes this a duty of the superintendents or persons in charge of hospitals, almshouses, lying-in or similar institutions. When sick persons are admitted, the nature of the disease and the place where contracted are to be noted. This provision is found in Arizona, Arkansas, Colorado, Florida, Idaho, Indiana, Illinois, Kansas, Kentucky, Louisiana, Maryland, Michigan, Minnesota, Mississippi, Missouri, Montana, Nevada, New York, North Carolina, North Dakota, Oregon, Pennsylvania, South Carolina, Virginia and Washington.

To facilitate the work and assist local registrars, as well as to secure uniformity, the model law provides that all blanks and forms used in registering, recording and preserving the returns shall be prepared, printed and supplied to the registrars by the state registrar. This provision has been adopted in Arizona, Arkansas, Colorado, Delaware, Florida, Georgia, Idaho, Illinois, Kansas, Kentucky, Louisiana, Maryland, Massachusetts, Michigan, Minnesota, Mississippi, Missouri, Montana, Nebraska, Nevada, New Hampshire, New Jersey, New York, North Carolina, North Dakota, Oklahoma, Oregon, Pennsylvania, Rhode Island, South Carolina, Tennessee, Utah, Virginia, Washington and West

Virginia. In Minnesota, however, the book for recording is to be paid for by the city, village or town. In Connecticut, the state registrar is by law to furnish death certificates and does furnish other forms. The same is true in Iowa. Doubtless, too, in some other states blanks are furnished by the state, though it may not be required in the statute, but in California it is expressly provided that the counties shall supply the blanks printed according to the forms prescribed by the State Board of Health. The model law, and practically those of all the states above named, as well as the statutes of Ohio and Texas, require the local registrars to distribute forms to all who need them.

For many reasons the preservaton of local records of birth, marriage and death is of much importance, though it has little relation to public health, and how and where they should be kept need not be discussed here. Whatever may be decided as to local records, the interests of public health demand that records of births, marriages and deaths be transmitted to the state registrar at the earliest moment. In Oklahoma and New Mexico there is no law. In Iowa, physicians report deaths to the State Board of Health monthly and the assessors report births annually. In West Virginia, county clerks send copies to the State Board of Health on the first of each July. In Rhode Island the returns are by law to be made by the first of March of each year, though the returns of death are in fact made monthly. In Massachusetts, returns of births and marriages are to be made annually. In all the other states the law requires that the original returns, or copies, shall be sent to the state registrar monthly. The model law fixes the date as the tenth of the month next succeeding. The time limit is the fourth of the month in Indiana and Michigan, the fifth in California, Kansas, Maryland (or earlier if required), Montana, Nebraska, New York, North Dakota, Ohio, Pennsylvania (for deaths), Utah, Washington and Wyoming; the seventh day in Connecticut (for deaths) and Wisconsin; twelfth to fifteenth day in Maine, the twelfth day in New Hampshire, fifteenth day in Connecticut (births and marriages) and South Dakota (births and deaths), and the thirteenth day in Vermont.

The original returns are to be sent to the state registrar in all the above except Connecticut, Maine, Baltimore, cities in Michigan, first-class cities in Nebraska, New Hampshire, New York City; Rhode Island, Vermont; first class cities in Washington and Wisconsin and in West Virginia. In all the above mentioned localities the original returns are to be retained and copies sent to the state registrar. Sometimes these copies are on sheets, or in book form, and sometimes on forms like the original returns, and sometimes on cards, as in Connecticut, Maine, New Hampshire and Vermont. In Maine and Rhode Island, though the original returns are kept by the townships, they are also copied into books for a permanent record.

With small registration districts it frequently happens that no certificates of any kind are received during a month. In order that the state registrar may keep run of the local registrars it is necessary that reports should be sent in every month from every registrar, no matter whether or not any records are to be forwarded to the central office. A report that no records have been received, if such is the fact, is required in all the states except Alabama, Iowa, New Hampshire, New Jersey, Oklahoma, Rhode Island, Texas, Vermont and West Virginia.

The success of registration, in a large measure, seems to depend on the stimulation of the registrar by an adequate compensation. Except in the larger cities, the fee system seems to be the best for this. This plan is followed in the majority of states. The fee is 10 cents for each record in South Dakota (marriages) and Vermont. It is 15 cents in New Hampshire and Wisconsin, 20 cents in Massachusetts (marriages), New Jersey and Rhode Island; 25 cents in Arkansas, California, Colorado, Connecticut, Delaware, Florida, Georgia, Idaho, Kansas, Kentucky, Louisiana, Maryland, Michigan, Mississippi, Missouri, Minnesota, Montana, Nebraska, New York, North Carolina, North Dakota, Ohio, Oregon, Pennsylvania, South Carolina, South Dakota (births and deaths), Virginia, Washington and West Virginia, and 50 cents in Massachusetts (births and deaths) and Wyoming (births and deaths). In several of these states, as Idaho, Michigan, Missouri and New Jersey, it is provided that the registrar may be given a salary instead of fees, and in Ohio a sliding scale of fees is provided, varying from 5 cents in cities of over 250,000 to 25 cents in cities of less than 25,000 inhabitants. In Illinois, if the returns number over 5,000 annually, the fee is 10 cents. In Pennsylvania, in cities in which the registrar receives a salary for other duties, his fee for each vital record is 5 cents. In Maryland, under the same conditions, where the county registrar receives a salary of $800, the fee is 10 cents. In Rhode Island, the minimum compensation of the town registrar (clerk) is to be $10 per year. In Utah, where the fee system is forbidden, the local registrars are paid at the rate of $3 per day, and the state registrar considers that six returns constitute a day's work. In Indiana, the registrars are salaried officers and receive no fees, and the subregistrars receive whatever the county commissioners choose to give them, which is very little.

As there is sometimes trouble in regard to the division of fees between registrars and subregistrars some states provide for this. In Delaware both deputies and subregistrars are to receive 10 cents, to be deducted from the fee of the registrar, for each return handled. In Montana the subregistrar receives the same fee as the registrar, but in this state he is "sub" only in name, reporting directly to the state registrar. In Maryland, where the local registrars transmit transcripts to the county registrar, and are to this extent subregistrars, they receive 10 cents for each transcript, as well as 25 cents for each original return received and sent to the state registrars. In California the subregistrar receives 15 cents, to be taken out of the registrar's fees. In Nebraska the subregistrar receives 10 cents, to be deducted from the fee of the registrar. In Arizona the local registrar receives fees, while the county registrar receives a salary of $300 per annum. In Nevada the deputy registrar receives $25 per month, and the county registrar the same.

In most states, where the local registrar is to report each month in which returns are received, he is to receive for this report the same fee as for a single return, usually 25 cents.

The registrar's fees are in most states to be paid by the counties, but in New England, New York and New Jersey they are to be paid by the township, or municipality, comprising the registration district. In a few states, as Colorado and Idaho, when cities make a primary registration district, the fees are to be paid by the city. In Florida the state pays the fee.

There has certainly been a very marked improvement in registration in the United States during the last few years, and there is every reason to believe that this advance will continue. From a public health point of view the purpose of collecting vital statistics is to show when and where, and under what conditions, fatal disease occurs, and to help solve, by means of these facts, the problems of disease causation and prevention. For the health officer the collection of vital statistics is valueless, unless the data are presented so that he can use them. Statistical material must be presented in tabular form. As much depends on comparison between different times, and between different places, uniformity is necessary. Blind conformity, however, is deplorable. Every thoughtful official will have problems of his own for which he will need a special arrangement of data. There ought, however, to be a number of standard tables in every report. The Section on Vital Statistics of the American Public Health Association has had a committee to suggest such tables, but as yet has done little. It is extremely urgent that steps be taken to prepare a set of standard tables, and in its preparation those should be consulted who use statistics, rather than those who compile them.

At present the tabulation of vital statistics and their analysis are the weakest points in registration, though the most important. There is little attempt at uniformity. Even in the same state, a registrar may discard the work of his predecessor without substituting anything better. In studying mortality, death rates are necessary, yet in many reports the deaths only are given, and the student cannot even calculate the rates, as the populations are not given. Every report should give the total deaths and the deaths from the principal diseases for as many years as they are available, together with rates. Yet if one opens a state registration report expecting to obtain these data, he is very likely to be disappointed. The distribution of data by locality, giving rates, is also of fundamental importance in state work. To decide on the most useful and important combinations of cause of death, season, sex, age, color, etc., is far outside of the scope of this report. It is high time for state officials to consider this subject seriously. They have a field of their own, distinct from that of the federal government and from that of the cities. It should be defined with great care.

In Table 7 is shown the states in the official registration area for deaths, and also in the next columns the states in which it is believed that 90 per cent. of the births are registered. This estimate is based on a comparison of the reported births with the number of children under 1 year of age, but this latter figure is also merely an estimate, as several years have elapsed since the 1910 census. Of course, such an estimate is very crude, but it serves to show approximately what states have made the most progress in birth registration.

The statement as to office force must not be considered as strictly accurate, as clerks are often employed at times for other than registration purposes. The expenses refer only to the expenses of the central office, and these, too, are unsatisfactory, for in many offices the accounts of divisions are not properly segregated, and approximations only are available. Also, in some of the states the figures include unusual expenses, such as the furnishing of record books, or new forms of blanks, which may not be necessary again for some time.

Whether a state has the "model" law or uses "standard" certificates, it is often difficult to decide. All sorts of deviations are found. What are permissible is a matter of judgment.

CHILD HYGIENE

Prevention of Infant Mortality

The possibility of effective work in promptly and greatly reducing the death rate of infants has been so well established, and so much has actually been accomplished in the larger cities, that the neglect of this field by state health officials is remarkable. Inquiry brings out the fact that, with very few exceptions, almost nothing is done except educational efforts of a general sort.

Most state health departments do, it is true, issue pamphlets or circulars of instruction to mothers for the care of babies. Some of these, as for instance, those issued by Indiana, New York and Virginia, are excellent. Doubtless others are equally good. The value of this literature is probably considerable, though the experience in eastern cities has been that it is very markedly inferior to personal instruction, but no doubt it is more effective among the better educated native population of other parts of the country. In most states, little effort is made to place this literature where it will do the most good. It is simply distributed as are other circulars, or sent out on call, or perhaps given to mothers' clubs. In Idaho, however, it was stated that a copy of the bulletin on the care of the baby, issued by the children's bureau, is sent to the mother of every child whose birth is reported. In North Carolina, the State Board of Health sends its excellent "Baby" booklet to accompany a congratulatory letter of the governor, to every mother. The same is done in Indiana where, indeed, the idea originated, but the money available provides only 8,000 booklets, whereas there are 20,000 births. Therefore, it is sent to primiparae only. In New York a letter from the health commissioner, instead of from the governor, accompanies the literature. In Utah and Wisconsin a bulletin is said to be sent to each mother. It is evident that in states where the births are poorly reported, or are not reported promptly, the value of this educational attempt is largely lost. Another useful means of stimulating interest on the part of the public is an exhibit. The first infant welfare and milk exhibit was organized by the State Board of Health of Maryland. Since then they have become very popular, and have been held in many cities under various auspices. Probably all of the general exhibits that have been held by state health departments have a section devoted to baby welfare. Lectures illustrated by lanterns and moving pictures are also added with good results.

So far as we know now, really effective work for the reduction of infant mortality depends on the intensive effort for the personal instruction of mothers by visiting nurses, supplemented when necessary by milk stations, consultations, baby contests and hospitals. Each community must do these things for itself, either through the local health department or some other agency. It is preeminently a field for local endeavor. It is a proper function of the state to stimulate each town

and city to take up this work. Only one or two states have so far
made any systematic effort to do this. For two or three years Pennsylvania has had a traveling exhibit with lecturers, for the betterment
of child life, which has gone from town to town through the state.
Effort is made in every place to induce the people to interest themselves
in the exhibit and make it their own show. It is said that much local
organization, for carrying on the usual methods of reducing infant
mortality, has resulted.

By far the best work seems to have been done in New York. It
began two years ago, or more, but was greatly extended in the summer
of 1914. Three exhibits were sent out, accompanied by lecturers and a
nurse, and a model consultation was set up. Every effort was made
to interest local people and arouse them to action. Forty-six cities
were visited, and afterward fifty-six county fairs. The exhibit stayed
in each city two weeks. Afterward, smaller exhibits were sent out
among towns, even as small as 1,500 in population. Many local consultations were established, so that by autumn there were sixty-eight
in thirty-nine cities outside of New York City. After the establishment
of the stations, they are visited by the nurse of the department to give
assistance and advice. In the state, outside of New York City, the
infant death rate fell from 141 during the summer months of 1913, to 117
in the corresponding period in 1914.

A division of child hygiene has just been organized in the Kansas
state health department, consisting at present of a chief at $2,400, a
stenographer, and a visiting nurse. The appropriation is $5,000.

A minor means of protecting infant life is the licensing and supervision of places for boarding infants. Probably a considerable number
of states have provision for this, but no effort was made to determine
how many. They are licensed by the State Board of Health in Minnesota, Ohio and Oregon, but apparently there is very little supervision,
though the experience of some cities is that regular supervision by
visiting nurses is very effective. One state health official thought his
department issued licenses, but was not sure about it. In a considerable
number of states, the entire control of these establishments is by the
board of charities.

Lying-in Hospitals are licensed by the state board of health in
Illinois, Iowa, Nebraska and Oregon, and formerly were in Colorado
where they were supervised by a special inspector.

The licensing, supervision and instruction of midwives may be made
a useful means of attacking the infant mortality problem. They are
licensed by the state health department in Colorado, Illinois and New
York. The latter is the only state where the matter is considered
seriously. Qualifications are prescribed and the licenses have to be
renewed annually. The most essential feature is that the midwives are
supervised by nurses employed by the department.

Ophthalmia Neonatorum

This subject which is of such great importance has received considerable attention from state health departments and legislatures. The
earliest type of law required the report of cases to the health officer

or a physician. Experience seems to show that the latter provision is unwise. Nevertheless this is required by the law in Idaho, Iowa, Maine, Maryland, Michigan, Missouri, Oregon, Pennsylvania, Tennessee and Texas. The model law recommended by the American Medical Association, and which ought to be made the basis of all legislation, requires reports to the local health officer. Such a provision is now found in California, Connecticut, Illinois, Indiana, Kentucky, Louisiana, Maryland, Massachusetts, Minnesota, New Hampshire, New Jersey, New York, North Dakota, Ohio, Oregon, Rhode Island, South Carolina, South Dakota, Utah, Vermont, Washington and Wisconsin. In Ohio the state pays 50 cents for each report. In addition to the regular form of report it is required in Arizona, California, Indiana, Michigan, New Jersey, New York, North Dakota and Wisconsin that the physician state on the birth return of every child whether prophylactic treatment was employed. In Indiana and New Jersey it is said that the question is usually answered. There was a similar question on the return in Minnesota and New York but it has been eliminated. In many states it is admitted that the notification law is sadly neglected. In others as Indiana, Maryland, Massachusetts, New Jersey and Vermont it is said that it is steadily improving. Very few states, however, give any facts in their annual reports. In Massachusetts in 1913 there were reported 2,304 cases.

Routine prophylactic treatment does not seem to be definitely required in any states except Michigan, Ohio, Rhode Island and Wisconsin though it is urged in many. In Ohio midwives must and in Illinois they may apply the prophylactic. The use of this means of prevention is greatly encouraged, and prompt treatment of the disease is facilitated if the silver solution is made easily accessible. It was first distributed by the state board of health in Rhode Island in 1909, and this is now done in California, Illinois, Kansas, Kentucky, Massachusetts, Nebraska, New Jersey, New York, Ohio, Oklahoma, Vermont and Wisconsin. In some of these states very little is used but in New York 24,660 packages were given out in 1914 at a cost of $3,731.25. In Massachusetts 3,236 packages were given out in May, 1915, as compared with 474 in May, 1914; in Rhode Island about 1,500 packages are distributed, and Vermont reports extensive use. As far as can be discovered by those most conversant with conditions blindness from ophthalmia has decreased one half in Massachusetts since the efforts of the state health department were directed to this end.

Medical Inspection of Schools

Outside of references to medical inspection in general educational work, not more than half a dozen state health departments have taken any active interest in this subject. Besides those here named few state boards of health have done much to advance school inspection. This does not mean that other departments of the state have done nothing. On the contrary, many laws relating to this subject have been enacted and the state department of education has often been active in securing their passage and enforcement. It has been impossible to report on the present status of school inspection in the United States and reference here is only made to the relation of state health officials to the movement.

In Florida the last legislature provided that every school child should have a physical examination each year. This is to be made by the county physician, under rules established by the State Board of Health. The inspection is to be paid for by the state department of health.

In Indiana where the health department has been exceedingly active in improving the conditions of school buildings, the law for the medical inspection of pupils provides that such inspection shall be made under rules promulgated jointly by the State Board of Health and the State Board of Education. Such rules have been made and issued by the two boards jointly, in a pamphlet with other instructions and information.

In Kansas the State Board of Health, in order to furnish an object lesson, made a thorough survey of a number of schools in Topeka.

Louisiana sends to every school the questionnaire issued by the United States Department of Education.

The Minnesota State Board of Health engaged a specialist to go to the smaller cities of the state and lecture and demonstrate methods of medical inspection. As a result systematic inspection was adopted in several of these cities.

In Pennsylvania the State Health Department carries on school inspection over a large part of the state outside of the larger cities. In all there are about 2,300 districts. The inspectors are appointed and paid by the department. There are 871 medical inspectors to inspect the buildings and pupils once each year in 11,684 rooms. They receive from $4.50 to $6.00 per room.

In Oregon the State Board of Health has recently had two nurses who are making the tour of the state, inspecting all schoolhouses and the children therein. They are sending children with obvious defects to physicians and reporting to the proper authorities unsanitary conditions in the school houses.

In Virginia the district health officers of the State Board of Health inspect thousands of schoolchildren and the department has been instrumental in organizing voluntary associations for the employment of school nurses to follow up the cases.

PUBLIC HEALTH EDUCATION

One of the most important functions of a state health department is to instruct the people in the science and art of sanitation. They must be taught how disease is caused and how it can be prevented.

There seems to be no immediate danger that health education will be neglected. Not only are state and local health officials hurrying to make use of every new device to attract the attention of the public, but numerous organizations, formed to promote some particular line of health work, as well as great corporations and universities, are flooding us with health leaflets, circulars, brochures, posters and postals. The press has been eager to publish catchy articles on sanitary matters, though there are signs that its capacity may become overtaxed. The magazine too, and the platform and the pulpit have been invaded by the health propaganda. It is now the quality rather than the quantity of health education which needs to be looked out for.

There are three main features of public health educational work which must especially be kept in mind. It must interest. It must reach all classes. It must be truthful.

By far the most important thing in public health education is to tell the truth. If sanitary science were an exact science, false teaching would be easily found out. Because it is not an exact science it requires the greatest care in teaching. It should not be made still more inexact by lapses from the truth. It is not necessary to be false to be interesting, though it is much easier. It takes some trouble to find out the truth. It is easier to guess at it. The hurried writer often does. There are enough things that are certain. There is no need of teaching what is uncertain. The great fault in health education today is that it does not always teach the absolute truth. In studying the efficiency of health education one should bear in mind especially its simplicity, attractiveness, truth and ability to reach people. Some of the more important means of education employed by state health departments are shown in Table 8.

Bulletins

The oldest form of attempt to reach the people is the periodical bulletin. It has been in use for thirty years or more, but it is only within a very few years that its use has become general. Bulletins are published in all the state health departments but Arkansas, Colorado, Delaware, Minnesota, Nevada, New Mexico, Oklahoma, South Carolina and Wyoming. In Nevada the publication is required but there is no appropriation, in Tennessee a food bulletin is published and in Minnesota a monthly report is printed by the county commissioners in a paper in each county and in Colorado bulletins were formerly published. At present monthly bulletins are published in twenty-two states and quarterly in seventeen. The regular bulletins vary in size from 8 pages to 124, though occasionally they may be larger still. The size is usually octavo though there are a few quartos and in Mississippi the bulletin is about the size of a small newspaper. It is believed in that state that this is the most attractive form, at least for country use.

As concerns subject matter and style there are several kinds of bulletins. One of the purposes in publishing periodical bulletins is to show health conditions in the state and what is being done by the department. More than half the bulletins contain statistical matter, in almost all mortality and perhaps morbidity statistics and statistics of the work of the laboratory, food divisions, etc. The amount of statistical material varies from one to twenty-four pages. The writer has found very little use for such monthly or quarterly statements. The bulletins in many states are delayed an inordinate time and at the best the publication is too late after the event to be of much interest. A monthly statistical bulletin was formerly published in Providence, R. I., and after its discontinuance there was only one inquiry made for it. Perhaps it is not unfair to consider this an index of the value attached to such literature. It is from annual statistical statements alone that much of value can be learned and it would seem that if the expense and labor involved in preparing and printing monthly or quarterly statements should be devoted to putting out promptly well analyzed annual reports much more would be accomplished. Sometimes as in Georgia, Illinois, Kentucky, Nebraska and Virginia one issue of the monthly bulletin may serve as an annual report or contain an annual report.

A few of the bulletins as those of California, Louisiana, Massachusetts, Ohio and Vermont are practically health officers' bulletins as the contents consist, besides the statistical part, chiefly of more or less technical papers on various phases of public health work or on epidemiology. The papers read at the meetings of the local health officers are published in this way, instead of in a separate volume, in Ohio, West Virginia and Vermont. Most of the bulletins, however, are designed apparently to reach educated lay readers such as clergymen, lawyers and especially teachers. Many of them are exclusively for this purpose while others contain occasional articles of a technical nature appealing to health officers or physicians. The New York publication is an example of a well balanced bulletin of this kind. Its vital statistics are of more than ordinary value, its technical and popular articles are well chosen and up to date, and it has useful suggestions to teachers for health lessons. The trouble with most of the articles found in the bulletins is that they frequently are carelessly prepared, do not contain the latest scientific truth, and are tiresome and uninteresting. Some attempt to overcome this latter fault by inserting a few jokes, poetry or articles having little or nothing to do with public health. Bulletins are made more attractive as well as effective if the subject is adapted to the season, or concerns any notable occurrence, or otherwise relates to matters of immediate interest.

In some of the states little or no effort is made to reach the technical reader, but much attention is given to secure the interest and attention of the great mass of intelligent people. This is particularly true in Florida, Indiana, Iowa, Michigan, Mississippi, North Carolina and Virginia. Sometimes this attempt is far from successful. More or less of the material is weak and inaccurate. On the other hand, if skilfully and honestly written, clear and simple language not only appeals to the masses, but secures the attention of the highly educated equally well. The truthfulness, and force, as well as the simplicity of the Virginia bulletins have been quickly recognized by health officers everywhere and these bulletins are the best examples of such publications.

The use of illustrations, especially cartoons, seems to meet with favor and they may be found in bulletins in Arizona, Illinois, Indiana, Iowa, Kentucky, Louisiana, Michigan, Mississippi, New York, North Dakota, North Carolina, South Carolina, Texas and Virginia and perhaps in other states. Another way of interesting the public in the bulletin has recently been adopted in North Carolina where a prize of $25 is offered for the best essay on each of six subjects relating to public health, the successful essays to be published in the bulletin.

In some states great effort is made to reach the public through the schools. Thus in Kansas some of the bulletins of the State Board of Health are used as textbooks on hygiene in the schools. In Maine a large number of leaflets for the schoolchildren have been prepared and are issued in editions of 10,000. If the department had the funds, it is said that a much larger number could be used. The schools are very glad to have them and it is believed by the executive officer that this is the most effective means of education he has.

Some of the state utilizes the monthly bulletin as a means of publishing bulletins on special subjects. Instead of filling the bulletin with articles, or notes on a variety of subjects, the whole of it is devoted to one subject as Scarlet Fever, The Sanitary Privy, Disinfection, Rural Water Supplies, etc. This plan is followed in Georgia, Pennsylvania, South Carolina and Virginia where all or most of the periodical bulletins deal with one subject only. These state board of health bulletins are usually entered at the postoffice as second-class matter, though in some states they are published too irregularly to admit of this. The circulation of the bulletins varies greatly. Among reported circulations are: Idaho, 1,000; South Dakota, 3,000; California, Missouri and Texas, 5,000; Florida, 7,000; New Hampshire, 7,500; Ohio and West Virginia, 8,000; Vermont and Wisconsin, 10,000; Mississippi, 15,000 to 20,000; Louisiana, Michigan and Virginia, 20,000; New York, 32,000, and North Carolina, 40,000. According to these figures the circulation according to population is far greater in Vermont than in any other state, which is surprising in view of the generally technical character of the bulletin. Bulletins are usually sent to health officers, physicians, and clergymen, often to teachers, to libraries and sometimes to nurses, and are distributed at state and county fairs. Lists are obtained in Mississippi from the circuit courts and from tax lists, in Vermont and Virginia from granges and farmers' clubs, in West Virginia from women's clubs; the postmasters are of much assistance in Vermont.

Health Almanacs

Since the first settlement in New England almanacs have been very popular and have always been used as a medium of education. The almanac is especially important in the country, but many of the dwellers in our north-eastern cities could not do without their "Old Farmers' Almanac." The Virginia Health Department seems to have been first to take advantage of this popularity and to issue a health almanac. This was in 1911. It proved very popular and health almanacs have since been issued in Kansas, North Carolina and New York. This almanac is usually sent out as the January number. In Kansas the health almanac is used in schools for its chronology of important events.

Special Bulletins

Probably every state issues bulletins on special subjects, such as the different communicable diseases, or other preventable diseases, or on various sanitary procedures, or indeed on any subject relating to the public health which is of interest to many people. These bulletins are kept in stock and may serve for a number of years without revision. Oftentimes they are made to serve too long. Often the edition of some of the special bulletins is very large, much larger than the periodical bulletins. Thus in Virginia while the usual issue of bulletins is 20,000 that on the sanitary privy rose to 45,000 and of the first aid manual to 100,000. In New Hampshire the issue of the quarterly bulletin is 7,500, that of the bulletin on tuberculosis 75,000. Sometimes these bulletins are obtained from outside sources as the American Medical Association, the United States Public Health Service and the Children's Bureau. There is of course great variety in the form of the bulletins as some are for health officers, some for physicians, some for other professional men, and some for the masses.

Posters

The poster has been used a good deal by state health officials, particularly in the South. Posters are the common means for preparing people for the lectures and the dispensary work in the campaign against hookworm. The grocery, the postoffice, the signpost, walls and fences are used as in other similar forms of advertising. So, too, posters are commonly used to announce tuberculosis, infant welfare, and general health exhibits. Besides these usual uses for posters many health departments have used them to set forth in a striking way important sanitary facts. A very popular subject in which the poster serves as a means of education is the fly. Various designs, notably with illustrations have been used. Another subject for which there have been printed a number of posters is vital statistics. "When is Your Birthday?" and "If You Owned a Thoroughbred" are catchy headings. Other posters which happen to be at hand deal with smallpox, tuberculosis, typhoid vaccine, rats, wood alcohol, pure food, and bad eggs. Recently the Virginia department has covered the state with enameled tin posters of excellent character. These were posted at remarkably low cost.

Press Service

Most persons are agreed that articles for the press afford the most effective means for reaching large numbers of persons. In North Carolina it was determined that the volume of printed matter reaching the public through news articles to about 200 newspapers was greater than that of the bulletins with a circulation of 40,000 copies of thirty-two pages. Reference to Table 8 will show the number of papers served in several of the states. The most important field for state board of health press service is the weekly country newspaper. It is true that the dailies, even the larger ones in great cities, occasionally make use of these articles but they are not so eager for them as are the smaller papers. Sometimes it is advisable to prepare special articles for the larger dailies or send to them only selected ones from the regular service to the weekly papers. Usually the articles are sent direct to the papers themselves, but sometimes, especially in the case of the dailies, it is done through a press association. Thus in Indiana the State Board of Health maintains a semi-weekly service for an association of about fifty dailies with an aggregate circulation of about 300,000. In California, Wisconsin and Texas the articles are given to a syndicate. Apparently in Texas the syndicate includes only the larger papers, but it is said that one or two of the larger papers always print and the smaller papers copy from them. This certainly is not a very effective way. In Texas, as in Indiana, the service is semi-weekly and also in Illinois. In the latter state many of the city papers, including those of Chicago, print. In California and Wisconsin representatives of a syndicate of dailies call each day at the office to receive whatever may be offered. Occasionally a state health officer will write articles exclusively for one paper, sometimes for pay. In the few instances where this has been done it is said to have caused no trouble, but it can readily be seen how it might. The smaller papers and many of the larger papers are generally very glad to get these health articles but occasionally, as in Louisiana, this service did not prove successful. In another state the papers were said to be unfriendly. In Indiana, besides the semi-weekly service to the dailies, weekly articles are sent to about 125 weeklies. In Oklahoma it is stated that about 400 of 600 papers print the articles.

Usually a multigraph copy of articles is sent to each paper, but, sometimes, plate matter is sent out in Pennsylvania, and it was done regularly for a time in New York. This of course is much more expensive, but in New York it is said to be more acceptable to the papers. In this state the double column article is prepared. It costs about $100 a week to send this to 400 papers reaching 1,500,000 people. In New York copy for several articles was sent at one time with the date of release over each. When copy is sent to the smaller papers it is well to have it with headings all ready for the compositor indicating the type to be used. The larger papers, it is said, prefer to write the headings.

To be successful press articles must be well written. There are few men who can do this. They must be clear and short. Too great length spoils many an article. It is said that in the north-eastern states somewhat more formal writing is necessary than in other parts of the country.

Doubtless more effective work can be done whenever local incidents can be worked into articles, but of course this requires much more labor, as it involves the writing of a special article, and can only be done occasionally. It is done, however, in Indiana and Virginia. Sometimes a special article may be sent to all the papers in one county. Some writers pride themselves on never using the name of the department, while others think it gives authority to have the article avowedly come from the state department of health.

Lectures

The lecture is a useful means of reaching people, but to directly reach many people in this way involves great labor and expense. Lectures to teachers, physicians and influential people are most useful because in this way teachers and leaders are being taught. Thus in Minnesota considerable attention is given to lectures in the Medical, Educational, and Agricultural Departments of the University and also at the meetings of county school officers. The latter is done in Kansas and Virginia. There are less than a dozen states in which it was reported that no lectures were being given. In many states the number of lectures is very large. One of the principal ways of enlightening the people in the hookworm campaigns has been by means of lectures which were given at various places in each county. The campaigns against tuberculosis and to reduce infant mortality have been largely carried on by means of lectures, as is the intensive work for the improvement of the sanitation of towns in Indiana and Louisiana. Lectures are often given in churches and schools, before women's clubs, granges, labor unions, the Chautauqua, at fairs and before Christian associations. In some instances, as in Massachusetts, New York and North Carolina, the syllabus of a lecture has been prepared and sent out in the way of suggestion to local speakers. Probably more lectures are given in connection with exhibits than anywhere else. Indeed, one of the functions of an exhibit is to draw people together so that they can be lectured to. The traveling exhibit, especially the train exhibit, gives an opportunity for large numbers of lectures. In Maine a woman lecturer has been giving 100 to 200 illustrated lectures to granges every year. The State Board of Health also employs other lecturers besides using its own staff. New York at present has lecturers on special subjects, on infant welfare, on the eye and ear and on the teeth, and these are sent all over the state. In Michigan extensive lecture trips are made by means of an automobile.

Lanterns and Moving Pictures

The non-illustrated lecture is said to be fast losing its power to draw and the "movies" have become so common that even the lantern is becoming obsolete. Probably this statement is rather an exaggeration and it is likely that lantern slides will for a long time to come prove a useful means of making lectures more interesting and instructive. Certainly many subjects connected with public health can be made very effective by the use of the lantern. At least seventeen state health departments have lanterns and some have several. About a dozen which are not provided with lanterns have sets of slides. Generally these slides are used by the lecturers of the department, but in some states they are loaned to outsiders. Stock slides purchased of the dealers are the cheapest and easiest to obtain, but when local conditions can be shown on the screen a far stronger impression is produced. In some states a very considerable effort is made to secure such slides. In Maine the department has eighteen sets of slides which are loaned. Much effort is made to get local views and an excellent camera is owned for this purpose. In Indiana, too, many local pictures are taken and after their use by the state board of health they are left with a local picture show. Moving picture machines are owned by the State Department of Health in Florida, Indiana, Kansas, Kentucky, Louisiana, Michigan, New Yorl Ohio, Rhode Island and Vermont, and one is occasionally hired in Utah and Washington, and most of these states own films. Films are also owned in Colorado, Illinois, Massachusetts, Maryland and North Dakota. In Indiana the machine is used in towns as far in the country as electricity can be obtained and wire has been run a mile in one place to reach the exhibit where the machine was used. So also in Ohio, the machine is in constant use in connection with intensive work of various kinds. In Rhode Island the machine is much used and very popular. In Vermont the moving picture machine is put on a wagon with electric generator and everything else needed and shipped on a flat car to different sections of the state and then run out to small places where there is no electricity and where they have not before had "movies." The machine was bought for tuberculosis work but is now used on many other subjects. It costs about $25 a night, but of course, when there is electricity, the machine alone is shipped and then the cost is much less.

Exhibits

The exhibit has become one of the most popular means of public health education. It usually is not used alone but is explained by lectures, illustrated by slides, and the lectures advertised by press notices, are made a means of distributing literature. Maryland was the first state to hold a tuberculosis exhibit (1904) and also the first to have a milk exhibit (1905). The latter was organized by the State Board of Health though the former was not. The efforts of the various tuberculosis associations, particularly the National Association, have been largely responsible for the development of the exhibit. But exhibits relating to milk, to infant hygiene and to health work generally soon followed. Individuals and firms make a business of preparing them and setting them up. Cartoons and diagrams, models and mechanical devices, photographs, pathological material and microscopical and bacteriological specimens, all have their place. The art of making everything tell and of securing durability, compactness and facility in setting up, is being highly developed. Exhibits may be temporary, or permanent, or traveling, and large enough to fill a hall, or small enough for a shop window. For state work the movable exhibit is by far the most important, as to provide for all parts of the state it must be continually on the move.

Although exhibits are of such recognized value they are not being used by the State Health Department in Alabama, Arizona, Arkansas, California, Colorado, Connecticut, Delaware, Georgia, Missouri, Montana, Nebraska, Nevada, New Hampshire, North Dakota, South Carolina, South Dakota and Wyoming.

Sometimes the exhibit is quite limited in scope. Thus it relates to tuberculosis alone in New Jersey, West Virginia and Vermont, to tuberculosis and food in Kansas, tuberculosis and milk in Maryland, tuberculosis and social hygiene in Oregon, tuberculosis and infant hygiene in Pennsylvania. General health exhibits are used more or less extensively in the other states. One of the most useful places for an exhibit is a state fair, for some of these are visited by great throngs of people from all over the state. Thus it is said that the combined attendance at the Rochester and Syracuse fairs where the New York exhibits were shown last year was 750,000. In several states, Idaho, Iowa, Mississippi, North Carolina and Utah, the state fair is the only place where the exhibit is shown. These are all general health exhibits. They are shown at many county fairs as well as the state fair in Indiana, Louisiana, Oklahoma, Michigan, Minnesota, New York, Tennessee and probably other states. In Indiana a small exhibit is kept on view in the State House. In this state a small exhibit, which can be packed in a trunk is sent about to be shown in shop windows.

In Illinois, Indiana, Kansas, Louisiana, Maine, Maryland, Michigan, Minnesota, New Jersey, New York, Ohio, Oregon, Pennsylvania, Rhode Island, Tennessee, Texas, Vermont, Washington and Wisconsin exhibits have made repeated and extensive tours of the state. In some the exhibits are general, but in others, as has been referred to, they are special. In a few, as will be noticed later, they are kept set up in a car and carried wherever there is a railroad. In most states the exhibits are designed so as to be packed readily and thus shipped from place to place.

The Health Car

So far as the writer knows the state departments of agriculture and the railroads were the first to use a car, or cars to carry exhibits and lecturers to the small communities of the state. The scheme has naturally appealed to public health workers. It is stated that a tuberculosis exhibit consisting chiefly of charts was sent out by the State Board of Health in Maryland in 1909. In March of the following year, the California car was started on its tour and this was the first health car with a general health exhibit and lecturers. The car was furnished and fitted up by the railroads and carried free and was also cleaned and kept in order without expense to the department. Dr. Snow, who later became secretary of the State Board of Health, was director and he and the demonstrators for the most part served without pay. The car was carried on some of the electric lines as well as on the steam roads and the exhibits were seen by 100,000 people.

In Louisiana the "train" started with one car in November, 1910. Another was added in 1911 to serve as an administration car in which the staff lived during the journeys. The cars were practically gifts, but it cost several thousand dollars to fit them up. A circuit of the state was made in 1910-11, as many places being visited as possible. The car aroused great public interest. A moving picture outfit was carried and was oftentimes taken to a hall in the town for evening lectures and sometimes these were given in the open air. Lectures were given for white and colored separately. Members of the staff were often taken in automobiles to lecture in places away from the railroad. The cars were always carried free by the railroads. Inspection work was vigorously carried on by the staff. Towns, villages, business places and public buildings were scored and much executive work in municipal sanitation was done. The staff consisted of about a dozen persons and the cost of maintaining them was about a dollar a day. Most of them were regular members of the department and carried on their routine work as well as they could. The first trip covered 7,000 miles. On the second trip, not so many small places were visited by the train which was left a longer time at the larger towns while some of the staff made short excursions to neighboring communities. It was stated (June, 1914) that 375,000 persons had seen the exhibits and 186,000 had attended the moving picture lectures. It is believed by the department that a great stimulus has been given to public health work, in the state. Towns have not only cleaned up but they have learned to keep clean. The position of the local health officers has been strengthened.

In Michigan the health car with its exhibit goes out with the agricultural car. These are loaned by the roads and are carried free. The exhibit is a general one and is accompanied by four members of the health department staff, different men going at different times. The first journey was made in 1913. In 1914 during a trip of twenty-eight days the exhibit was seen by 40,000 persons.

In Tennessee the State Board of Health sent out a health car with a general exhibit in 1913, in conjunction with the car of the department of agriculture. A diner and sleeper were attached to the train. The cars were loaned by the railroads and carried free. The cost to the State Board of Health the first year was $2,750. Last year it was $400. The tour covered two and a half months and it is stated that by actual count the car was visited by 400,000 persons.

In Texas an appropriation of $10,000 was made for a health train which became available in September, 1914, at which time the car was sent out. It was intended to be run in cooperation with the Committee on Public Health of the State Medical Association. No details of the work are at present available. For a time a car was used for the anti-tuberculosis campaign in West Virginia. A health train is in preparation in Florida.

Intensive Campaigns

The greatest value appears to be obtained from the exhibit when it is used in conjunction with other features as a part of an intensive campaign to develop interest and give popular instruction in general sanitation or in relation to some specific subject. This type of aggressive campaign centering around an exhibit was first developed and popularized in connection with anti-tuberculosis work and in most states a tuberculosis exhibit was the first type set up. Baby saving and child welfare, milk, food, social hygiene and other specialized exhibits have also been shown and the general health exhibit has been a development from them. The special exhibits have been designed to help the special campaigns and the general exhibits have been part of a general campaign for health betterment. In all such campaigns preliminary work has to be done, and the local health officials and prominent persons interested. Press announcements are secured, posters distributed and perhaps banners strung across the street and other advertising methods employed. Illustrated lectures are given and local talent is engaged. Literature is distributed. Special times are set apart for different classes, as the schools, or labor unions, or women's clubs. Sometimes schools are dismissed to allow the children to attend and they are made to write essays about it. In some lines, as in baby welfare and anti-tuberculosis campaigns, the public health muse has an important place. At times the methods are quite sensational. This of itself does not matter, if it does not offend the public taste, but unfortunately sensational methods are apt to go with careless and inaccurate teaching. On the whole the intensive campaign appears to be the most effective means of securing results, but every detail of the instruction must be based on the established truths of sanitary science and not on the hastily developed theories of enthusiastic reformers. While as a rule the intensive campaign centers around the exhibit it does not necessarily do so, and the widespread work of the Rockefeller Commission was largely carried on without this aid.

Health Days

The setting aside of a day or week for arousing public sentiment on health matters is often done. "Tuberculosis Day" or "Babies Day" have been utilized by associations organized for the promotion of these special lines of health work. State health departments, in a similar manner, have planned health days in schools, as in Louisiana and North Carolina, or in the granges, as in Michigan. Indiana has had a health day which under the guidance of the State Board of Health effectively stimulated the interest of large numbers of persons in general health problems. The teachers in every school were asked to give a health lesson. Processions were arranged for in many places. The one in Indianapolis was very elaborate, with many floats, and was said to have been viewed by more people than ever assembled for any parade in that city. The store windows were decorated. There were many public meetings with addresses on health topics. It was almost as successful in a dozen or more of the other Indiana cities. Health days have been organized in many Michigan cities and counties by the State Board of Health. Minnesota also has had a most successful health week.

Persons in Charge of Education

In most state health departments there is no special person or separate bureau in charge of the educational work. The executive officer is most likely himself to do most of the writing and directing, though of course he frequently calls on the other members of the staff and on outside parties. In Rhode Island a committee of the State Board of Health has charge of the bulletin, while the executive officer has charge of exhibits and other means of education. In California and Texas the vital statistician has charge of the publication of the bulletin. In Pennsylvania a physician is employed to edit but he is in no sense a "publicity" man. In Florida a newspaper man comes to the office weekly and writes the press notices, receiving his public health ideas and his directions from the executive officer. In Virginia also a newspaper man is employed to write press articles and get them in proper shape for sending out. Scientific and technical information is furnished by members of the department, particularly by the assistant commissioner. This combination has been particularly successful in that state. Many articles and bulletins are of course also prepared entirely by members of the staff.

In Georgia a man devotes all his time to educational work, and has been engaged chiefly in lecturing. In Louisiana a woman, called Instructor in School Hygiene, has charge of a large part of the educational work and publications, though the president of the board is the real director and also attends to much of the detail himself. In Massachusetts the educational work is carried on by the Division of Hygiene with a part time director. In North Carolina it has come about that the engineer gives most of his time to education and may properly be considered the educational man of the department. In Wisconsin there is on paper a Bureau of Publications, Information and Education, but it has not yet been organized. In New York one of the six divisions of the department already established is the Division of Publicity and Education. Ohio has the most elaborate bureau, but it covers the tuberculosis work as well as general health work. The director is also secretary of the state tuberculosis association though for this he draws no salary. There is also a superintendent of publications, a supervising nurse, a visiting nurse, a superintendent of exhibits, a statistician and assistant statistician and three stenographers.

This formal cooperation of the state department of health with other organizations is seen in other states. Thus the education man of the North Carolina department is secretary of the Social Service Association. The president and secretary of the Oregon board have been active in the management of the Social Hygiene Society and the department does some of the printing for the society and helps it in other direct ways. In Minnesota the State Board of Health for a time paid a part of the salary of the secretary of the Minnesota Public Health Association and also for some of the printing. In Louisiana Miss Morris of the State Department of Health is chairman of the Sanitation Committee of the Federation of Women's Clubs.

FOOD

In the popular mind it is believed that nothing affects health more than food. The pseudo-sanitarian of a half a century ago laid the foundation for this popular error which in recent times has been well fostered by the magazine writer and the sensational lecturer. It is doubtless true, though we know altogether too little about it, that health may be unfavorably affected by an ill-balanced ration, by improperly prepared food, or by disregarding its digestibility. The popular mind, however, gives little heed to this, but wants to blame adulterated food for general bad health and infected food for many specific diseases. It is now well recognzed by those conversant with the subject, that adulteration is, except rarely, an economic problem, and that with the exception of milk, foods are only very occasionally the bearers of infection. It is true, also, that a good deal of the effort made to prevent what little disease transmission does occur in this way is quite ineffective, is often misdirected and lays emphasis on the least important points. The unesthetic receives more attention than the dangerous. Marble and white paint in the restaurant do not prevent the typhoid carrier in the kitchen from infecting the food. While it is true that cases of food poisoning (popularly called ptomaine poisoning) do, from time to time occur, the ordinary methods of market inspection accomplish absolutely nothing for their prevention.

There are two kinds of food control. Prevention of adulteration and promotion of cleanliness. In less than a quarter of the states is work being done by the health department along these lines. In this brief survey it was, of course, impracticable to go into the details of the work of other departments, even if it had been desirable, and it therefore seemed unnecessary to do so in regard to the health department. It is, perhaps, desirable to note in a general way what is being done.

Adulteration

The first state to enact a comprehensive law for the prevention of food adulteration was Massachusetts in 1882. The execution of the law was placed with the State Board of Health, partly, perhaps, because at that time more importance was attached to the relation of adulteration to health, but largely, doubtless, because of confidence in the scientific ability of the department. This law, with some modification, has been adopted in a number of states and its principles served as the basis of federal legislation. In some states, the duty of enforcement is placed on the health department for reasons similar to those advanced in Massachusetts. At present, the health department has the enforcement of these laws in Arkansas, California, Colorado, Delaware, Idaho, Indiana, Kansas, Louisiana, Maryland, Massachusetts, Montana, New Hampshire, New York, Oklahoma, Tennessee and Vermont, only sixteen in all. In two of these, Idaho and Tennessee, the connection between the food commissioner and the state board of health is exceedingly tenuous, so that the commissioner is pretty nearly an independent

officer. In Arkansas, Delaware and New York practically nothing is
done owing to lack of funds, so that there are only eleven states in
which the state health department is actually enforcing the "pure food
law." It should, however, be mentioned that in Arizona the execution
of these laws is with the director of the laboratory at the state university,
though the State Board of Health meets a small portion of the expenses
and publishes bulletins. In Kansas, the food work, though directed by
the State Board of Health, is done at the university and paid for by
the university.

Nearly all the states have officials to enforce food laws and in some
they are independent commissions; in others, they combine the control
of general adulteration with dairy work, and in others they are attached
to the state department of agriculture. As the health department in
so few states administer these laws, and as they have practically no
relation to the public health, they are not considered in this report, and
their enforcement is not credited to the health activities of the states.

Various opinions are held by state health officers as to the advisability
of including the control of food adulterations in the activities of the
health department. Quite a number, who do not have it in the department, desire it, some for the opportunity it would give to enforce cleanly
methods of food handling, others because they believe that it appeals to
the people, advertises the department and helps to increase the appropriation. On the other hand, some believe that the economic importance
and volume of food work tends to divert attention from really effective
lines of health work. Others fear the opposition of large commercial
interests. It seems to be a matter the decision of which must depend
on local conditions. If for certain reasons it appears that the control
of food adulteration would be more efficient and economical if it were
in the health department, there is no sufficient reason why it should
not be so placed, even if it has no connection with health.

Cleanliness, or Sanitation, of Food

Most health officials believe that uncleanly methods of handling food
are a cause of a good deal of disease transmission which could be
avoided. Exposure of food to dust and flies, and the handling of it,
are believed to make it often a carrier of disease germs. It is thought
to be important health work to prevent as much of this infection as
possible. It is not necessary here to discuss the relative importance
of this mode of infection, or the merits of the usual remedies. It is
sufficient to note activities in this direction. The essentials which are
aimed at in the "sanitary laws" and enforced by inspectors are general
cleanliness, fresh paint and whitewash, clean floors and woodwork, proper
toilet arrangements, the protection of food from dust, and screening
to prevent the ingress of flies. Sometimes reference is made to the
cleanliness, or healthfulness, of food handlers, but under present conditions, all that can be hoped for is to make them look a little more
tidy. It is useless to expect to inculcate those habits of cleanliness
which alone can prevent infection, or to eliminate any but the merest
fraction of those who are infected with transmissible disease. Everybody knows that half-way habits of cleanliness in the bacteriologic
laboratory, or the wards of a hospital, accomplish very little, and it

is doubtless somewhat so in the handling of food. Good is doubtless accomplished by the campaign of cleanliness, but there is some suspicion that, as the results of the control of adulteration are economic, so the results of sanitary inspection are more esthetic than disease reducing.

In all of the states in which the control of adulteration is in the health department, this department does something in the way of sanitation. In only one state, where the control of adulteration is in another department, does the health department interest itself in the sanitary side. This is in Mississippi. In most of the others, the food commissioner, or dairy commissioner, or whatever office may be charged with the maintenance of food standards, makes an effort to secure sanitary conditions also, as well as the freshness of food material, such as fruit, vegetables, meats and eggs. In a few states this is not so, notably Pennsylvania, where the food commissioner has not been able to secure a "sanitary law." A note, however, has just come that the state department of health has adopted regulations requiring the protection of food and the exclusion of all diseased persons from handling food.

One field of sanitary endeavor is the market, grocery, fruit stand, peddler's wagon, restaurant or dining room where food is handled and delivered, to the consumer. These places have received little attention from the state health departments in the northeastern states, as New England, New York, New Jersey, Pennsylvania, Ohio and Michigan, but in the South are considered of great importance. In Louisiana, the inspection and scoring of these pla es has been carried on by the inspectors of the State Board of Health, and during the tour of the health train much attention is given to conditions in all the towns where stops are made. Screening, especially, is insisted on, for there is reason to believe, that under present conditions in the South, the fly is an important factor in the spread of typhoid fever. The Mississippi health department is equally insistent on this sort of food control, and its sanitary inspector is largely occupied in seeing that the county health officers do their duty in this respect. In many other states, the food department gives a great deal of attention to these matters, often requiring their inspectors to devote much time to this kind of inspection. This is true, especially, in Colorado, Connecticut, Georgia, Idaho, Indiana, Iowa, Missouri, Montana, Nebraska, New Hampshire, Nevada, North Dakota, Tennessee, Utah, Virginia, Wisconsin and Wyoming.

The sanitation of places where food is prepared, or manufactured, also receives attention, and in many states some state department exercises control over slaughter houses, canneries, oyster houses, ice cream factories, candy factories, bakeries, bottling establishments, and the like. Slaughter houses, particularly, have come under supervision, though this is largely on account of the nuisance they are likely to cause, rather than for securing a satisfactory condition of the product. A slaughter house is so often a nuisance to an adjoining town, when it is not to its own town, that local control has never been very successful. Some states, which pay little attention to the retailing of food, pay much to slaughter houses, as Massachusetts and New Jersey. In the former state, the health department pays especial attention to the inspection of the animals and meat. Local inspectors must be appointed and must be approved by the state health department, which keeps up a constant supervision and requires reports of work done. Through the local inspectors the sanitation is controlled. A great deal of slaughter house inspection and reconstruction has been done in Idaho, Kansas, Louisiana, Maryland, Mississippi, Montana, Nebraska, New Jersey, Tennessee and Wisconsin, and in most states the health department finds it necessary, more or less frequently, to go to the assistance of local officials who find themselves unable to cope with special cases. Many of the states have rules governing the construction and conduct of slaughter houses, and in Oklahoma, Mississippi, and perhaps other states, standard plans and specifications have been provided.

Probably the majority of the states have laws relating to bakeries. In Rhode Island this law, which also covers the supervision of ice cream and candy factories, is executed by the factory inspector. In most states, the food department has charge of bakery inspection and it is only in the few states where general food control is placed in the health department that the latter has anything to do with bakeries, and in some of these states it does not, as in Massachusetts and New Jersey.

Canneries receive special attention in Delaware, Indiana, Maryland and Georgia. Ice cream and candy factories, too, are subjects of legislation.

The regulation of cold storage is a matter which has received much attention, though its relation to health is still uncertain. Nevertheless, most persons, including the cold storage people, believe that some sort of supervision is desirable. Hence, in several states, laws have been passed to regulate the manner and length of storage and to provide for inspection. In Delaware, California, Indiana, Massachusetts, New Jersey and New York, the enforcement of the law depends on the state health department, and, in all but Delaware, a considerable sum is spent in an earnest endeavor to execute it properly. Nebraska, North Dakota and Pennsylvania have similar laws, but their enforcement is with the state food commissioner.

Danger from the spread of typhoid fever by oysters is real, though not very great. The pollution of the water must be very considerable or infection does not result. If there is no regulation, the danger is likely to increase with the increasing amounts of sewage which are being discharged. A number of states have undertaken such regulations. Among the seaboard states, Alabama, California, Delaware, Florida, Georgia, Maine, New Hampshire, North Carolina, Oregon, South Carolina, Texas and Washington, have no legislation and have taken no action. In some of these states there is little or no pollution of shellfish. In Connecticut a study was made by the State Board of Health of certain infected grounds and there was an effort to secure legislation, but without avail. In Louisiana the State Board of Health has made regulations, but there is no effort to enforce them. The Mississippi health department began an investigation similar to that in Connecticut, which at its request was completed by the United States Public Health Service. In New York extensive investigations were carried on by the State Board of Health, at the request of the Conservation Commission, but nothing has since been done.

In Maryland the State Board of Health has ordered, but apparently without authority, that oysters shall not be shipped from above a certain line in the bay.

The statutes in Massachusetts provide that the State Board of Health shall, on complaint, investigate instances of shellfish pollution, and may forbid the taking of such shellfish. This has been done, and also polluting sewers have been removed in several places. These activities have been for the protection of clams rather than oysters. In New Jersey it is forbidden to empty sewage (except by municipalities) into streams where there are shellfish. The State Board of Health is to inspect beds annually and issue certificates. Much has been accomplished. Careful surveys are made and much pollution has been removed. Probably Rhode Island has the best law. It is administered by the Shellfish Commission. The beds are to be inspected and certificates issued. The sanitation of the opening houses is provided for, and they are regularly inspected and scored. Careful inspection of the beds is maintained, many original investigations have been made, and a great deal has been accomplished. In Virginia the State Board of Health, the State Board of Agriculture and the Federal Department of Agriculture cooperate in the survey of beds. The use of many of the polluted beds has been stopped. The Shellfish Commission has recently begun the supervision of the opening houses after the Rhode Island plan.

MILK

The subject of milk control is one of the most complicated and difficult in the whole field of public health. There are some who feel that it is a local problem and should be left to the municipalities to work out for themselves. The majority believe theoretically in uniform state laws and state control, but these are difficult of attainment. In agricultural states, with small cities, the difficulties are not so great, and they are most acute in the northeastern states, where there are many large cities and less good agricultural land. Theoretically, the State Board of Health should be entrusted with the enforcement of milk laws, as well as consulted in their framing. Actually, state legislatures have not given the State Board of Health much authority, owing to fear on the part of the farmers. In some states it is claimed that authority over milk has been given to the department of agriculture, to keep it away from the health department, or a special dairy department has been created for a similar purpose.

Nearly all of the state health departments which are charged with the prevention of adulteration, attempt something in the way of improving the milk supply, and in only one of the states which are not so charged, namely, Connecticut, does this department do anything of consequence with milk.

The laboratory of the Connecticut State Board of Health has been doing much to improve conditions in the smaller towns where there is no inspection. The health officer sends iced samples to the laboratory, which are examined chemically and bacteriologically. The work is followed up in each place until improvement results. Seven thousand seven hundred and fourteen samples were examined in 1911-12. A good deal of effective work seems to have been done. The food commissioner formerly inspected many dairy farms, 5,366 in 1911-12, but this inspection is now somewhat in abeyance.

In Idaho the food commissioner, who is appointed by the State Board of Health, but is under no control by it, stated that much attention is given to milk, that all producers are inspected and scored, all milk must be sold in bottles or sealed cans, that there is a bacterial standard of 500,000, and that numerous samples are taken from delivery wagons, even in cities where there is an inspector. The claim is made that the "milk supplies are in first class condition," but as only ninety-five chemical analyses, and fewer bacteriological, were made in a biennial period, it may be suspected that much more remains to be done to improve the milk supply of Idaho.

Illinois has a dairy inspector, who is chiefly occupied in seeing that milk which is excluded from Chicago does not go elsewhere, and in summer four other inspectors are employed to assist the local inspectors in other parts of the state in inspecting dairies.

In Indiana it is stated that the food inspector takes about 1,000 samples a year for chemical analysis. They are also tested for visible dirt and offenders are prosecuted. Dairies are inspected to some extent and scored.

The Kansas health department tries to assist local health officials by taking the towns one by one and sampling and testing the milk. From the laboratory reports, however, it would appear that very little work is really done. The department has just completed a milk and cream survey of the state. Every town of 3,000 inhabitants has been visited and 800 samples of milk, and many samples of cream, have been taken and analyzed.

In Louisiana, rules for the sanitation of dairies are included in the code enacted by the State Board of Health, and the department inspects and scores dairy farms, of which there are about 1,000 in the state. Two thousand cows have been tested with tuberculin. Samples of milk are tested chemically, but not bacteriologically. Efforts seem to have been rather centered on New Orleans, though that city has local inspection. As only 421 analyses were reported for the year 1912-13, evidently little stress is laid on this part of the work.

Although there are a large number of cities carrying on local milk inspection in Massachusetts, the food division of the State Board of Health has long given considerable attention to the maintenance of the chemical standards. Most of the work is done in the towns where the facilities for local work are lacking, or scanty, though occasionally samples are taken in other places as a check. During 1913, 6,702 samples were analyzed. The veterinary division of the department has charge of the inspection of farms. There are three inspectors, who inspect all farms yielding over 20 quarts. A score card is used and all animals are examined and tuberculous cows reported to the state department of animal industry. There are about 20,000 dairy farms subject to inspection, and 4,492 were visited in 1913. A letter is sent to the physicians of the towns, giving a list of clean dairies, and one to the health officials, showing the poor dairies, and the dairymen also are notified by letter. Such dairy inspection is, by the present department, not considered the most effective line of work and has, to a large extent, been abandoned, and the veterinary division has been merged in the food division.

In Mississippi a rule of the State Board of Health requires that no milk can be sold except under a license issued by the county health officers, who are appointed by the State Board of Health. Before the license is issued, the cows must be tuberculin tested. In 1913 about 3,000 were tested. Infected animals are killed without compensation. This law has recently been declared constitutional.

In Montana all dairy farms must be licensed by the State Board of Health. They are inspected monthly by the county health officer, though recently the state dairy commission inspects farms supplying creameries.

The food inspectors of the New Hampshire board of health collect samples of milk for chemical analysis. Five hundred and eighty-four were taken in 1911-12. Local inspectors are shown about dairy inspection. Under a recent law milk can be sold as "certified milk," or "inspected milk," when produced under rules made by the State Board of Health and under inspection by the department. About twenty farms are selling "inspected milk."

The dairy division of the New Jersey board of health consists of a chief and six inspectors, who are supposed to inspect the 10,000 dairy farms of the state annually. They can, however, visit only about one third of this number. Five thousand, four hundred and forty-two inspections were made of 3,603 farms in 1913, and attention was devoted to the poorer ones. The division also tries to help local health officials by going out with them to inspect the farms supplying the town. As in Massachusetts, the chemical laboratory examines many samples of milk; 3,713 in 1913, and in this work makes every effort to cooperate with local officials.

In New York the state health department has, as yet, done no executive work, but last summer enacted an addition to the sanitary code providing that in municipalties no milk shall be sold except under license, that all dairy farms shall be inspected and scored, and that milk shall be sold in "grades" which are defined by the code.

The other state health departments do very little in the way of milk control. Some examine a few samples, and in Tennessee there is a little scoring. The Utah department at one time cooperated with the United States department of agriculture in an effort to eliminate tuberculosis. In Vermont some inspection of farms is carried on by the state appointed local health officers.

It was impossible to study the other state departments which are charged with the supervision of milk, but a cursory examination of their reports does not indicate that much is really being accomplished. One might suspect that the alleged attempt by the farmers to prevent effective control has been successful. Some of these departments do nothing at all. In a few no statement of the amount of work is given in the reports. Most of them do very little. The analysis during a year of 550 samples of milk in Georgia, 639 in Minnesota, 50 in Missouri (in six months), 103 in North Carolina, 40 in North Dakota, 518 in Ohio,

10 in Virginia, and 24 in Washington, does not indicate a serious attempt to prevent adulteration. In Connecticut 527 samples were taken by the dairy and food commission, as compared with 7,714 by the State Board of Health.

The inspection of 83 farms in Nebraska, of 28 in Nevada, of 103 in North Carolina, of 423 in Ohio, and 739 in Virginia, does not compare favorably with the more efficient health departments. Even Wisconsin, with 1,317 inspections, is far behind Massachusetts and New Jersey. The food and dairy department in Kentucky seems to have done some good work in assisting local officials, and reports 3,000 bacteriologic examinations. In Pennsylvania 2,951 chemical tests were made, and the health department in Philadelphia reports that the state dairy and food commission has been of much assistance. In Oregon 4,352 farms were inspected in 1913-14, and in Washington 3,522.

ENGINEERING

Water and Sewage

The supervision of water supplies, so that only water which is free from the danger of causing disease may be used by the public, is an exceedingly important function of the state. It is peculiarly the business of the state, as distinguished from the municipality. The latter, it is true, has to build and operate water works, but the relations of communities to one another have such an important bearing on the purity of water supplies, and the cleanliness of streams and lakes, that the central authority of the state is needed to prevent the trespass of one community on the rights of another. Moreover, the state is in a position to secure expert advice for the smaller communities, which they would not, or could not, obtain for themselves.

Massachusetts seems to have been the first state to adopt a plan for central water supervision, placing it under the State Board of Health in 1886. The law was not far reaching at first, and, in fact, never has been as stringent as is now thought desirable. The investigations and extensive experimental work of the department was so important, and its advice so good, that a vast improvement has been made in conditions in the state, particularly in regard to potable waters. The influence of this work was felt beyond the confines of Massachusetts, and much of the improvement in the water supplies of other New England states has been due to the example set by Massachusetts cities, and much assistance has been given through the published reports of the department and in other ways. The comparatively low typhoid death rate from typhoid fever, of the New England states, is probably largely the indirect results of the activities of the State Board of Health of Massachusetts.

The supervision of water and sewerage is largely health work. The supervision of potable water is almost entirely so, and of sewage disposal to a considerable extent. Many of the problems of sewage disposal, however, are not health problems, but have to do only with nuisances. It is impossible, in practice, to make any distinction in administration and so in this, as in other lines, health officials are obliged to deal, often to a large extent, with matters which do not particularly affect health.

A table has been prepared (Table 9) to show what is being done to protect the waters of the various states, salient or suggestive features being indicated in different columns. Not much over a third of the states appear to be taking active interest in this matter, and it may be asked whether some of these, as Connecticut, Louisiana, Maine, Montana, New Hampshire, Oregon and West Virginia, really belong in the list, but Louisiana and West Virginia have engineers who are working on the problems which arise. Maine, with a very small appropriation, has studied its water supplies and keeps up regular analyses. Connecticut, Montana, New Hampshire and Oregon, have laws which can doubtless be made effective.

It is also true that in Colorado, Delaware, Nebraska, Oklahoma, South Carolina, and at times in other states, more or less analyses are made of public supplies, and in Nevada the laboratory proposes to seriously undertake such work.

Massachusetts, New York and New Jersey have been longer engaged in this work than have the other states, and it is notable that New England, and New York and New Jersey, have the lowest typhoid rates of any part of the country. Pennsylvania and Ohio have been doing effective work for some years, and the typhoid rate in those states has been markedly decreasing. At present good work is being done along effective lines in Illinois, Indiana, Kansas, Maryland, Michigan, Minnesota, Rhode Island and Virginia, but it has not continued long enough or the vital records are too imperfect for the results to be as apparent as in the other states.

Legislation

Nearly every state has some sort of law, usually dating back a great many years, forbidding in a general way the pollution of potable and other waters, but these are of little value. So, too, some of the laws provide that the state department of health shall have oversight, or care, of the waters of the state, as in Massachusetts, North Carolina and Vermont, or power to prevent pollution, as in California. In some states, as Massachusetts, Washington, West Virginia and Vermont, the State Board of Health is to advise with local authorities, or the latter are to consult the state board. In most states the health department, by virtue of its general powers, would feel authorized to investigate the condition of rivers, lakes and wells. Such general provisions are of little practical use. Something more specific has been found to be necessary. Among the more useful means of statutory control have been found:

1. **The Approval of Plans for Water Supply and Sewage Disposal.**— Such approval is virtually required in California, Connecticut, Iowa, Kansas, Louisiana, Maryland, Massachusetts, Michigan, Montana, New Hampshire, New Jersey, New York, North Carolina, Ohio, Oregon, Pennsylvania and Wisconsin. In Iowa and Louisiana, however, the requirement is by rule of the State Board of Health, which has the force of law. In Massachusetts this approval is not formally required, but towns can rarely get authority from the legislature to carry out their plans unless they are approved by the State Board of Health. In Michigan the law does not apparently call for a formal approval, but the State Board of Health has power to order changes and this amounts to the same thing. In California and Michigan those who apply to the department for advice concerning their plans must pay the cost of investigation.

The approval of plans presupposes their submission, and in all these states the law or rules so prescribe. To facilitate the preparation and consideration of these plans and specifications several states have adopted very explicit rules. In most instances these provisions apply only to works to be undertaken after the enactment of the law, but in Maryland, Michigan, North Carolina and Pennsylvania, plans of existing works, also, had to be filed after the passage of the law. In Kansas and Pennsylvania the state department of health has not been given full authority in these matters, for, in Kansas, although all sewerage works must have the approval of the State Board of Health, sewage may be discharged if the approval is secured of the governor, the attorney-general and the secretary of the State Board of Health. In Pennsylvania all plans are approved by the governor, attorney-general and commissioner of health.

In New Jersey, water projects must be approved by the water board and the public utilities board, as well as by the State Board of Health.

In New York, plans for water works must be approved by the conservation commission.

2. **Changes May Be Ordered.**—The submission and approval of plans for intended work is probably the most important measure for improving the condition of the waters of a state. It does not, however, in itself, bring about the correction of existing abuses, or remove existing dangers. Hence, some states have gone further and given to the state health department authority to order changes in the construction, or operation, of existing water or sewerage systems. This is true in Kansas, Maryland, Michigan, Minnesota, New Jersey, Ohio and Pennsylvania. In New Hampshire when the State Board of Health is satisfied that a water supply is dangerous it may prohibit its use. In New York the commissioner of health, and in Wisconsin the State Board of Health, with the approval of the governor, may order pollution to cease. In Ohio the State Board of Health may order the installation of a sewer system. Nevertheless, in Ohio, changes in water and sewerage systems are not to be ordered by the State Board of Health, except with the approval of the governor and attorney-general. In Missouri the public service commission claims great power, though it has not exercised its authority, "to order such reasonable improvements as will best promote the public interest, preserve the public health" of the users of water supplies.

In Maryland and Ohio, if water and sewerage works are not operated properly after due notice, the State Board of Health may order the appointment of a person, approved by it, to operate them.

Several laws provide for appeals to the courts, but two states have provisions of special interest, and which have received the approval of many engineers. In Ohio and Wisconsin, in case of dissatisfaction with the orders of the State Board of Health, an appeal may be had to a board of experts. A case in Ohio is now being decided in this way.

3. **Protection of Water Supplies by Rules.**—Many state boards of health have broad authority to make rules for the preservation of the public health and some, as those of Iowa and Louisiana, have not hesitated to attempt to control the whole water and sewerage situation in this way. In a number of the states, which have the best control of water pollution, specific authority is given in the statute for making rules for this purpose. Such states are Massachusetts, Michigan, Minnesota, Montana, New Hampshire, New York, North Carolina and Vermont. In many instances great care is given to the preparation of these rules. Usually a different set of rules is made for each watershed, but sometimes, as in North Carolina, general rules are adopted for the protection of all water supplies. Penalties are provided in all states but Michigan.

Department in Charge

Except in Missouri, where the public service commission has jurisdiction, though it as yet has done nothing, and in New Jersey and New
York, where other departments of the state government have a share
in the control, the state health department is charged with the administration of the laws relating to the protection, or purification, of the
waters of the state. In certain of these, however, as Kansas, Ohio,
Pennsylvania and Wisconsin, the approval of the governor and the
attorney-general has to be obtained in certain instances, as well as that
of the health officer, and, indeed, it is possible for the two laymen to
override the opinion of the sanitary expert. If adequate legislation for
water protection could be secured in each state, nearly every state
would require at least the full time service of an engineer, and many
would require, as indeed a number now have, much more than this.
In a few of the smaller states, as Arizona, Nevada, Delaware, and
some of the New England states, this is probably not necessary, and
a laboratory man with engineering training might be able to give such
engineering advice as is needed, or at least to show when it is needed,
and how it can be obtained, and at the same time he can do the laboratory
work needed by the department. As a matter of fact, at the present
time, the chemist, or bacteriologist, is doing what water work is done
in Connecticut, Maine, Montana, Nebraska, Nevada, New Hampshire,
North Dakota, Rhode Island and Wisconsin.

While a single engineer may suffice for quite a number of states,
those which are most populous, particularly if the population is largely
urban, will find it necessary to have several employees grouping them
into a division or bureau. The following have such a bureau or engineer: Alabama, California, Illinois, Kansas, Indiana, Maryland, Louisiana, Massachusetts, Michigan, Minnesota, New Jersey, New York, North
Carolina, Ohio, Pennsylvania, Vermont, Virginia and West Virginia.
In Alabama, Louisiana, North Carolina and West Virginia there is,
however, only an engineer. In Indiana and New Jersey the supervision
of water and sewerage is combined with the supervision of foods
and drugs, and in New Jersey the bureau of bacteriology is in the
same division. The arrangement in these two states seems to be unwise.
It would be much better to keep the engineering and food divisions
separate.

In Illinois up to the present time, and in Kansas, the engineering
work of the state, in the supervision of water and sewerage, has been
carried on by the state university. In Kansas this plan seems to have
worked very well. While there may be some difference of opinion as
to the desirability of a state university bearing a considerable part of
the burden of such a service, it is after all a matter of no real importance
which department pays the bills. There can, however, be no doubt whatever, that it is of great advantage to a state department of health to
have such a university connection. It is stimulating to the former and
enables it to keep in touch with scientific men and to know where they
are to be found when it wants them. Such a connection should be of
equal value to the university, for it affords a splendid opportunity of
making its students acquainted with the applications of science and

it is possible to fit them thus to become at once of practical use to the community. In the case of Kansas, although the engineering work is done at, and by, the university, the relation between the State Board of Health and the university is close and intimate. In Illinois the state water survey is more exclusively a division of the university, and because the State Board of Health has had little connection with it, it has operated to the disadvantage of the latter and of the state. Very recently, under a new law, the State Board of Health of Illinois has organized an engineering bureau which is to have charge of the administrative side of water protection. The laboratory work, as before, is to be done at the university. In Iowa the engineer of the State Board of Health has been relieved of hotel inspection and devotes all his time to the supervision of water and sewage. The laboratory work, which before had been done in part at Drake College, is, in the future, to be done by the laboratory at the state university. In North Dakota the state public health laboratory at the university, having little or no connection with the State Board of Health, has done excellent work in making a preliminary survey of the water supplies of the state.

In Illinois, Kansas, Massachusetts and Minnesota, the laboratory in which the necessary chemical and bacteriologic analyses are made, is maintained by the engineering division, and this seems to be an excellent arrangement. If the amount of work is large, as it is in all the larger states, it does not seem to be an uneconomical arrangement. Besides its laboratory in Boston, Massachusetts State Board of Health also maintains an experiment station at Lawrence, the valuable work of which is well known to everybody.

The largest engineering division by far is that of the Pennsylvania department of health. It consists of a chief and about twenty engineers, as many clerks, a number of draftsmen and fifty-five inspectors.

Operation of the Division

The work of an engineering division is varied.

1. Perhaps its most important function is the examination and approval, or criticism, of plans for public water supplies and sewerage. This, of course, occupies a great deal of time and labor, and often involves long and laborious investigations.

2. The giving of advice to communities, or officials. Thus, in Massachusetts in 1913, 211 such applications for such advice were made. In New York, 2,163 matters were referred to the division, of course, many of them of very minor importance.

3. Supervision of water supplies and sewage treatment works. Companies and municipalities should be induced, or compelled (as in Pennsylvania), to provide adequate laboratory facilities for such continuous control, at least of all suspicious water supplies. In Illinois the state water survey has, without compulsion, induced the installation of nineteen of these laboratories in that state. Even when such laboratory control is maintained, it is the duty of the State Board of Health to make observations from time to time to see that it is properly done. The knowledge that there is some such outside supervision is a desirable stimulus for local officials. When there is no local laboratory control, it is the business of the state to exercise control by means of frequent

analyses and inspections. Analyses are made quarterly, monthly, or weekly, according to the urgency of the need of supervision.

The inspection, at intervals, of water purification plants, sewage treatment works, polluted streams and dangerous water sheds, is important and is systematically carried on in Massachusetts, New Jersey, New York, Pennsylvania, and in some other states.

4. Surveys. Quite a number of states are making, or have made, more or less extensive surveys. Probably Pennsylvania is doing this more extensively than any other state. Detailed plans have already been prepared covering a large portion of the water sheds of the state, and showing the location of every house, barn, privy, cesspool or any other possible source of pollution.

5. Experimental work. The volume of experimental work in Massachusetts far exceeds that of any other state. It began nearly thirty years ago, and was made necessary by the lack of knowledge of water and sewage purification at that time. Many other states have found it necessary to study peculiar problems of their own, as the disposal of sugar refinery wastes in Louisiana, and creamery wastes in the Middle West. Local problems are continually arising, which can only be settled by experimental work, and the engineering departments of all the larger states must be prepared to undertake such as may be necessary.

6. Inspection of private wells. In some parts of the country, where the soil is sand and gravel, and drainage is good, the dwelling house well is rarely dangerously polluted. This is true of large portions of New England, and of regions in the Northwest and doubtless in other parts of the country. Where, however, the soil is of a limestone formation, or where drainage is poor, shallow wells are more often a source of disease. There is difference in attitude, in the different states, as to the inspection and analysis of private wells. Many states refuse to receive and analyze samples from private sources of water supply, on the ground of labor and expense. Most·believe that mere analysis of samples of water, without inspection of premises, is of little value, and to send inspectors hither and thither on such errands is impracticable. Others find that physicians and untrained health officers flood the laboratory with specimens, simply to satisfy some persistent client, or nervous citizen, not from well grounded suspicion. In some states systematic examinations are made of all the wells in certain communities, as in Kansas. In North Dakota the state laboratory examined a number of representative wells in each county. In Massachusetts it is the policy of the State Board of Health to systematically study the wells in any community in which it believes that the installation of a public water supply is needed.

7. The sale of bottled spring waters has become a business of considerable importance in some communities, and its supervision has been considered desirable. The incident which led to this in Rhode Island was the discovery that water was sold from a spring flowing directly beneath a main sewer. In that state analyses and inspections have been made of all commercial springs, and will be made annually. In Connecticut, by the act of March 11, 1913, spring water dealers must be licensed by the State Board of Health. Analyses and inspections of springs and bottling plants have been made and a number of dealers

have been refused a license. The recent Maryland water law has a similar provision in regard to the licensing and supervision of the sale of spring waters.

8. The regulations of the United States Public Health Service requiring water and ice used by interstate carriers, to be reported on by state or local health officials has, in some states, thrown quite a burden on the State Board of Health, for it is much more properly the duty of the state, than of the local health officers, to do such work. In most states the analyses are made by the state health department, and are made without charge, though this is not true of Kansas where a fee of $15 is charged.

In Minnesota advantage was taken of this demand of the railroads for certificates, to make a thorough investigation of all the supplies used by the intrastate, as well as the interstate, carriers. The results of this survey were published in United States Public Health Reports, May 15, 1914.

Ice

Those who have given most attention to the subject are agreed that the danger of infection by means of ice is negligible. Nevertheless, there has been a good deal of popular interest in the question and, rather from popular demand than on the opinion of experts, there has been considerable legislation. In California, Connecticut, Massachusetts, New Hampshire, New Jersey, Ohio and Washington local health authorities are given control of the cutting or sale of ice. Statutory provisions forbidding the cutting or sale of impure ice are found in California, Connecticut, Idaho, Maryland, New Hampshire, New Jersey and Wisconsin, and in Nevada the United States Public Health Service rules in regard to the use of water and ice by interstate carriers, by action of the State Board of Health, have been made to apply to intrastate carriers.

In California, Maryland, Massachusetts and New Hampshire the State Board of Health may make rules concerning ice, but in Massachusetts and New Hampshire this is only to be done on complaint and after a hearing. In Maryland no new source of ice supply can be used without a permit from the State Board of Health. In Wisconsin the State Board of Health may forbid the use of dangerous ice. In Montana and Vermont the State Board of Health is to have supervision of sources of ice supply.

In most states ice is examined by the State Department of Health for interstate carriers and occasionally on request, but besides this little is done. Sometimes, as in Minnesota, this involves the inspection of the source.

Other Engineering Activities

While the supervision of water and sewerage works is by far the most important line of engineering from a public health standpoint, and occupies most of the engineer's attention, in some states other matters are considered. Thus, in Louisiana, the engineer of the State Board of Health has given much attention to the sanitary construction of schools, jails and courthouses. In Minnesota considerable time has been devoted to a study of garbage disposal in the different cities and to advice about the sanitation of public buildings. In Michigan the engineer

also has to examine plans for public buildings, and is called on for
advice in regard to nuisances. The engineering division of the New
York department is frequently called on to investigate offensive trades,
smoke and other nuisances, the drainage of swamps, etc. The time
of one man is nearly occupied in examining public buildings. A special
investigation was made of oyster beds for the conservation commission.
In Massachusetts, too, the engineering division of the health department
looks after shellfish protection, as it does also in New Jersey. A vast
amount of work has been done by the Massachusetts State Board of
Health in connection with such projects as the improvement of the
Charles, Concord, Neponset and Sudbury rivers. In Pennsylvania a very
considerable amount of time is given by the engineering division to
offensive trades and other nuisances. About one half of the time of
the engineer in Vermont is devoted to the sanitation of schoolhouses and
other public buildings.

MISCELLANEOUS DUTIES

Hotel Inspection

A number of states, especially in the South and West, have enacted a "hotel law." These laws are very similar in nature, though some go much further than others, and have more "sanitary" features. The administration of most of these laws is self supporting, or partly so, as a license fee is charged. Among sanitary features touched on are the common towel, common glass for drinking, condition of toilets, freedom from vermin, cleanliness of bedding, length of sheets, cleansing, disinfection, screening, etc. While the appointed inspectors do much to enforce the laws, the traveling men do a great deal too, and in Louisiana they are appointed inspectors of the health department.

Among the states which have such a statute are Florida, Idaho, Illinois, Indiana, Iowa, Kansas, Minnesota, Mississippi, Missouri, Montana, Nebraska, Nevada, New York, North Dakota, Oklahoma, South Dakota, Tennessee, Utah, Virginia, Washington, West Virginia and Wisconsin. The inspection is the duty of the health department only in Idaho, Iowa, Mississippi, Montana, New York, Tennessee, Virginia and Wisconsin. In the other states the inspector is an independent official, or in the food department, as in Utah. In most states the law seems to be quite vigorously enforced, while in others, as Indiana, Illinois, Minnesota, Oklahoma and South Dakota, less attention is paid to it. Some of the state health officers think well of the law and believe that it is productive of much good, others think that its enforcement causes an undue amount of trouble. In Kansas the law was as first enforced by the health department, and when it was transferred to another department the former was well pleased.

Summer Hotels

Several state health departments have made some effort to improve the sanitary condition of summer hotels and cottage colonies. The sewage disposal is often very defective at such places, and typhoid outbreaks are not rarely traced to them. It was such an outbreak which led the Rhode Island legislature to pass an act in 1888 to provide for inspection by the State Board of Health. These inspections have been made at irregular intervals since. California also has an inspection law, but only one inspector, to cover this and other fields which, if properly done, would occupy the time of many men. The Connecticut State Board of Health has at times inspected summer hotels and cottage colonies. In Delaware this is done every summer. During the last summer a special inspector was employed in Illinois for this purpose. Summer resorts have also been inspected in Ohio, and more will be done in the future. The same is true of New York, Vermont and, to some extent, of Wisconsin.

Camps

The methods of living, and particularly the methods of excreta disposal, in camps, are a fertile source of trouble to the occupants of the camps and also to others, for streams are frequently polluted by them. Ordinary pleasure camps, the popular camps for boys and for girls, and the various types of industrial camps, are all in need of supervision. The importance of the problem is very generally appreciated, but very little has as yet been done to overcome the danger. In California there are many thousands of camps and single tents, but only the part time of one inspector is given to their supervision. In Connecticut there has been a desultory inspection. In Kansas the department did make earnest effort to improve the condition of the railroad construction and maintenance camps which are the greatest menace in that state, and much good was accomplished. Something has also been done in Illinois and Louisiana. In the latter state elaborate rules have been adopted and approval required. The new sanitary code of the New York state health department provides that labor camps for over ten persons shall be licensed by the local board of health. Rules are given for the privies, washing arrangements, garbage, manure, drainage, protection of nearby water supplies and other matters. The local health officers are to enforce the rules, but, of course, the supervisors will probably have much to do with it. South Carolina has rules for camps but no inspection. Considerable inspection is done in Vermont and Wisconsin. Special effort has been made in Washington to improve conditions in the very numerous lumber and construction camps and a great deal has been accomplished, largely owing, apparently, to the tact and practical judgment of the inspector.

School Houses

Although the importance of the school house has always loomed large in the eyes of health officials, comparatively little is being done by state health officials to improve or control conditions. Doubtless most health officers have talked and lectured on the subject and issued descriptive pamphlets on the sanitary school house. Undoubtedly good has been accomplished in this way. Nevertheless, when asked if they had any real authority over school houses 'construction, or could exercise any control, or were carrying on any systematic efforts for improvement, most state health executives answered in the negative. The states which exercise the most direct control through the health department are Indiana, Maine, Montana, South Dakota and Vermont. The department in Indiana has taken great interest in this subject. Under its grant of authority the board has made a series of rules governing the construction and care of school houses. Under a recent act in Illinois the superintendent of schools, with the advice of the State Board of Health, the state architect, and the fire marshal, is to draw up minimum specifications for the heating, ventilation and sanitation of school houses. These cover nineteen octavo pages. The legislature, in 1913, also passed a law covering many other points. The poorer school houses, with many defects, have been condemned. It is said that during the last two years 393 houses have thus been reconstructed or remodeled at a total cost of about $4,000,000. The State Board of Health of Maine has for years given much attention to school houses. Years ago a great many houses were inspected and useful bulletins on construction were published. At the present time the department of education has certain standard plans which are recommended, but many buildings are constructed according to other plans. All except the standard plans have to be approved by the State Board of Health, amounting to 150 or 200 per year. In Minnesota, plans formerly had to be approved by the health department, but this is now done by the board of education. In Montana and South Dakota, school house plans must be approved by the state health department, but in neither are there sufficient funds to do it. The Vermont board, like that of Indiana, has done much to improve the school houses of the state. The board has authority to make rules, which it has done, and, also, to condemn unsanitary houses. An engineer connected with the university is employed to give advice. A very great deal has been accomplished in improving the heating, ventilation, lighting and plumbing, as well as other matters. In Ohio the plumbing has to be approved by the health department. In Wisconsin, while the plans for school houses are approved by the board of education, the State Board of Health makes rules in regard to such matters as heating, cleaning, ventilation, water, etc. In those states where the state health department has sanitary inspectors of its own, as in Louisiana, Massachusetts, Mississippi, Utah, Washington and Wisconsin, a certain amount of school house inspection is done. In Kansas it was stated that a great deal was accomplished by a campaign of education among the teachers, and then leaving it to them to get the improvements made. A great many boards of education have taken up the matter of school house construction, or have had duties in regard to it placed on them by statute, but it has been impossible to go into this. The medical school inspectors in Pennsylvania are required to give careful attention to the house as well as to the pupils, and much good has been accomplished by them.

In the South the hookworm work has incidentally been of great assistance to the schools. Great numbers of privies have been built, and poor privies made "sanitary." It is surprising how often the individual cup has taken the place of the common dipper. In other ways, too, the campaign has stimulated the local school authorities to try for better things.

Public Institutions

In at least a dozen states the laws authorize the state health department in general terms to advise in regard to the sanitation of public buildings, and power to make rules is conferred in California, Florida, Indiana, Minnesota, Oklahoma, South Carolina, Utah, Vermont and

West Virginia. The department is also directed to inspect buildings
and institutions in Idaho, Massachusetts (jails), Mississippi, Montana,
North Carolina, Oklahoma, South Carolina and Wyoming. In California,
Michigan, Minnesota, Montana, New York and Vermont plans must be
submitted to the health department for approval.

In most of the states authorized to make rules, they have been
made, and also in some others, under the general grant of legislative
power, as in Kansas, Louisiana and Mississippi.

As regards the approval of plans, though required, this is not done in
California and Minnesota, in California because there is a state archi-
tect, and in Minnesota because the board of control fails to submit plans.
Approval is given in Michigan, Montana, New York and Vermont.

Regular inspection of public institutions is made by the members of
the State Board of Health in Kansas, Missouri and South Carolina,
and by the state health officer in Oklahoma and North Carolina. In
Louisiana, New York and Vermont an engineer does much of the
inspection work. In all of these states a great deal has been accomplished. In Louisiana particular attention has been given to jails, a
great many of which were in a deplorable condition and have been
rebuilt. The work in Vermont, too, has been very effective. In Idaho
and Montana, inspections are made by the county health officers under
the direction of the state health department.

Industrial Diseases

Very few states do much about this class of diseases, though the
subject is of much importance. For several years the State Board of
Health of Massachusetts had large powers in relation to factory inspection and the supervision of the health of operatives, but these have
since been transferred to another department. Occupational diseases
are reportable in Florida, Illinois, Kansas, Maine, Maryland, Mississippi,
Missouri, New Jersey, Ohio and Pennsylvania. Lead poisoning is
reportable in New Jersey. Very little seems to be done in any of these
states except Ohio. Here the State Board of Health was directed
by the legislature, in 1912, to make a survey of industrial diseases, and
a bureau was organized with a director and five inspectors. It is
hoped that after the survey is completed, the bureau will be made
permanent.

Narcotic Law

New York and Tennessee have a narcotic law which is to be
enforced by the state department of health. It was not learned that
much was done in New York, but in Tennessee the administration of
the law throws a good deal of a burden on the department. It is
believed that its enforcement is accomplishing much good. During the
legislative sessions of 1915, narcotic laws were passed in California,
Colorado, Connecticut, Idaho, Illinois, Maine, Massachusetts, Minnesota,
New Hampshire, New Jersey, New York, Nevada and Vermont.

Nostrums

The use of nostrums is certainly a very great evil and in more ways than one profoundly affects the public health. Many health departments occasionally issue literature on the subject and those of Indiana, Kentucky, Louisiana, North Carolina and Tennessee have been particularly active in fighting this evil.

Sex Hygiene

A number of state health officers have issued bulletins, or press notices, or they, or some other member of the staff, have lectured on this subject. This must be done with great care and tact, or very bitter hostile criticism may be aroused, as has happened in some instances. The only state in which organized effort seems to have been made is Oregon. Here the state appropriated $5,000 a year for two years for the use of the Social Hygiene Association, of which the executive officer of the health department is an active member. The appropriation for the next biennial period is $7,500.

Licensing

Physicians.—In Alabama, Connecticut, Illinois, Iowa, Maryland, Mississippi, Missouri, Nebraska, Rhode Island and West Virginia the state department of health is authorized to examine and license physicians. In Nevada and Pennsylvania the executive of the health department is, *ex officio,* a member of the examining board. There is a difference of opinion as to whether this is desirable. Many health officials seem to think that it is not. They feel that it is such an important subject, and requires so much time and attention, that it is unfavorable to the full development of the purely health activities of the department. Instead of helping the department to gain the good will of physicians, the duty of enforcing the medical practice act sometimes has the reverse effect, and often the physicians blame the health officials for failures due to defects in the laws, or negligence of prosecuting officers, or the hostility of the courts. It is, perhaps, unwise to say that a state department of health should not have charge of the licensing of physicians, but there are decided objections to having the department burdened with this duty.

Embalmers.—The department of health licenses embalmers in Florida, Idaho, Illinois, Iowa, Louisiana, Maryland, Michigan, Minnesota, Montana, North Dakota, Utah and Wisconsin. In Colorado, Connecticut, Maine, North Carolina, South Carolina, South Dakota, Tennessee, Washington and Wyoming, one or more members, usually the executive officer, ex officio, serve on the embalmers' board.

Midwives.—In Colorado, Connecticut, Illinois and New York the department licenses midwives, though in Connecticut they are examined by a special board.

Nurses.—Nurses are registered by the state department of health in California, Iowa and Maryland, and in Michigan and Wisconsin the executive officer serves on the board of registration.

Plumbers.—Plumbers are licensed by the state department of health in Massachusetts and Wisconsin.

Dentists, Pharmacists and Veterinarians.—These are licensed by the health department in Maryland.

Optometrists.—These are licensed by the board of health of Iowa.

Contagious Diseases of Animals

The older laws establishing the State Board of Health often conferred on it authority in relation to the contagious diseases of animals. As special departments for this were from time to time established in the different states, this function has generally fallen into disuse except in Florida. Here the state department of health has a well organized veterinary division which absorbs a considerable share of the income of the department. The legislature of 1915 in Texas appropriated $4,000 for the control of anthrax by the State Board of Health.

Illuminating Oils

The State Board of Health has charge of inspection in Iowa, Louisiana and New Jersey, and in Louisiana the license fees are the chief source of revenue of the department.

Inspection of Plumbing

In Ohio the secretary of the State Board of Health with some other officials constitute a building code commission, and drew up a code governing plumbing and drainage, which serves as the plumbing code of all cities. There is a state plumbing inspector, appointed by the State Board of Health, whose duty is to inspect the plumbing in all buildings where people congregate, but it is entirely impossible for him to cover the field.

In Wisconsin the State Board of Health enacted a plumbing code applicable to the whole state. Cities of the first, second and third class must have local inspectors and some of the cities of the fourth class do. The department supervises these inspectors, and outside of these cities is to do all plumbing inspection throughout the state.

Lodging House Inspection

The State Board of Health in Illinois is charged with the purely local duty of inspecting the lodging houses in cities of 100,000 inhabitants, of which Chicago is the only one. About $10,000 a year is expended for this purpose. In Pennsylvania the last legislature appropriated $14,000 to establish a division of housing in the state department of health. A director has been appointed and is making a survey of the state.

Operation of Hospitals

The management of the state sanatoria for tuberculosis in North Carolina, Pennsylvania, South Carolina and Virginia has already been referred to. In Florida the State Board of Health has constructed and operates four smallpox hospitals in different parts of the state.

Care of Crippled Children

In Florida the State Board of Health is authorized to provide care for crippled children. These are boarded in different hospitals at $10 per week and their treatment is under the direction of a physician employed by the board for this purpose. In 1914, there was expended $5,172.47. Fifty-one children were treated during the year.

FINANCIAL STATEMENT

It is necessary, for the proper appreciation of the successes or short-comings of public health work in the different states, that there should be available a statement of the amount of money expended. To simply show the gross amount, while of some interest, is not nearly so important as to show how much is expended on each of the chief activities of the department. This is especially necessary, as the functions of the department vary so in the different states. Again, some lines of work are carried on by other departments, as laboratory work by the state university, or the collection of vital statistics by the secretary of state. An attempt has been made to prepare a financial statement in the form suggested above and this is shown in Table 10, but it is far from satisfactory. In a considerable number of states it was impossible, even with much correspondence, to obtain a statement of expenses properly classified. State health officials rarely classify their expenditures according to function. In many reports the financial statement is far from clear, in others it merely separates salaries and other expenses, and in others still, a list is given of those to whom money is paid, but no attempt is made at classification, and in still others, when such an attempt is made, evidently little thought is given to it, so it is of no value for the present purpose. If a proper classification involved great labor, or expense in bookkeeping, there might be some excuse, but the labor involved is negligible when once the system is established. So, too, if a proper classification of expenses were only to be used in some comparative study like the present, there might be no justification for thus criticizing, but a classification of expenses according to the uses to which the money is put is absolutely essential if the health officer expects to have any clear idea of the cost of the different activities of his department. To know costs is just as essential in public health work as it is in manufacturing. Moreover, it is due the legislature and the taxpayers that they should know how their money is expended. It is not surprising, when one learns how difficult it is to find out for just what the health department money is expended, that legislators doubt the wisdom of increased appropriations.

A uniform plan of statement ought to be worked out and should then be used by every state health department. The principles followed by the census bureau should serve as the basis. Administrative or overhead charges should be carefully separated and nothing included which belongs under other headings. Thus, the salary of a clerk employed in receiving and tabulating morbidity statistics should be charged to the communicable disease account, and traveling expenses should not be placed together, but distributed to the divisions to which they properly belong. The expenses of each state health department should be distributed somewhat as follows:

Administration.
Vital statistics.
Control of communicable diseases.

Diagnostic laboratory.

Distribution of vaccine and sera and anitrabic treatment.

Food and drug supervision.

Milk supervision.

Engineering.

Sanitary inspection.

Public health education.

Other functions (specified).

There should be many subdivisions and it is desirable, under each heading, to separate salaries from other expenses.

The census bureau and certain groups of municipal health officers have worked out comprehensive schemes for a statement of municipal expenditures for health. State health officials have a strong organization and it is not to their credit that they have not long since done the same. The present chaos in their accounts is most disheartening. A carefully selected committee should be appointed to draw up a form of statement, but only after consultation with those who have had experience in their use. This form should then be followed by every state. The two things coming within the scope of this report, in which uniformity is most desirable, are the financial statement and tables of vital statistics. With all the current talk about standardization, one would think that state health officers would attempt to apply it here. As it is, these statements and tables are useless for comparative purposes and are often not much better for local use.

In preparing Table 10 expenditures for health purposes such as water control, the diagnostic laboratory, and the distribution of antitoxin, are included, even if they happen, as in certain states, to be charged to another appropriation. An important exception has been made in the case of state sanatoria for tuberculosis. The cost of these is so great, and they are so rarely managed by the health department, that it was feared that this inclusion would so overshadow other expenses as to defeat the purpose of the comparison. Unfortunately it was found impossible to obtain, in all cases, the cost of health work when carried on by the university, or a separate department, so that the totals do not in all states cover exactly the same lines of work, but the figures certainly come nearer to this than they would if the health department figures only had been used. In some states it was found impossible to get any useful distribution of expenses. In some states it is impossible to obtain any statement until months after the close of the fiscal year, and even then it is likely to be unintelligible until explained by a considerable correspondence. This is the reason why Table 10 is not brought up to date as nearly as one might expect. Many of the details of expenditures are far from accurate, often being mere approximations. Nevertheless, one can obtain a better idea of how the states spend money for health purposes from this table than from any other compilation with which the writer is acquainted.

It was planned to show, also, the ratio of expenditures for health in each state to the total expenditures in each state, but after a great deal of labor and several scores of letters, it was found to be impracticable, as, owing largely to the different treatment of interest charges in different states, and the existence of various distinct funds and grants, it is impossible to obtain figures which are at all comparable.

The following shows the states arranged according to expenditures for health, and also according to per capita expenditures for health purposes:

Expenditures for Health		Per Capita Expenditure	Cents
Pennsylvania	$1,047,431.66[1]	Florida	15.21
New York	284,676.85	Pennsylvania	12.70
Massachusetts	180,219.14	Maryland	10.54
Maryland	142,600.00	Vermont	9.27
Illinois	133,919.60	Nevada	7.59
Florida	129,012.03	Montana	5.45
New Jersey	125,942.15	Idaho	5.22
California	112,953.48	Massachusetts	4.95
Ohio	91,736.25	Louisiana	4.93
Louisiana	87,491.20	New Hampshire	4.81
Minnesota	72,013.31	New Jersey	4.47
Indiana	64,719.00	Delaware	4.04
North Carolina	61,031.78[2]	California	3.96
Texas	48,200.00	Arizona	3.76
Kansas	46,430.00	Minnesota	3.25
Virginia	45,000.00[3]	Rhode Island	3.14
Michigan	44,872.07	Utah	2.93
Wisconsin	38,205.63	Kansas	2.60
South Carolina	36,112.52[4]	New York	2.87
Vermont	33,385.50	North Carolina	2.60
Georgia	33,311.90	Indiana	2.32
Oklahoma	32,700.00	South Carolina	2.27
Iowa	32,568.32	Connecticut	2.24
Kentucky	30,002.45	Colorado	2.19
Missouri	29,206.19	Virginia	2.09
Connecticut	27,000.00	Maine	1.95
Alabama	25,000.00	Ohio	1.80
Montana	23,600.00	Illinois	1.78
Mississippi	22,975.43	Oregon	1.78
New Hampshire	21,200.00	Oklahoma	1.61
Idaho	19,820.00	Wisconsin	1.56
Colorado	19,980.00	North Dakota	1.48
Rhode Island	18,569.18	Michigan	1.48
Tennessee	16,552.49	Iowa	1.46
Washington	15,240.99	South Dakota	1.43
Maine	14,893.24	Kentucky	1.27
Oregon	14,000.00	Wyoming	1.24
West Virginia	14,000.00	Georgia	1.21
Utah	12,150.00	Texas	1.13
Nebraska	10,640.00	Alabama	1.11
North Dakota	10,569.38	Washington	1.08
South Dakota	9,730.00	Mississippi	1.20
Arizona	9,300.00	West Virginia	1.02
Arkansas	8,970.00	Missouri	.86
Delaware	8,492.02	Nebraska	.85
Nevada	7,500.00	Tennessee	.73
Wyoming	2,100.00	Arkansas	.53

1. Also $1,183,542.07 for tuberculosis sanatoria.
2. Also $52,376.79 for tuberculosis sanatoria.
3. Also $45,000 for tuberculosis sanatoria.
4. Also $10,000 for tuberculosis camp.

RATING OF THE STATES

Table 1 is intended to show the rating of the states in health work. Reference has been made in the introduction to the difficulties connected with such a scheme.

Perhaps some of the headings in the table may need explanation. Under supervision of local health officers is the subdivision "supervision" which means personal direction by some one from the central office. This appears to be the most important means of improving the local service and is given the highest rating. The value of conferences or "schools for health officers" is apparent. The regular bulletins in some states are popular and give little information to health officers. In other states, they are an important means of education for local health officials. Under communicable diseases, completeness of notification is important. In a registration state the score depends on the ratio of cases to deaths. In a non-registration state it is a matter of judgment. The direct control of communicable diseases by the state involves the routine control through supervisors, or inspectors, or advice from the central office of the cases as they are reported day by day, as well as the more usual "epidemic work" or control of outbreaks, which nearly every state health department does, though in some it is small in amount and inefficient. Intensive work is all too rare and means such work as that of Freeman in Virginia on rural typhoid, or the hookworm campaign in the South. Under tuberculosis, intensive work means going into a community and stimulating the people and officials so that something is done, an association formed, a nurse employed, notification improved and cases followed up by one agency or another. If a disease is not reportable, or if no report could be obtained, "reports" score zero. Where reportable the score depends on the ratio of cases to deaths. If the state is earnestly seeking to establish local hospitals and dispensaries for tuberculosis and especially if success is attending the effort, credit is given.

Under the diagnostic laboratory credit of two is given for each additional disease if the laboratory is prepared to examine for diseases other than diphtheria, tuberculosis and typhoid fever. The score for amount of work depends on the ratio of the examinations for diphtheria, typhoid fever and tuberculosis to the deaths from these diseases but cities with local laboratories are deducted from the computation. If more than two vaccines or sera are distributed, credit of two is given for each additional one. The credit for the amount of serum distributed refers only to diphtheria antitoxin. When the use of typhoid vaccine is more systemized it would be desirable to give credit for the amount of this also, but at present conditions vary so, and it was so difficult to obtain comparable data that it is not thought best to do so. Perhaps credit should be given for anti-rabic treatment, but after all, this disease, though serious enough, is insignificant in amount as compared with the other communicable diseases.

Under vital statistics a credit of forty is given for deaths if the state is in the registration area, and for births if it is probable that ninety per cent. are reported. If the state has a good law, even if it is not as yet enforced, a credit of ten is given, but if the law is poor and less than ninety per cent. of the deaths and births are reported, or if no data could be obtained from reports, or otherwise, no credit is allowed. Credit for tables is largely a matter of judgment but tables for a series of years and tables for localities, with rates in each, are considered of special importance.

Under child hygiene so little is being done that it may perhaps be argued that it should not have a place in the rating but the subject is so important that it was thought best to emphasize its neglect by the low score. The medical inspection of schools is omitted, chiefly because this is more often encouraged by the educational authorities than by the health authorities and data could not easily be obtained, but extra credits are given to those states where the health department has shown some activity in this important health problem. Intensive work on infant mortality, by which communities are taken one by one and actively stimulated, is considered of the most importance though little has been done. Nevertheless the prompt distribution of good literature to mothers is of value and deserves credit. The instruction and supervision of midwives is also important, as is the prevention of ophthalmia neonatorum. States which require reports of this disease to health officers receive a credit of ten, as notification, here as in other diseases, seems to be the most necessary step in prevention.

The items under education do not need explanation.

While the prevention of most adulterations is of little sanitary moment, the protection of milk, both from chemical and bacterial injury, is of great importance and should receive due credit. So, too, the protection of foodstuffs in general from dirtiness is worthy of credit and doubtless there are some who would give it a higher rating than is shown in the table.

It is doubtless true, also, that many would give to sanitation a higher rating, yet if one compares it with matters of such preponderating importance as the control of communicable diseases and aggressive work against tuberculosis it will scarcely be maintained that the sanitation of schools and other public buildings and of hotels and camps is of more than one fourth the value of either.

In considering the control of water and sewerage, it was thought that the investigation and approval of new projects, or the extension of old ones, is the most important duty of the engineer, while continued supervision of existing works and systematic surveys are each given an equal though slightly lesser credit.

Extra credits are given as follows: To Indiana, Kansas, Louisiana, North Carolina and Tennessee, ten each for fighting nostrums. To Maryland, Minnesota, Montana, New York, Pennsylvania, Vermont, Virginia and Washington, ten, and Massachusetts fifty, for research. To Ohio twenty for the study of occupational disease, to Oregon twenty for social hygiene work and Pennsylvania twenty and Florida ten for school inspection. To Pennsylvania ten for housing control.

Every one who has had experience in marking students in school and college knows full well that marks are of little value as indicating differences between those of nearly the same standing.   The difference between a student and his nearest neighbor in rank may often be a matter for argument.   The fallibility of man's judgment here shows out clearly. Nevertheless it is generally true that marks will rarely if ever put a student in the first third who ought to be in the last third of a class. Probably the same principle holds in the present rating.   There are few if any who would gainsay that the first three states in rank are Massachusetts, New York and Pennsylvania, though there will be very decided opinions as to the relative standing of the three.   So also few will demur at placing in the next group of six, Minnesota, New Jersey, Indiana, Maryland, Kansas and Vermont.   Passing to the other extreme, all will admit that the proper rating for New Mexico is zero and that Wyoming is not much better.   Counting up the next seventeen in order are Arizona, Nebraska, Arkansas, Nevada, Oklahoma, South Dakota, Alabama, Colorado, West Virginia, Texas, Tennessee, Idaho, Delaware, North Dakota, Missouri, Georgia and Utah.   While this order might be changed somewhat by further study and discussion, it is doubtful if a single one of these states ought to be moved out of the group.   Moreover, if 745 is admitted to be a fair rating for Massachusetts there are few who would claim that Oklahoma, South Dakota and Colorado are not generously treated by rates of 97, 101 and 106, respectively, though doubtless there may be room for argument as to the accuracy of the relative values assigned to the three states.

TABLE 1.—RATING SHEET

	Supervision of Local Health Officers			Communicable Diseases			Tuberculosis						Diagnostic Laboratory		Distribution of Sera and Vaccines		Vital Statistics			Child Hygiene				Education				Food		General Sanitation			Control of Water and Sewage			Ratia Credits	Total
	Personal Supervision	Conferences	Bulletins	Notification	Direct Control	Intensive Work	Notification	Sanatoria	Hospitals	Dispensaries	General Education	Intensive Work or Direct Control	Scope of Work	Amount	Varieties	Amount	Deaths	Births	Tables	Intensive Work	Literature to Mothers	Prevention of Ophthalmia	Supervision of Midwives	Newspapers	Bulletins	Exhibits	Lectures	Milk Supervision	Sanitary Handling of Food	School Construction	Public Institutions	Hotels and Camps	Approval of Plans	Surveys	Supervision		
	60	20	20	30	80	50	20	20	20	20	30	30	10	70	10	40	40	40	20	40	10	10	10	30	30	30	10	40	20	20	10	10	40	30	30		1000
Alabama	0	0	0	7	0	0	10	10	10	10	0	0	10	10	0	8	0	0	0	0	0	0	0	0	10	0	10	0	0	10	0	0	10	0	10		105
Arizona	0	8	0	3	0	0	10	10	0	0	0	0	0	0	0	0	10	10	0	0	0	0	0	0	8	0	0	0	0	0	0	0	0	0	0		39
Arkansas	0	6	5	0	10	0	10	10	10	10	0	0	8	5	0	0	10	10	0	0	0	5	0	0	0	0	10	0	0	10	0	0	0	0	0		74
California	0	0	0	15	10	0	12	10	10	12	30	0	10	40	0	10	40	10	20	0	0	0	0	0	20	20	0	0	12	0	0	0	30	10	0		342
Colorado	0	0	5	23	10	0	0	0	0	0	0	0	8	15	0	30	40	10	0	0	0	0	0	0	0	0	0	0	8	0	0	0	0	0	10		106
Connecticut	0	10	0	19	10	0	0	15	15	0	0	0	4	60	6	12	40	40	10	0	0	5	0	0	10	0	0	30	10	0	0	8	20	20	0		393
Delaware	0	0	0	0	30	0	0	10	0	12	8	0	10	0	0	10	10	10	5	0	0	0	0	0	25	0	0	0	10	0	0	8	0	0	0		131
Florida	0	0	0	0	5	10	0	0	0	0	8	5	10	60	0	40	10	10	0	0	0	0	0	20	8	25	0	0	5	0	0	0	0	0	0	22	253
Georgia	0	0	0	0	0	0	0	0	0	0	8	0	4	5	0	0	10	10	0	0	8	5	0	18	8	0	0	5	10	0	0	0	0	0	0		156
Idaho	0	0	10	4	0	0	0	10	0	0	0	0	10	15	0	40	10	10	0	0	0	0	0	24	25	10	10	10	12	10	8	0	0	0	0		127
Illinois	5	0	10	17	30	0	0	10	0	0	10	0	2	10	10	40	10	10	10	0	10	10	0	24	20	20	8	10	10	5	0	10	0	30	30		346
Indiana	5	20	10	13	20	15	5	10	10	0	20	5	6	60	6	22	40	40	13	0	10	5	0	24	20	30	10	10	12	20	10	10	10	15	10	20	526

State	Total
Iowa	225
Kansas	499
Kentucky	393
Louisiana	315
Maine	280
Maryland	507
Massachusetts	745
Michigan	370
Minnesota	574
Mississippi	297
Missouri	152
Montana	246
Nebraska	66
Nevada	94
New Hampshire	320
New Jersey	555
New Mexico	0
New York	730
North Carolina	411
North Dakota	139
Ohio	462
Oklahoma	97
Oregon	227
Pennsylvania	716
Rhode Island	432
South Carolina	165
South Dakota	101
Tennessee	122
Texas	116
Utah	161
Vermont	486
Virginia	397
Washington	262
West Virginia	113
Wisconsin	392
Wyoming	10

TABLE 2.—ORGANIZATION OF STATE DEPARTMENT OF HEALTH

State	No. of Members of Board	Qualifications	By Whom Appointed	Terms	Expiration of Terms	Compensation
Alabama	10	Censors of State Medical Association	Delegates and Councilors of Association	5 years	2 annually	Expenses.
Arizona	3	Governor, Attorney General, Superintendent of Public Health	Superintendent of Public Health by Governor and Senate	2 years	Together	10 cts. mileage, expenses.
Arkansas	7	Physicians of seven years' practice in state, one from each congressional district, secretary	Six appointed by Governor	2 years	Together	Traveling expenses.
California	7	Physicians practicing in state	Governor and Legislature	4 years	Together	Traveling expenses.
Colorado	9	Not specified	Governor and Senate	6 years	3 every 2 years	None
Connecticut	7	Three physicians, one lawyer, secretary	Governor and Senate	6 years	3 every 2 years	Expenses.
Delaware	7	Physicians representing ten counties	Governor and Senate	4 years	3 every 2 years	Expenses.
Florida	3	"Discreet citizens"	Governor and Senate	4 years	Together	$6.00 per day, 5 cts. mileage.
Georgia	13	One for each congressional district, majority physicians, secretary	Governor	6 years	2 every year	$5.00 per day, traveling expenses.
Idaho	5	Two physicians, Attorney General, State Engineer, Secretary	Physicians by Governor	4 years	1 every 2 years	$10.00 per day, expenses.
Illinois	7	Not specified	Governor and Senate	7 years	1 every year	Expenses.[1]
Indiana	5	Not specified	Board of Appointment[2]	4 years	1 every year	$10.00 per day, expenses.
Iowa	9	Four physicians,[3] 1 engineer, Governor, Secretary of State, Auditor of State, Treasurer of State	Appointive members by Board of Appointment[4]	5 years	1 every year	$900.00 per annum.[5]
Kansas	9	Eight physicians of seven years' practice[6]	Governor and Senate	3 years	3 every year	$5.00 per day, traveling expenses.
Kentucky	8	One homeopathic, one eclectic, one osteopath, five regular physicians, secretary[7]	Governor and Senate	6 years	2 every year	Expenses.
Louisiana	7	Physicians from different parts of state	Governor and Senate	7 years	2 or 3 every 2 years	$10.00 per day, 5 cts. mileage.
Maine	7	Not specified, secretary	Governor and Council	6 years	1 every year	Expenses.
Maryland	7	Health Officer of Baltimore, Attorney General, one engineer, three physicians, secretary	Governor	4 years	2 every 2 years	$5.00 per day, expenses.
Massachusetts	7	Three physicians, Commissioner of Health[8]	Governor and Council[12]	3 years	2 every year	$10.00 per day, traveling expenses.
Michigan	7	Six not specified, secretary	Governor and Senate	6 years	2 every 2 years	Expenses.
Minnesota	9	Learned in sanitary science	Governor	3 years	3 every year	Traveling expenses.
Mississippi	13	Eight, one for each congressional district, five nominated by Medical Society	Governor	4 years	Together	$3.00 per day, expenses.
Missouri	7	Physicians, five years' resident	Governor and Senate	4 years	3 or 4 every 2 years	Expenses.
Montana	7	Three physicians, Governor, Attorney General, State Veterinary, Secretary	Governor and Senate	4 years	2 every 2 years	$5.00 per day, expenses.
Nebraska	3	Governor, Attorney General, Superintendent of Public Instruction. Board of Secretaries consists of two regular physicians, one homeopath, one eclectic, seven years' practice	Governor	4 years	1 every year	None.[9]

State	No.	Composition / Qualifications	Appointed by	Term	Meetings	Compensation
Nevada	3	Physicians of five years' practice in Nevada	Governor	4 years	Together	$20.00 per day, traveling expenses.
New Hampshire	6	Governor, Attorney General, three physicians, one engineer	Governor and Council	4 years	Together	Expenses.
New Jersey	8	Three physicians, two engineers, one veterinarian	Governor and Senate	4 years	2 every 2 years	Expenses.
New Mexico	7	Physicians, five years' resident	Governor	4 years	3 or 4 every 2 years	Fees.
New York	7	Three physicians, one sanitary engineers	Governor	6 years	1 every year	$1,000.00.
North Carolina	9	Four physicians, one engineer	Physicians by Medical Society, others by Governor	6 years	Together	$4.00 per day, expenses.
North Dakota	3	Attorney General, Vice President, Superintendent of Public Health	Governor and Senate	2 years	Together	5 cts. mileage, expenses.
Ohio	8	Seven, not specified, Attorney General	Governor and Senate	7 years	1 every year	$5.00 per day, expenses.
Oklahoma	4	Advisory, not provided by law	Commissioner	4 years	3 every 2 years	Expenses.
Oregon	1-6	Physicians, different parts of state	Governor and Senate	4 years	Together	Expenses.
Pennsylvania	6	Majority physicians, 10 years' practice, one engineer	Governor and Senate	4 years		Expenses.
Rhode Island	7	One from each county, four members of some medical society	Governor and Senate	6 years	1 every year	$10.00 per meeting, traveling expenses.
South Carolina	9	Seven members State Medical Association, Attorney General, Comptroller[10]	Recommended by State Medical Assn., appointed by Governor	7 years	Together	$4.00 per day, 10 cts. mileage.
South Dakota	5	Physicians must be five years in state[11]	Governor and Senate	2 years	2 or 3 every year	$5.00 per day, 5 cts. mileage, expenses.
Tennessee	4	Three physicians of ten years' practice, representing the three divisions of state, Commissioner of Agriculture		6 years	1 every 2 years	Traveling expenses.
Texas	7	Physicians of ten years' residence	Governor	2 years	Together	$10.00 per day, 3 cts. mileage.
Utah	1-3	Majority physicians, one engineer	Governor and Senate	7 years	1 every year	Expenses.
Vermont	3	Not specified	Governor and Senate	6 years	1 every 2 years	$4.00 per day, expenses.
Virginia	12	Members of State Medical Society, one each congressional district and two from Richmond	Governor	4 years	3 every year	$8.00 per day, mileage.
Washington	5	Not specified, Commissioner of Agriculture	Governor and Senate	5 years	1 every year	Expenses.
West Virginia	1-	Physicians of five years' practice[8]	Governor and Senate	4 years	2 or 3 every 2 years	$10.00 per day, traveling expenses.
Wisconsin	7	Not specified	Governor and Senate	7 years	1 every year	$10.00 per day.
Wyoming	3	Qualified electors, one physician	Governor and Senate	4 years	Together	$200.00 per year, traveling expenses.

1. Also $10.00 per day as examiners.
2. Consists of Governor, Secretary of State, Auditor of State.
3. Not more than three of same political party nor more than two of the same school of practice.
4. Consists of Governor, Secretary of State, Auditor of State.
5. Includes services on examining board.
6. Majority not to be of one school of practice.
7. Physicians to be selected from list furnished by their respective state societies.
8. Public Health Council.
9. Fees as examiners.
10. These are the Executive Committee, the Medical Association; together with the two state officials are the State Board of Health.
11. Homeopathic school to be represented.
12. Governor's Council, not Public Health Council.

TABLE 3.—EXECUTIVE OFFICER

State	Executive Officer	Election or Appointment	Elected from Board or Outside	Membership in Board	Salary	Term	Full Time
Alabama	State Health Officer	Elected by Association Nominated by censors	Not specified	Status not changed by election	$5,000	Indeterminate	Full time
Arizona	Supt. of Public Health	Governor, Senate	Outside	Member	2,000[1]	Two years	Part tim
Arkansas	Secretary	Elected by Board	Not specified	Member	1,800	Two years	Part tim
California	Secretary	Elected by Board	From the Board	Member	4,500	Indeterminate	Full time
Colorado	Secretary	Elected by Board	From the Board	Member	1,500	Two years	Part time
Connecticut	Secretary	Elected by Board	From the Board	Member	3,000	Indeterminate	Full time
Delaware	Secretary	Elected by Board	Not specified	Status not changed by election	1,500	Indeterminate	Part tim
Florida	State Health Officer	Elected by Board	Outside	Status not changed by election	3,000	Four years	Full time
Georgia	State Health Officer	Elected by Board	Outside	Member	2,000	Six years	Part tim
Idaho	Secretary	Elected by Board	Outside	Member	2,400	Indeterminate	Part tim
Illinois	Secretary	Elected by Board	Not specified	Status not changed by election	3,600[3]	Indeterminate	Full time
Indiana	Secretary	Elected by Board	Outside	Not member	3,000	Four years	Full time
Iowa	Secretary	Board of Appointment	Not specified	Not member	3,000	Five years	Full time
Kansas	Secretary	Elected by Board	Not specified	Not member	4,000 as Dean	Indeterminate	Also Dea_ of Med. Sel_ool
Kentucky	Secretary	Elected by Board	Not specified	Member	1,200	Four years	Part tim
Louisiana	President	Governor	From the Board	Member	5,000	Four years	Full tim
Maine	Secretary	Elected by Board	Not specified	Member	2,500	Indeterminate	Full tim
Maryland	State Health Officer	Elected by Board	Not specified	Member	3,000	Indeterminate	Full tim
Massachusetts	Commissioner of Health	Governor and his Council	Not specified	Member	7,500	Five years	Full tim
Michigan	Secretary	Governor (recommended by board)	Not specified	Member	2,500	Six years	Full tim
Minnesota	Secretary	Elected by Board	Not specified	Status not changed by election	4,500	Indeterminate	Full tim
Mississippi	Secretary	Elected by Board	Not specified	Member	1,500	Four years	Part tim
Missouri	Secretary	Elected by Board	From the Board	Member	2,400	One year	Full tim
Montana	Secretary	Elected by Board	Not specified	Member	3,000	Four years	Full tim
Nebraska	Secretary	Board of Secretaries	From the Board	Member	500 to 800[2]	Four years	Part tim

State	Title	Appointment	Residence	Board membership	Salary	Term	Service
Nevada	Secretary	Governor	Outside	Member	1,500	Four years	Full time
New Hampshire	Secretary	Elected by Board	Not specified	Status not changed by election	2,500	Indeterminate	Full time
New Jersey	Director of Health	Elected by Board	Not specified	Member	5,000	Four years	Full time
New Mexico	Secretary	Elected by Board	From the Board	Member	Fees	Four years	Part time
New York	Commissioner of Health	Governor	Not specified	Member	8,000	Six years	Part time
North Carolina	Secretary	Elected by Board	Not specified	Not member	3,000[9]	Six years	Full time
North Dakota	Supt. of Public Health	Governor	Outside	Member	1,200	Two years	Part time
Ohio	Secretary	Elected by Board	Not specified	Not member	3,000	Indeterminate	Full time
Oklahoma	State Commissioner of Health	Governor		Not member	1,800	Four years	Full time
Oregon	Secretary	Elected by Board	Outside	Member	4,000	Indeterminate	Part time
Pennsylvania	Commissioner of Health	Governor, Senate	Outside	Not member[3]	10,000	Four years	Full time
Rhode Island	Secretary	Elected by Board	Not specified	Not member	3,000	Indeterminate	Part time
South Carolina	State Health Officer	Recommended by Executive Committee, Appointed by Governor	Not specified	Not member	2,500	Indeterminate	Full time
South Dakota	Superintendent	Governor	From the Board	Member	2,000	Two years	Part time
Tennessee	Secretary	Elected by Board	Not specified	Not member	3,500	Five years	Full time
Texas	State Health Officer	Governor, Senate	From the Board	Member	2,500	Two years	Part time
Utah	Secretary	Elected by Board	From the Board	Member	4,000	Indeterminate	Full time
Vermont	Secretary	Elected by Board	Not specified	Status not changed	2,500[4]	Indeterminate	Full time
Virginia	State Health Commissioner	Governor	Not specified	Member	3,500	Four years	Full time
Washington	State Health Officer	Elected by Board	Not specified	Status not changed by election	3,600	Five years	Full time
West Virginia	Commissioner of Health	Governor, Senate	Outside	Member	3,000[5]	Four years	Full time
Wisconsin	State Health Officer	Elected by Board	Not specified	Member	3,250[8]	Indeterminate	Full time
Wyoming	Secretary	Governor	From the Board	Member	200[7]	Four years	Part time

1. Also $1,000 as registrar.
2. Fees as examiner.
3. Entitled to vote.
4. Also $200 as registrar.
5. Also about $500 as registrar.
6. Also about $500 fees for licensing embalmers.
7. Also about $300 fees for inspections.
8. Also $1,800 for services on examining board.
9. Also a small sum as registrar's fees.

TABLE 4.—CONTROL OF COMMUNICABLE DISEASES

State	Person or Division in Charge	Executive Authority	Legislative Authority	Reports of Cases — From Whom Received	Reports of Cases — Frequency	Department in Control of Quarantine — Inland	Department in Control of Quarantine — Maritime
Alabama		None	None	Local Health Officers	Promptly	Governor on advice of State Board	Federal government
Arizona		Complete	General	Local Health Officers	Immediately	State Board	Federal government
Arkansas	Bureau of tuberculosis only	Probably	General	Local Health Officers	Monthly	State Board	
California	One medical inspector at $10 per day (about $900 a year)	Complete	General	Local Health Officers	Immediately	State Board	Federal government
Colorado		On failure of local	None	Local Health Officers	Monthly	State Board	
Connecticut		None	None	Local Health Officers	Monthly	Local Health Officers	Local Health Officers
Delaware		Complete in incorporated portions, on failure in unincorporated	General	Physicians	Immediately	State Board	Local in Wilmington Federal government
Florida	Seven assistants, 2 agents of State Health Officer[1]	Complete	General	Physicians	Immediately	State Health Officer	Federal government
Georgia		In communicable diseases	General	Physician where no health officers	Promptly	State Board	Federal government
Idaho	Epidemiologist, $2,400; four district health officers	Complete	Doubtful	Local Health Officers	Monthly	State Board	
Illinois	Epidemiologist at laboratory	In communicable diseases	Doubtful	Local Health Officers	Immediately	State Board	
Indiana	Part time of four men	Complete	General	Local Health Officers	Monthly	State Board	
Iowa	Epidemiologist at laboratory	Complete	General	Local Health Officers	In 24 hrs.	State Board	
Kansas	Chief, $2,400; two clerks	Complete	General	Local Health Officers	Immediately	State Board	
Kentucky	Part time of two inspectors	Complete	General	Physicians	Immediately	State Board	
Louisiana	Part time of one man		General	Local Health Officers	Weekly	State Board	Federal government
Maine		In communicable diseases	General	Local Health Officers	Weekly	State Board	Federal government
Maryland	Chief $1,800, one inspector, four clerks	Very limited	General	Local Health Officers	Daily	State Board	Federal government
Massachusetts	Director $4,000, acting epidemiologist $2,000, part time of eight inspectors	Coordinate with local board of health	General, no penalty	Local Health Officers	Daily		Local Board of Health; Federal government in Boston
Michigan	Small part of time of 25 inspectors, five clerks	On failure of local	General, no penalty	Local Health Officers	Immediately	State Board	
Minnesota	Director $3,500; two field men, four clerks	Complete	General	Local Health Officers	Immediately	State Board	
Mississippi		Complete	General	Local Health Officers	Monthly	State Board	Federal government
Missouri		Perhaps in communicable disease	General	Local Health Officers	Monthly	State Board	

State							
Montana		Complete	General	Local Health Officers	Monthly	State Board	
Nebraska	Part time of one inspector	On failure of local	General	Local Health Officers	Monthly	State Board	
Nevada		Possibly	General	Local Health Officers	Monthly	County Commissioners	Local Board of Health
New Hampshire		In unincorporated portions	Limited	Local Health Officers	First case immediately	State Board	Local Board of Health
New Jersey	Bureau of communicable diseases. Chief $2,750. One inspector, clerks	On failure of local. Can compel local action	General	Physician when on dairy farm	Weekly	State Board limited	State and Federal government
New Mexico	Director $4,000. Part time of ten supervisors	Complete	General	Physicians	Immediately	State Board	Separate state department
New York	Part time of bureau of county health work	None	General	Physicians		Local Board of Health	Federal government
North Carolina		On failure of local in towns	None	Local Health Officers	Monthly	Local Health Officers	
North Dakota	Chief $2,250, one epidemiologist, one clerk, small part time eight inspectors	Complete	General	Local Health Officers	Monthly	State Board	
Ohio		Complete	General	Local Health Officers	Twice a month	State Board	
Oklahoma		Complete	General	Local Health Officers	Monthly	State Board	Federal government
Oregon		Complete	General	Local Health Officers	Monthly	State Board	Separate state department and federal government also.
Pennsylvania	Part time of chief and assistant. Acts through state appointed local officers	Complete in townships and some boroughs, may take charge in all	General	Local Health Officers	Weekly	State Board	
Rhode Island		None	General	Local Health Officers	Monthly	Governor may direct State Board	Federal government in Providence. Towns.
South Carolina		Complete	General	Physician where no health officer	Monthly	State Board with advice of governor	Federal government
South Dakota		Complete	General	Local Health Officers	Immediately	State Board	
Tennessee		On failure of local	None	Local Health Officers	Monthly	State Board	
Texas		Very little	None	"Pestilential" diseases by physicians	Monthly	State Board	State Board of Health and federal government
Utah		Coordinate with local	General	Local Health Officers	Monthly	State Board	
Vermont	Part time of one man	Coordinate with local	General	Local Health Officers	Weekly	State Board	
Virginia	Assistant of commissioner	Complete	General	Local Health Officers	Weekly	State Board	Separate state department and federal government. Federal government
Washington	Epidemiologist, $2,000	Complete	General	Local Health Officers	Monthly	State Board	
West Virginia		Complete	General	Local Health Officers	Quarterly	State Board	
Wisconsin	Clerk $900, part time of five deputies	Complete	General	Local Health Officers	Weekly	State Board	
Wyoming		None	General	Local Health Officers	Immediately	State Board	

1. Have full charge except in a few cities.

TABLE 5.—DIAGNOSTIC LABORATORY

State	Laboratory Force	Where Located	Diphtheria	Gonococcus	Fecal Worms	Malaria	Rabies	Tuberculosis	Widals	Anthrax	Plague	Wassermanns	Cerebrospinal Meningitis	Pathological	Water	Miscellaneous
Alabama	Chief, $2,400; assistant, clerk, helper....	State Health Dept.	877	48	1,194	543	386	1,346	1,071	—	—	395	34	1,067	632	303
Arizona	Assistant in chemical laboratory	State University	+	—	—	—	+	+	+	—	—	—	—	—	—	—
Arkansas	Director is state health officer no salary, students do most of work..		—	—	—	—	—	—	—	—	—	—	—	—	—	—
California	Chief, $3,000; 3 assistants, clerk, helper and students[1]	Medical School	39	117	431	56	42	418	122	1	—	419	6	—	239	700
Colorado	Bacteriologist, $1,000; part time	State University	2,928	—	9	109	337	587	929	54	2	—	4	—	429	300
Connecticut	Chief, $1,500, part time; 2 assistants, helper	State Health Dept.	+	20	—	80	68	2,536	716	—	—	2,181	+	—	—	3,299
Delaware	Chief, $2,000; assistant, helper	Delaware College	8,397	85	—	—	28	442	449	+	—	—	—	1,147	667	21
Florida	Chief, $2,500; 3 assistants, 3 helpers[3]	State Health Dept.	334	1,577	5,079	5,409	117	3,066	4,593	—	2,131	—	+	—	349	—
Georgia	Chief, part time; 4 assistants, 3 helpers, 2 clerks[2]	State Health Dept.	5,653	114	4,433	199	319	2,120	235	—	—	—	11	621	226	94
Idaho	Chief, $2,400[1]	State Health Dept.	749	150	—	—	—	344	107	—	—	142	12	277	255	12
Illinois	Chief, $1,800; 1 assistant, 1 helper	State Health Dept.	147	—	—	—	—	2,328	1,199	—	—	70	—	—	—	71
Indiana	Chief, $2,000; 3 assistants, 2 helpers, 2 clerks	State Health Dept.	875	691	—	139	311	4,947	1,603[12]	—	—	—	—	365	—	48
Iowa	Chief paid by university, 2 assistants, helper, clerk[7]	State University	11,064	—	—	—	25	4,014	2,725	—	—	—	18	106	—	1,325
Kansas	Chief, $1,200; 1 assistant.	State Health Dept.	9,885	61	—	—	13	1,862	443	—	—	—	5	—	78	146
Kentucky	Chief, $2,400; 4 assistants	State Health Dept.	1,390	271	98,622	302	99	3,597	957	—	—	—	—	377	—	100
Louisiana	Chief, $1,599.96; also $2,500 from city	New Orleans Lab.	378	—	1,716	481	—	693	588	—	—	—	—	—	260	170
Maine	Bacteriologist, $1,200[4]	State Health Dept.	4,406	—	—	—	—	1,824	564	—	—	—	—	—	1,596	206
Maryland	Chief, $1,800 ($1,800 from city); 5 assistants, 1 clerk	Baltimore Lab.	1,574	78	—	—	—	—	1,202	—	—	—	2,692	—	2,507	—
Massachusetts	Chief, $1,800; assistant, 3 helpers	State Health Dept.	984	—	—	301	10	1,261	1,611	—	—	+[13]	—	—	—	500
Michigan	Chief, $2,500; 1 assistant, 1 clerk, 1 helper.	State Health Dept.	6,371	159	—	59	6	2,620	778	—	—	—	—	—	—	293
Minnesota	Chief, $2,800; 1 assistant, 4 helpers, 2 clerks[2]	State University[5]	4,353	—	—	2	49	3,105	3,023	—	—	—	19	227	1,82_	311
Mississippi	Chief, $2,000; 2 assistants	State Health Dept.	23,761	—	2,060	1,142	—	2,004	1,902	—	—	—	—	—	—	530
Missouri	Chief, $1,800; 1 helper.	State Health Dept.[6]	779	157	+	136	+	2,059	1,321	—	—	+	—	+	+475	4,289
Montana	Part time bacteriologist, $900	State Health Dept.	631	—	—	—	16	2,456	—	—	—	—	—	—	—	198
Nebraska	Chief, $3,000; 1 assis-	State Health Dept.	259	3	—	—	—	182	332	—	—	—	3	—	—	3

State	Staff	Administered by														
New Jersey	Chief, $4,000; 1 assistant, 1 helper	State Health Dept.	10,802	—	—	—	399	—	6,589	3,205	—	—	—	—	—	—	1,277
New Mexico	Chief, $4,000[7]	State Health Dept.	14,528	105	—	+	+	18	3,193	1,191	—	—	+	—	—	2,091	61
New York	Chief, $3,000; 5 assistants	State Health Dept.	896	1,117	—	—	340	297	1,605	1,382	—	—	—	18	250	4,669	50
North Carolina	Chief, $3,000 to $3,500; 5 assistants,[19] 1 clerk	State Health Dept.	965	—	7,285	—	—	3	1,255	989	—	—	—	25	1,971	1,400	911
North Dakota	Chief, $3,000; 3 assistants, 3 helpers, 1 clerk[20]	State University	4,725	—	43	—	32	196	3,314	1,039	—	6	—	—	17	2,249	302
Ohio	Professor of bacteriology at university, 1 assistant	State Health Dept.	98	—	40	—	11	109	600	374	—	—	—	—	—	163	39
Oklahoma	Chief, $2,700;[26] 1 assistant	State University	617	—	—	—	+	59	455	213	—	53	—	—	—	742	—
Oregon	Chief, $3,000; 8 assistants, 4 helpers, 4 clerks[22]	State University	—	+	—	+	52	23	7,612	1,171	—	—	—	—	1,005	6,691	682
Pennsylvania	Chief, $4,000; 1 assistant, 1 helper, part time of clerk	State Health Dept.	2,296	115	121	—	41	262	1,943	1,017	7	—	—	10	161	220	59
Rhode Island	Chief, $2,500; 1 assistant, part time of clerk	State Health Dept.	200	62	1,257	—	228	2	852	4,188	—	—	—	12	—	54	369
South Carolina	Chief, $1,500 plus $1,500 from university	State Health Dept.	1,135	—	10	—	2	—	569	585	—	—	—	—	—	135	204
South Dakota	Chief, $1,500; 2 assistants	State University[24]	120	—	382	—	44	—	804	92	—	—	—	20	251	224	—
Tennessee	Chief, $1,800	Medical School	147	—	—	—	251	—	308	62	—	—	—	16	—	73	13
Texas	Professor of bacteriology; 1 assistant, paid by university	State Health Dept.	36	—	—	—	9	—	50	46	—	—	—	3	—	1,217	—
Utah	Chief, $3,000; 1 assistant, part time of helper and clerk[15]	State University[25]	4,051	546	—	—	+	—	1,842	1,162	—	408[26]	—	—	—	178	—
Vermont	Chief, $2,500; 1 assistant, part time of clerk	State Health Dept.	2,367	—	10,262	—	—	—	2,209	1,486	—	—	—	+	—	1,159	1,872
Virginia	Part time bacteriologist, $820; part time clerk	State Health Dept.	325	+	—	—	+	28	116	163	—	—	—	+	—	256	43
West Virginia	Director paid by university; assistant, $1,500, by board of health	State Health Dept.	66	4	—	—	—	8	156	99	—	—	—	4	—	—	—
Wisconsin	Director, no pay; bacteriologist, $1,750; part time assistant, helper, clerk[3]	State University	1,729	+	—	—	—	55	3,168	987	—	—	+	—	—	889	1,422

+ indicates that the laboratory offers to make the examinations, — indicates that it does not or that no figures are available.

1. Branch laboratories in three cities.
2. Makes antitoxin.
3. Also engineering work.
4. Does chemical work also.
5. Work of branch laboratories at Duluth and Mankato not included in table.
6. There is also a Hygiene Laboratory at the University.
7. Included in the examinations here given are 1,364 made at the seven "branch" laboratories which are really merely municipal laboratories

8. Five branch laboratories:
9. Milk specimens, 3,196.
10. At Department of Animal Industry, cow.
11. Branch laboratory at University of Mos-
12. 1,148 tested for paratyphoid.
13. About one thousand per month.
15. Does much chemical work.
16. Does chemical work also.
17. Employees in serum and hygienic laboratories not separated. Has arranged with laboratory in New York to do state work in south part of state.
18. At State Veterinary College.

19. Two of these in charge of branch laboratories at Bismarck and Minot.
20. Does chemical work.
21. Gives half time to epidemiological work.
22. Makes tuberculosis and other vaccines.
23. By Live Stock and Sanitary Board.
24. University furnishes room, etc., health department directs work, special appropriation for laboratory, $3,500.
25. Independent of the State Board of Health, to do work for State Board of Health.
26. University at $2 each.
27. During last year for which data could be obtained.

TABLE 6.—DISTRIBUTION OF VACCINES AND SERA

State	Diphtheria Antitoxin, Units Distributed	Cost	Mode of Purchase and Distribution	Free or Otherwise	Number of Stations	Typhoid Vaccines, Amount	Made or Purchased	Persons Treated for Rabies	Where and How	Other Vaccines and Sera
Ala.	.....	$1,000.00	Contract with manufacturer to sell at discount	State gives to poor	170	0	.....	415	Laboratory	0
Ariz.	0	.....	.....	.....	.....	0	.....	0	Health Department	0
Ark.	0	.....	.....	.....	.....	0	.....	42	.....	0
Calif.	0	.....	.....	.....	.....	500 immunizations per month	Made	249	Prepares vaccines, treatment at University Laboratory, also 10 branch laboratories	.....
Colo.	.....	.....	.....	.....	.....	0	.....	0	By towns, payments from dog tax	Tetanus, smallpox
Conn.	20,000,000	8,000.00	Purchased	Free to all	168[2]	0	.....	25	Laboratory or elsewhere, towns pay for poor	0
Del.	.....	500.00	Purchased and sold at cost	Counties give to poor	27	0	.....	89	.....	0
Fla.	Not available	644.90[1]	Purchased	Free to poor	3	400 pks.	Purchased	0	Purchases vaccine for indigent persons	Tetanus, smallpox
Ga.	12,719,500[3]	6,647.98[6]	Manufactures	Practically free to all	.....	30,224 doses[7]	Made	59	Laboratories	Tuberculosis, smallpox, meningitis
Idaho.	.....	.....	.....	.....	.....	1,500 pks.	.....	.....	.....	0
Ill.	120,467,000	29,000.00	Purchased	Free to all	375	6,878 pks.	Purchased	.....	Pasteur Institute, Chicago	Tetanus, smallpox
Ind.	3,386,500	.....	Contracts with several makers to sell at discount	Towns or counties give to poor	3	1,079 ampules / 10,000 doses	Made	231	Health Department	0
Iowa.	.....	1,064.13	Contracts with makers to sell at discount	None free	241	.....	.....	77	Laboratory, free to residents	Smallpox
Kan.	2,984,000	1,209.60	Contracts with makers to sell at discount	State gives to poor	115	300 doses	Purchased	78	Medical School	Tetanus, meningitis, scarlet fever
Ky.	For convenience keeps many kinds of sera and vaccines on hand, none free	.....	.....	Many counties give to poor	In each county	11,787 immunizations	Purchased	161	Laboratory	Many varieties
La.	.....	2,383.00	Purchased and sold at cost	.....	90	0	.....	315	Charity Hospital, free	0
Me.	0	.....	Contracts with manufacturers to sell at discount	Towns give to poor	.....	0	Made	0	.....	0
Md.	0	.....	Manufactures	.....	.....	.....	Made	24	State Board of Health pays Pasteur Institute $60 per case	Smallpox
Mass.	482,539,000	21,286.02[4]	Manufactures	Free to all	400[2]	21,014 ampules	Made	.....	Health Department inspectors	Smallpox, meningitis
Mich.	0	.....	.....	Towns give to poor	.....	0	.....	.....	University Hospital, a charge is made	0
Minn.	.....	5,000.00[5]	Purchased	.....	65	36,820 c.c.	Made	74	Laboratory free to residents, makes vaccine	0
Miss.	.....	.....	Contracts with manufacturers to sell at discount	None free	Every town over 500	.....	Purchased	0	.....	Smallpox

State										
Mo.	0	0	……	Counties give to poor	1[9]	0	……	……	Free at laboratory	0
Mont.	0	0	Contracts with manufacturers to sell at discount	……	……	……	Made	0	……	0
Neb.	0		……				……	0	……	0
Nev.	0		……			Very little	……	0	……	0
N.H.		5,000.00[11]	Purchased	Free to poor	110	248 doses	Purchased	0	……	0
N.J.	0		……			0	……	0	……	0
N.M.			……			0	……		……	Tetanus
N.Y.	76,482,000	16,825.23	Manufactures	Free to poor	1,300[10]	679 pks.	Made		By supervisors, free.	0
N.C.	9,254,000		Purchased of manufacturers, sold 10% above cost	Towns give to poor		10,000 immunizations	Made	259	Laboratory, mostly free.	
N.D.	0		Contracts with manufacturers to sell at discount			0	……		Laboratory	0
Ohio			……	Counties give to poor	700[10]	7,000 pks.	Made		Counties provide treatment free	0
Okla.		7,500.00[8]	Contracts with manufacturers to sell at discount	Free to poor	2 or 3 in each county		Purchased		Distributes virus	Smallpox, meningitis, whooping cough
Ore.	0		……			Small amount	Purchased	18	Health Department gives treatment	Smallpox
Pa.	108,445,000		Purchased		550		Purchased		Local charity departments	Tetanus, smallpox, tuberculosis
R.I.	6,145,000	2,638.00	Purchased	Free to poor	41	150 pks.	Purchased		Towns only	Tetanus, meningitis
S.C.	23,822,000	9,944.75	Purchased	Free to all	152	39,374 ampules	Made	286	Virus made at laboratory sent to physicians, some patients treated	Smallpox, tetanus, meningitis
S.D.	0		……			0	……		……	0
Tenn.	0		……		[9]	234 pks.	……	94	Laboratory,	Meningitis
Texas	2,213,000		Contracts with manufacturers to sell at discount	Counties give to poor		500 pks. per year	Made	357	By State Hospital for Insane, free to the poor	
Utah			Purchased	Free to all	68	0	……	0	……	0
Vt.		2,385.50	Contracts with manufacturers to sell at discount	Many towns give to poor	17	0	……	97	Laboratory, free to poor.	Smallpox
Va.	12,302,000		……			2,621 pks.	……			
Wash.	0		……	Counties give to poor		13,536 c.c.	Made	0	Distributes P. H. S. virus, gives treatment at laboratory	0
W. Va.	0		……				……			Smallpox
Wis.	7,002,000		Contracts with manufacturers to sell at discount	Towns give to poor	240	13,385 doses	Made		Laboratory	Smallpox, tetanus
Wyo.	0		……			0	……	0	……	

1. Includes diphtheria, tetanus and typhoid.
2. With local health officers.
3. Drug stores.
4. Includes smallpox vaccine.
5. Appropriation, 1915-16. New law.
6. 1913. Amount slightly larger in 1914, but cost not given.
7. 1914.
8. Appropriation for sera and vaccines.
9. With local health officers.
10. Drug stores.
11. Appropriation.

TABLE 7.—REGISTRATION OF VITAL STATISTICS

State	In Registration Area for Deaths	Probably 90% of Births Reported	Department in Charge	Registry Deaths	Registry Births	Registry Marriages	Registry Divorces	Office Force	Expenses	Model Law Deaths	Model Law Births	Standard Certificate Deaths	Standard Certificate Births
Alabama	0	0	Health Department	+	+	+	+	Chief, $2,400; four clerks....	$9,000	0	0	0	0
Arizona	0	0	Health Department	+	+	0	0	Superintendent Public Health, $1,000 as registrar; 1 clerk....	Not separated	+	+	+	+
Arkansas	0	0	Health Department	+	+	+	0	One clerk	3,920	+	+	+	+
California	+	+	Health Department	+	+	+	0 [2]	Chief, $2,400; assistant, three stenographers....	Not separated	+	+	+	+
Colorado	+	0	Health Department	+	+	+	0	Part time of two clerks....	1,200	+	+	0	+
Connecticut	+	+	Health Department	+	+	+	0	Two clerks....	4,800	+	+	0	0
Delaware	0	0	Health Department	+	+	+	+	Part time of clerk....	1,994.50	+	+	+	+
Florida	0	0	Health Department	+	+	+	+	Chief, $1,200....	613.69	+	+	+	+
Georgia	0	0	Health Department	+	+	0	0	No appropriation	......	+	+	+	+
Idaho	0	0	Health Department	+	+	+	0	One clerk....	800	+	+	+	+
Illinois	0	0	Health Department	+	+	+	0	Registrar, $1,500; two clerks, one stenographer....	Not separated	+	+	+	+
Indiana	+	+	Health Department	+	+	+	+ [3]	Chief, $200; eight clerks....	5,570.79	0	0	+	0
Iowa	0	0	Health Department	+	+	+	0	Assistant registrar, $900; four clerks....	2,842.26	0	0	+	+
Kansas	+	0	Health Department	+	+	+	0	Chief, $2,400; five clerks....	8,150	+	+	+	+
Kentucky	+	0	Health Department	+	+	+ [1]	0	Chief, $2,400; statistician, $1,000; nine clerks....	9,886.17	+	+	+	+
Louisiana	0	0	Health Department	+	+	0	0	Registrar, $1,800....	894.60	+	+	+	+
Maine	+	+	Health Department	+	+	+	+	Four clerks....	Not separated	0	0	+	+
Maryland	+	+	Health Department	+	+	0	0	Chief, $2,400; five clerks, one stenographer....	7,800	+	+	0	0
Massachusetts	+	+	Secretary of State	+	+	+	+	Nine clerks....	Not available	+	0	+	+
Michigan	+	+	Secretary of State	+	+	+	+	Registrar, $1,500; twelve clerks....	Not available	+	+	+	0
Minnesota	+	0	Health Department	+	+	0	+ [4]	Assistant registrar, $1,500; seven clerks....	8,187.68	+	+	+	+

State	1	2	Agency	3	4	5	6	Statistical staff	Expenditure	7	8	9	10
Mississippi	o	+	Health Department	o	+	+	+	Deputy registrar, $2,000; four clerks	4,879.92	+	+	+	+
Missouri	+	+	Health Department	o	+	+	+	Statistician, $1,800; ten clerks	Not separated	+	+	+	+
Montana	o	+	Health Department	o	+	+	+	One clerk	Not available	+	+	+	+
Nebraska	o	+	Health Department	o	+	+	+	Two clerks	2,900	+	+	+	+
Nevada	+	+	Health Department	o	+	+	+	Part time of one clerk	Not separated	+	+	+	+
New Hampshire	o	+	Health Department	+	+	o	+	Three clerks	1,653.95	o	o	o	o
New Jersey	o	o	Health Department	o	o	+	+	Registrar, $2,250; five clerks	7,000	o	o	o	o
New Mexico	+[6]	o	0	o	o	+	+	0	0	o	o	o	o
New York	o	+	Health Department	+	+	+	+	Director of division, $4,000; thirteen clerks	30,000[7]	+	+	+	+
North Carolina	+[6]	o	Health Department	o	+	+	+	Deputy registrar, $2,500; five clerks	17,312.52	+	+	+	+
North Dakota	o	o	Health Department	o	+	+	+	Part time of clerk	Not separated	+	+	+	+
Ohio	o	o	Secretary of State	o	+	+	+	Registrar, $2,000; twenty-four clerks	Not available	+	+	+	+
Oklahoma	o	o	Health Department	o	+	+	+	Part time of clerk and stenographer	2,400	o	o	o	o
Oregon	o	+	Health Department	+	+	+	+	One clerk	Not separated	+	+	+	+
Pennsylvania	+	+	Health Department	o	+	+	+	Registrar, $4,000; twenty-four clerks; morbidity statistics also	31,960.70	+	+	+	+
Rhode Island	+	o	Health Department	+	+	+	+	One clerk	1,000	o	o	o	o
South Carolina	o	o	Health Department	o	+	+	+	Chief clerk, $1,200; four clerks, one part time	3,0268	+	+	+	o
South Dakota	o	o	Dept. of history	o	o	+	+	No data	Not separated	+	+	o	o
Tennessee	o	o	Health Department	o	+	+	+	Registrar, $3,000; three clerks	8,000 appropriation	+	+	+	+
Texas	o	+	Health Department	o	o	+	+	Registrar, one clerk	1,800	+	+	o	o
Utah	+	+	Health Department	o	o	+	+	Part time of two clerks	1,250	+	+	+	o
Vermont	+	+	Health Department	+	+	+	+	One clerk	Not separated	o	+	o	+
Virginia	+	o	Health Department	o	+	+	+	Director of bureau, $2,000; four clerks	10,000	+	+	+	+
Washington	o	o	Health Department	o	+	+	+	Two clerks	3,292.73	+	+	+	o
West Virginia	o	+	Health Department	o	o	+	+	Commissioner of health is registrar, no clerk	Not separated	o	o	o	o
Wisconsin	+	o	Health Department	o	o	+	+	Statistician, $2,100; seven clerks	6,411.50	o	+	+	o
Wyoming	o	o	Health Department	o	o	+	+	Secretary is registrar, no clerk	Not separated	+	+	o	o

1. State Auditor.
2. Commissioner of Bureau of Labor Statistics.
3. Bureau of Statistics.
4. Commissioner of Statistics.
5. Bureau of Agriculture, Labor and Industry.
6. For municipalities of 1,000 and over.
7. Approximately.
8. First eight months of law. Appropriation, $5,000.

TABLE 8.—PUBLIC HEALTH EDUCATION

State	Bulletins Regular	Bulletins Special	Press Service	Lectures	Lanterns and Slides	Moving Pictures	Exhibits	Health Car
Alabama	Monthly	Few	0	Hookworm, Vital Stat.	Slides	0	0	0
Arizona	Quarterly	Few	0		0	0	0	0
Arkansas	0	0	0	Hookworm		0		?
California	Monthly	Many	0	Few	Slides		Formerly	Car
Colorado	Formerly	Few	0	Few	Slides	Films	0	0
Connecticut	Monthly	Very few	0	Very few		0	0	0
Delaware	0	0	0	0			0	in preparation
Florida	Monthly	Many	225 papers weekly	Very few	Lantern and slides	Films	Just formed	
Georgia	Quarterly	Many	Press service	Many	Slides	0	0	0
Idaho	Quarterly (Food)	Few	109 papers weekly	Few	Slides		State fair only	0
Illinois	Monthly	Many	Bi-weekly, 375.	Many	Slides	Films	In constant use	0
Indiana	Monthly	Many	Semi-weekly, Associated Press	Very many	Lantern and slides	Machine, eight films	Very frequent	0
Iowa	Quarterly	Many	0	Few	0	0	State fair	0
Kansas	Monthly	Many	500 papers weekly	Many	Lantern and slides	Machine, films	Tuberculosis and food	0
Kentucky	Monthly	Few	450 bi-weekly	Very many	Several lanterns, slides		State fair	
Louisiana	Monthly	Many	Formerly	Very many	Lantern and slides	Machine, films	County, state fair	Two cars
Maryland	Monthly for health officers	Many	0	Many	Four lanterns, many slides	0	Frequent	
Vaine	Quarterly	Very many	0	0	0			Car
Massachusetts	Monthly	A number	0	0	Lantern and slides	Films	Tuberculosis and milk	0
Michigan	Monthly, formerly quarterly	Many	0	Many	Lantern and slides	Machine, films	A few times	Car
Minnesota	0	Many	Formerly	Few	Lantern and slides	0	State fair and elsewhere formerly constant	0
Mississippi	Monthly	Some	0	Many	Lantern and slides	0	State fair	0
Missouri	Quarterly	Few	0	0	0	0		0
Montana	Quarterly	Few	0	Few	0	0		0
Nebraska	Quarterly	0	0	0		0		0
Nevada[1]	0		0	0		0		0

State								
New Hampshire	Quarterly, formerly monthly	Few	0	0	Lantern	0	0	0
New Jersey	Monthly	Many	0	Few	0	0	Tuberculosis only	0
New Mexico	0	0	0	0	0	0	0	0
New York	Monthly	Many	400 papers weekly	Very many	Lantern and slides	Machine, films	In constant use	0
North Carolina	Monthly	Many	250 papers weekly or oftener	Few	Slides	0	State fair	0
North Dakota	Quarterly, formerly monthly	Few	0	0	0	0	0	0
Ohio	Monthly	Many	0	Many	Lantern and slides	Machine, films	Frequent	0
Oklahoma	Formerly	0	400 papers weekly	Few	Three lanterns and slides	0	Small, county fairs	0
Oregon	Quarterly	Few	0	Many	Slides	0	Social hygiene, tuberculosis	0
Pennsylvania	Monthly	Many	1,000 weekly	0	Lantern and slides	0	Tuberculosis and infant welfare	0
Rhode Island	Quarterly, formerly monthly	Few	papers	Few	Many slides	Machine, seven films	Large and small	0
South Carolina	Formerly monthly	Few	0	Hookworm	Slides	0	0	0
South Dakota	Monthly, formerly quarterly	Very few	0	0	0	0	0	0
Tennessee	Quarterly (Food)	0	0	Hookworm chiefly	Four lanterns and slides	0	State fair and car	With Dept. of Agriculture Two cars
Texas	Monthly	Few	Semi-weekly Associated Press	Hookworm	Lantern and slides	0	0	0
Utah	Vital statistics only, monthly	Few	0	Few	Lantern and slides	Hires machine and films	State fair	0
Vermont	Quarterly	Very few	0	Many	Slides	Machine, films	Tuberculosis	0
Virginia	Monthly	Many	Weekly	Very many	0	0	At county fairs	0
Washington	Quarterly, formerly monthly	Many	0	Many	Many slides	Hires machine and films	County fairs and elsewhere	0
West Virginia	Quarterly	Few	0	Very few	0	0	Tuberculosis	0
Wisconsin	Quarterly	Many	2	Very few	Slides	0	Tuberculosis, small general	0
Wyoming	0	0	0	Very few	0	0	0	0

1. Required by law, no appropriation.

2. Syndicate reporters call daily.

TABLE 3.—WATER AND SEWERAGE CONTROL

State	Legislation	Filing of Plans	Division of Department of Health in Charge	Activities of Division
Alabama	General prohibition of pollution, health officer to abate. State Board of Health may order changes in water works and advertise neglect. Plans of new works must be approved		Engineer, $1,560	Laboratory examined 298 samples in 1913. Waters to be analyzed quarterly
Arizona				
Arkansas	General prohibition of pollution		Chemist also inspects sources. Bureau organized 1915; engineer, $4,000; chemist, $2,100; stenographer	Laboratory examined 239 specimens. No work on water. Investigation of sewage disposal on application. Applicants pay from less than $100 to $300. Ninety-five analyses in 1913. Appropriation, $30,000, 1915.
California	Permit for discharge of sewage or furnishing water. Cost of investigation to be paid by petitioners. Applicable to old works	Plans and description for sewerage. Description for water. 29 plans 1911-1914		
Colorado	General prohibition of pollution			Laboratory examined 77 samples in 1912. Analyzes samples from water supplies, follows up poor, has inspected 61 watersheds. Is making a survey of pollution by sewerage. Analyzes from 600 to 700 samples a year.
Connecticut	State Board of Health to investigate pollution. Compels operation of works. May order pollution stopped. Water plans to be approved	Plans to be filed	No bureau. Full time chemist at Wesleyan University; salary, $2,000	
Delaware	General prohibition of pollution.			Analyzed 249 samples in 1914.
Florida	Pollution forbidden. State Board of Health to regulate disposal of sewage near towns. Discharge of sewage into deep wells forbidden			
Georgia	General prohibition of pollution			Analyzed 295 samples in 1913. Occasionally goes out to advise and inspect
Idaho	General prohibition of pollution. Water companies must supply clean water			A few specimens examined in laboratory and advice given.
Illinois	General prohibition of pollution		State water survey in connection with the university. Director, engineer, consult. engineer, two asst. engineers, chemist and bacteriol., consult. bacteriol., five asst. chemists, inspector, five assistants, five clerks; bureau organized in Health Department, 1915. Engineer, $3,500; two assistants, $1,200; stenographer	$27,000 appropriated in 1914 for survey. Appropriation for bureau, $11,500.

State	Law and control	Plans	Organization	Activities
Indiana	Purification plants to be approved by State Board of Health. On petition may order purification or pollution stopped. May compel improved operation of works	....	Division of food, drugs and water. One engineer-chemist; one or two assistants in winter, four in summer.	In 1912, analyzed 217 samples from public supplies. Investigations or surveys of a dozen plants. Survey of Wabash River with floating laboratory. Emergency chlorin plant. Quarterly analyses of a few supplies. Many wells examined.
Iowa	No statute, but by rules of Board which have the force of law the department claims to have complete control. Would secure compliance by mandamus	Plans must be filed and approved	Engineer who is member of board, inspector, stenographer. Laboratory at State University	Chemist is supposed to analyze all public supplies monthly. Inspector makes surveys, perhaps twenty in year. The bacteriological laboratory at University also has made analyses and investigations. $599.91 expended in year ending June 30, 1914.
Kansas	No sewage may be discharged without permit from the State Board of Health. Applicable to old works if pollution dangerous. Permit required for water works. State Board of Health may order changes in existing water and sewerage works. Penalties. Appeal to governor, attorney general and secretary State Board of Health who can grant permit to discharge sewage	Plans must be filed and approved	Bureau at State University. Three engineers, five chemists and other employees. Has its own laboratory	First portable chlorin plant (1910). Routine inspection of all water and sewage plants. Bacterial tests of surface supplies monthly. Survey of all wells in Lawrence. Advice in regard to 89 water plants and 36 sewage plants in 1914. Detailed survey of Neosho and Verdegris rivers. Located all privies. Formerly did epidemiological work. Paid in part by University. $12,400 expended in year ending June 30, 1914.
Kentucky	No statute, but by rules of Board....	Plans must be filed and approved; 25 or 30 in 1915	Chief sanitary inspector in charge. Engineer, $1,800; two inspectors (part time); two analysts. Has its own laboratories, also consulting engineer	$6,348.50 expended in 1914; 1,439 analyses in 1914. Portable chlorin plant. Portable laboratory. Inspects reservoirs and filters twice a year.
Louisiana	No statute. Control is exercised through rules of the State Board of Health. Plans for water and sewerage works to be approved by the State Board of Health	Plans to be filed	Engineer at $1,500 does much other work, small part of time on water and sewage. Analyses by food laboratory	Has studied special sewage problems. One hundred to two hundred samples of water analyzed. $2,000 expended in 1913.
Maine	No effective laws. Pollution forbidden	....	The chemist of the department makes the analyses and advises	Analyzes samples from public supplies quarterly, 1,144 in years 1912-1913.
Maryland	One of the most modern and strongest laws gives complete control through rules, or orders for existing, or future water, or sewerage works. None to be installed without permit. Orders may be issued for changes in construction and operation and funds must be provided as specified by the act. This section has been sustained by the court. State Board of Health may require appointment of suitable operators of works. State Board of Health may make rules	Plans of existing and future works to be filed	Bureau organized May, 1911. Engineer and five assistants. Four district engineers.	Began June, 1912. Is making a survey of water and sewerage systems of the state. Much attention given to private wells. Is doing technical work of Sewerage Commission of Washington District. Six hundred to seven hundred analyses in 1912. $25,000 appropriated in 1914.
		Plans to be filed		

TABLE 9.—WATER AND SEWERAGE CONTROL—Continued.

State	Legislation	Filing of Plans	Division of Department of Health in Charge	Activities of Division
Massachusetts.....	Little direct or positive control, but legislature rarely authorize water or sewerage works except on advice of State Board of Health. Makes rules. On petition may, after hearing, order pollution stopped		Bureau with chief engineer at $5,000. Eleven assistants, four clerks. Laboratory chief chemist at $4,000. Eight assistants, two clerks. Experiment station, two chemists, two bacteriologists, two assistants	Prepared plans for Metropolitan sewerage system, Charles River improvement. Metropolitan water supply and several other large undertakings, and carried on as well as planned improvements for the Concord, Sudbury and Neponset rivers and other undertakings. Up to 1912 2,372 applications from towns for advice have been acted upon. Monthly analyses of principal rivers and all public water supplies. Annual examinations of sewer outlets and analyses. Analyses of effluent from sewerage works monthly. Frequent analyses of water filter effluents. In some localities examines wells. Investigates pollution of shell fish and controls taking of shell fish. Has done and is doing a large amount of experimental work. $54,972.69 expended in 1914.
Michigan.........	State Board of Health can order changes in water and sewerage works, and make rules with penalty. Cost of investigation to be paid by petitioner. Orders to be enforced in court	Plans to be filed of existing and future water and sewerage works	Chief engineer, $3,000; three assistants, two stenographers. Analyses by laboratory division	Bureau was established in June, 1913 and has been chiefly occupied with answering requests for advice. Is studying creamery and other trade wastes. Advises about private sewage disposal. Does other engineering work. $6,992.4 expended in year ending June 30, 1914.
Minnesota........	No effective law. May issue orders to prevent pollution of potable waters. Makes rules with penalty	Plans to be filed of existing and future water works. No penalty, advice at times not taken	Division of sanitation, four engineers, chemist helper, two clerks. Some are part time and do other work. Laboratory is under division	On request or complaint investigations and surveys are made. Keeps up supervision of treated water supplies, especially chlorin plants. Has three potable chlorin plants. Makes all investigations with own men, using portable laboratory. Investigates sewage disposal on request; follows up advice; 117 investigations of water supplies and 46 of sewage problems in 1913. Does work on trades wastes, garbage, public buildings, etc. $15,135.26 expended year ending July 31, 1914.

State	Legal powers	Plans to be filed	Laboratory	Work done
Mississippi	General prohibition of pollution.			
Missouri	Public Service Commission have power to order improvements in water works. Perhaps other powers		Public Service Commission does nothing. State Board of Health laboratory examines samples. Investigations and analyses at University also	About 400 samples in 1913. Mostly wells.
Montana	May make rules with penalties. New water and sewage works and extensions to be approved. Appeal to courts. Special control of watersheds	Plans to be filed	Consulting engineer without pay. Laboratory work at Agricultural College. Paid for by health department. Chemist is in charge of water and sewage work	A number of river surveys have been made. Supervises chlorin plants; 836 analyses in 1913-1914.
Nebraska	General prohibition of pollution		State Board of Health bacteriologist does a little field work at local expense	Two hundred to three hundred analyses in 1914.
Nevada	General prohibition of pollution		Hygienic laboratory now prepared to undertake investigations along modern lines	
New Hampshire	Approval required for sewerage or water works or extension. Makes rules with penalties. May prohibit use of supply	Plans to be filed	Chemist, $2,000; assistant and helper. Does some food work	Analyzes samples from all supplies once or twice a year, poor ones oftener. Survey of poor supplies. Supervise chlorin plants but not filters. Advises in regard to sewage on request. 710 samples in two years, also many samples from wells.
New Jersey	Plans for water and sewage have to be approved by State Board of Health, water plants also by Water Board and Public Utilities Board. May issue orders and enforce in courts	Plans and descriptions to be filed	Bureau of food, drugs, water and sewerage. Chief, $3,000; six engineers, four inspectors. Chemical and bacteriological work done in general laboratory of bureau	Samples and analyzes all water supplies quarterly. Inspects purification plants monthly. Has surveyed all supplies. Inspects suspicious ones annually. Has done much sewage work to protect oysters. In 1913, 369 water supply inspections, 80 watershed inspections, 526 sewerage systems inspected. Stream pollutions reinspected 2,133, abated 948, referred to attorney general 279. 1,705 water analyses and 218 sewage analyses in 1913.
New Mexico	General prohibition of pollution.			
New York	Permits to discharge sewage. May order pollution stopped. Penalties. Plans for water supplies to be approved by Conservation Commission. Commissioner of health makes rules, penalties. Sewerage plans for villages to be approved. Difficult for municipalities to sell bonds unless State Department of Health approves	Certain plans to be filed	Chief, $4,500; assistant, $3,000; five engineers, four stenographers. Other work besides water and sewage	Has surveyed 175 watersheds since 1908. In 1912, 57 examinations of water supplies completed. 232 cases of stream pollution investigated, 16 investigations of sewer systems, 2,163 matters referred to division, 2,400 chemical and 2,800 bacteriological analyses of water. $15,008.53 expended in 1914. Emergency chlorin plant.

TABLE 9.—WATER AND SEWAGE CONTROL—Continued.

State	Legislation	Filing of Plans	Division of Department of Health in Charge	Activities of Division
North Carolina	Makes rules, penalty. No new water or sewerage works or extensions without approval. Inspection of watersheds required quarterly and when asked	Plans to be filed, also of existing works if asked for	Part time of one engineer. Analyses in general laboratory	Comparatively little is done with public supplies. Every water company pays $64 a year, amounting to about $5,000. Advice to thirty-three cities in 1914.
North Dakota	General prohibition of pollution. Forbidden to discharge sewage into lakes unless treated		State Public Health Laboratory bacteriologist makes inspections and analyses	Director of laboratory made complete water survey of state by inspection and analyses. Special studies on life of typhoid bacillus in water. Over 600 analyses in 1913. Special water investigations and advice.
Ohio	Permits from State Board of Health for water supplies and sewerage works or extension, State Board of Health, with approval of governor and attorney general, may order changes in existing works. Appeal to experts. May require appointment of suitable operators of works. May order construction of sewer system	Plans to be filed	Chief, $3,000; three engineers, three stenographers; student assistants. Analytical work in general laboratory	Has made surveys of all public supplies. Visits three or four times a year and usually takes samples. Has traveling laboratory. Has inspected many watersheds. Inspects sewerage works three or four times a year. Is making sanitary survey of state by counties with special reference to water and sewerage. 2,000 analyses, $15,463.81 expended in 1914
Oklahoma	General prohibition of pollution. Laboratory at University to analyze samples from water supplies quarterly	Not required, but many filed		Analyzed 150 samples in 1912, about half from wells.
Oregon	General prohibition of pollution. Is testing law in court. New water and sewerage plans to be approved	Plans to be filed		Has employed engineer to make a few special investigations. 1,553 bacteriological analyses in 1913.
Pennsylvania	No water or sewerage works shall be constructed without a permit from the commissioner of health. Latter may order abatement of pollution. Permit to discharge sewage also requires approval of governor and attorney general	Plans and descriptions to be filed of existing and proposed works must be complete. Has 20,000 plans	Chief, $6,000; office work, one engineer, two clerks; installations, seven engineers, eight clerks; operating section, five engineers, two clerks; stream inspection, fifty-five trained men, six clerks; design and construction, twelve engineers and draftsmen, one clerk. The stream inspectors do other work	Large force of inspectors are making very detailed survey of all watersheds. Thousands of these plans filed. Continual supervision of watersheds. Monthly reports from all water supplies. Local analyses required. Frequent inspection of water and sewage purification works. Much attention to private water and sewage problems. Much other work on nuisances, general sanitation, and the epidemiology of typhoid fever, 8,873 analyses in 1913, many from wells. $173.-70.40 expended year ending May 31, 1915.

State	Legal provision	Plans to be filed	Personnel	Work done
Rhode Island	Potable water to be of standard fixed by State Board of Health. Latter may order removal of pollution. Penalties. Courts may enjoin.		Chemist, who is also engineer and biologist, $2,200. Works exclusively on water and sewage	Monthly or bimonthly analyses of all water supplies and sewage effluents, 1,165 in 1914. Frequent inspections. $3,854.10 expended in 1914.
South Carolina	Rule of State Board of Health forbids discharge of sewage without permission		Employs chemist to analyze samples of water	One hundred and fifty-one samples analyzed in 1913.
South Dakota	General prohibition of pollution		State Health Laboratory analyzes samples of water. Inspects if paid	Forty samples analyzed in 1913.
Tennessee	General prohibition of pollution.			
Texas	Forbids discharge of polluting material on watershed for live stock or human beings. Offenders given three years to remove such		Governor to appoint inspector to enforce law to act under State Board of Health	The State Board of Health laboratory analyzes samples.
Utah	General prohibition of pollution		Sanitary inspectors give advice	Sixty-three analyses in 1913 in the University laboratory.
Vermont	State Board of Health makes rules for protection of water. May stop delivery of polluted water. May on complaint order removal of pollution. Towns to consult in regard to water and sewerage. Lakes of over 1,000 acres not to receive sewage	To be filed on request	Perhaps two months' time of consulting engineer	Samples from all public water supplies sent in quarterly by local health officers and analyzed. In 1910-1911, 1,435 analyses. $2,500 expended in 1913.
Virginia	General prohibition of pollution		Engineer, $2,500. Analyses in bacteriological laboratory	Investigates, analyzes samples (400 in 1913). Makes surveys and advises. Eighty-five inspections 1914. Often consulted by towns. Portable chlorin plant. $3,000 expended in 1914.
Washington	General prohibition of pollution. Municipalities to enforce. May ask for injunction		Sanitary inspector investigates and gives advice. Has employed engineer for large projects. Analyses by State Board of Health laboratory and by chemical laboratory of University	In 1914, 1,151 samples of water analyzed.
West Virginia	General prohibition of pollution		Hygienic laboratory at University does a little work. Engineer, $2,000 in Health Department.	
Wisconsin	Plans for sewerage and water works to be approved by State Board of Health. On complaint State Board of Health to investigate and with approval of governor may issue orders in regard to sewage. Appeal to experts. May forbid use of dangerous water	Plans and descriptions to be filed. 300 on file	Part time consulting engineer. Much work done by chemist	Chemist is out two or three days a month on water and sewage inspection. About 400 sewage analyses and 900 water analyses in a year. Half of latter from private wells.
Wyoming	General prohibition of pollution.			

TABLE 10.—STATEMENT OF EXPENDITURES OF STATES FOR HEALTH

Year Ending	State	Expenditure for Health	Amount per Capita, Cents	Administration	Vital Statistics	Diagnostic Laboratory	Food and Drugs	Engineering	Epidemiological Work	Antitoxin Vaccines, Etc.	Other Expenses
April 11, 1915	Alabama	$25,000.00	1.11	$7,000.00	$6,000.00	$8,000.00		$2,000.00		$2,000.00	
June 30, 1915	Arizona	9,300.00	3.76	4,800.00		4,500.00[1]					
Mar. 31, 1915	Arkansas	8,970.00[2]	0.53		3,920.00	250.00					$3,640.67[6]
June 30, 1915	California	112,953.48	3.96	9,736.60		9,985.99	$25,662.73		$4,040.68[3] / 51,044.53[4]	2,516.50[5]	6,325.73[7]
Nov. 30, 1915	Colorado	19,980.00[8]	2.19	5,200.00	1,200.00	1,000.00	11,680.00		900.00		
Sept. 30, 1914	Connecticut	27,000.00	2.24	3,200.00	4,800.00	9,000.00				10,000.00	1,159.4[9]
Jan. 11, 1915	Delaware	8,492.02	4.04		1,994.50	3,498.32		100.00	37,483.90	2,970.80	28,521.2[10]
Dec. 31, 1914	Florida	129,012.03	15.21	20,837.33	2,442.39	30,324.46					5,172.4[11]
Dec. 31, 1913	Georgia	33,311.90	1.21			21,657.10				6,647.98[12] / 5,006.82[5]	
Dec. 31, 1913	Idaho	19,820.00	5.22	10,200.00	800.00	1,000.00	7,520.00			2,900.00	10,745.00[14]
Sept. 30, 1914	Illinois	133,919.60	1.78			5,200.00		27,000.00[13]		3,209.10[5]	25,000.00[15]
Sept. 30, 1915	Indiana	64,719.00	2.32	15,000.00	5,000.00	10,000.00	20,000.00 / 5,000.00[16]			4,719.00[5]	5,000.00[17]
June 30, 1914	Iowa	32,568.32[18]	1.46	11,332.57	2,842.26	5,552.54		599.91		1,064.30	3,003.85[19] / 1,388.53[20] / 5,430.13[21] / 124.3[22] / 1,229.5[23]
June 30, 1914	Kansas	46,430.00	2.60	5,800.00	8,150.00	3,200.00[24]	10,880.00[25]	12,400.00[26]	4,500.00	1,500.00	15,943.4[27]
Dec. 31, 1914	Kentucky	30,002.45	1.27	7,155.71	9,836.17	6,662.07	8,747.67	6,348.50	22,336.51[4]		5,406.2[28]
Dec. 31, 1914	Louisiana	87,491.20	4.93	17,065.22	5,893.56	2,500.00		2,500.00			7,098.5[29]
Dec. 31, 1914	Maine	14,893.24	1.95	6,836.42	3,056.00	5,000.82[30]	13,575.00	18,600.00	10,800.00	2,500.00[5]	11,080.00[28]
1915	Maryland	142,600.00[8]	10.54	23,245.00	7,800.00	7,900.00		54,972.69	2,989.85[33]	20,968.85	47,000.00[34]
Nov. 30, 1914	Massachusetts	180,219.14	4.95	27,555.87		4,472.00	17,468.21 / 4,980.30[31] / 6,620.62[32]				34,895.79[35] / 285.60[34] / 5,009.85[36]
June 30, 1915	Michigan	44,872.07	1.48	25,869.40		5,629.92		13,372.75 / 6,955.40 / 8,179.86[37]	14,316.16	7,456.53[5]	1,888.13[9]
July 31, 1914	Minnesota	72,013.31	3.25	11,438.71	8,187.68	13,589.79					3,195.1[38]
Dec. 31, 1914	Mississippi	22,975.43	1.20	10,482.30		3,300.00					
Dec. 31, 1914	Missouri	29,206.19	0.86	9,600.00	5,997.89						
Feb. 28, 1915	Montana	23,600.00	5.45				9,000.00		5,000.00[39]		
Apr. 30, 1915	Nebraska	10,640.00[8]	0.85	2,500.00		3,500.00					
1915	Nevada	7,500.00	7.59	12,000.00	2,800.00	5,000.00					
Aug. 31, 1914	New Hampshire	21,200.00	4.81		7,000.00	6,400.00[40]	23,357.52 / 12,000.00[41] / 2,598.00[32] / 3,331.87[42]				1,580.8[43]
Oct. 31, 1914	New Jersey	125,942.15	4.47	16,015.00		8,647.96		28,500.00	13,022.85		9,888.0[44]
Sept. 30, 1914	New Mexico										
Nov. 30, 1914	New York	284,676.85	2.87	9,320.65	17,312.52	17,693.79		8,120.87[46]	7,102.87[47]		1,481.5[48]
June 30, 1915	North Carolina	61,081.78[45]	2.60	2,569.38		8,000.00[40]					
Feb. 15, 1915	North Dakota	10,560.38	1.48					15,388.74	9,215.59		6,752.0[50]
	Ohio	91,736.25	1.80	21,901.38		14,905.32[40]			16,753.62[49]		7,012.0[51]

Date	State	[1]	[2]	[3]	[4]	[5]	[6]	[7]	[8]	[9]	[10]	[11]
June 30, 1915	Oklahoma	32,706.00[8]	1.61	5,300.00	......	2,400.00	12,500.00	......	......	5,000.00	7,500.00	5,000.00[54]
Sept. 30, 1914	Oregon	14,186.00[52]	1.78	......	......	......	......	......	......	......	394.00[53]	2,112.00[55]
May ..., 1915	Pennsylvania	1,047,481.66[56]	12.70	97,759.55	31,360.70	21,309.81	......	173,170.40	326,895.90[57] 396,335.30[58]	......	......	......
Dec. 31, 1914	Rhode Island	18,569.18	8.14	4,893.09	1,000.00	5,029.08	......	3,854.10	223.16	2,848.00	......	721.75[9]
Dec. 31, 1914	South Carolina	36,112.52[59]	2.27	9,876.95	1,500.00	4,428.13	......	1,136.32	9,984.75[60]	1,500.00[28] 1,430.00[5] 6,306.87[61]	......	......
June 30, 1915	South Dakota	9,730.00	1.43	......	......	3,500.00[62]	......	......	......	......	......	10,660.00[63]
Dec. 17, 1914	Tennessee	16,552.49	0.73	......	......	1,800.00	......	......	......	......	......	......
Aug. 31, 1914	Texas	48,200.00	1.13	......	2,700.00	500.00[64]	......	......	......	......	......	......
Nov. 30, 1914	Utah	12,150.00[8]	2.93	......	1,250.00	15,000.00[65]	......	2,500.00[66]	......	2,385.50[66]	......	5,800.00[67] 2,000.00[68]
Dec. 31, 1913	Vermont	33,385.50	9.27	3,700.00	......	......	......	......	......	......	......	2,000.00[69]
Sept. ..., 1914	Virginia	45,000.00[70]	2.09	12,500.00	10,000.00	5,500.00	......	3,000.00	......	......	......	4,500.00[71] 6,000.00 3,500.00[72]
July 31, 1914	Washington	15,240.99	1.08	5,456.07	3,292.73	2,510.59	......	......	......	......	......	307.62[9]
June 30, 1915	West Virginia	14,000.00[52]	1.02	......	......	......	......	......	3,673.98	......	......	......
June 30, 1914	Wisconsin	38,205.63[52]	1.56	4,583.32	6,411.50	8,000.00[72]	......	193.84	8,404.34[73]	......	......	3,458.64[74] 7,203.99[75]
Sept. 30, 1914	Wyoming	2,100.00	1.24	......	......	......	......	......	......	......	......	......

1. State University appropriates $400 of this. Remainder is special appropriation, mostly food work.
2. One-half of appropriation for biennial period ending March 31, 1915.
3. Tuberculosis.
4. Bubonic plague.
5. Rabies treatment.
6. Sanitary inspections.
7. Registration of nurses.
8. Appropriation.
9. Education.
10. Veterinary division.
11. Crippled children.
12. Antitoxin.
13. Appropriation in part special and in part by University.
14. Lodging house inspection, Chicago.
15. Examination of physicians, midwives, embalmers.
16. Water laboratory.
17. Weights and measures.
18. Half of expenses for biennial period, June 30, 1914.
19. Examination of physicians.
20. Examination of embalmers.
21. Hotel inspection.
22. Examination of optometrists.
23. Examination of nurses.
24. $1,000 provided by State University.
25. $2,000 provided by University, $2,000 provided by State Agricultural College.
26. $10,400 provided by University.
27. Special medical, school hygiene department, medical and sanitary inspection, printing, general sanitation.
28. Chemical laboratory.
29. Health train and moving pictures.
30. Also examines water chemically, and dairy products for department of agriculture.
31. Meat inspection.
32. Cold storage.
33. Poliomyelitis.
34. Ophthalmia.
35. Supervision of local work.
36. Examination of plumbers.
37. Water and sewage laboratory.
38. Municipal sanitation.
39. Rocky Mountain fever.
40. Also chemical laboratory.
41. Creameries and dairies.
42. Shell fish protection.
43. Contagious diseases of animals.
44. Tuberculosis exhibit.
45. Also the Health Department expends $20,000 for tuberculosis.
46. Mostly education.
47. Hookworm.
48. Bureau of county health work.
49. Education and tuberculosis.
50. Plumbing inspection.
51. Occupational diseases.
52. Approximately.
53. Special fund.
54. Sex hygiene special fund.
55. School inspection.
56. Also the health department expends $449,151.16 for the construction of sanatoria for tuberculosis and $734,390.91 for maintenance.
57. Includes supervision.
58. Tuberculosis division, dispensaries.
59. Also the health department expends $10,000 for construction of tuberculosis camp.
60. Diphtheria antitoxin.
61. Smallpox vaccine.
62. Provided by University.
63. Exhibit car.
64. Printing only.
65. Includes chemical laboratory.
66. Not charged to health department appropriation.
67. School for health officers.
68. Inspection and supervision.
69. Tuberculosis education.
70. Also the health department expends $45,000 for maintenance of tuberculosis sanatorium.
71. Rural sanitation.
72. Bureau of inspections.
73. Deputy health officers also largely occupied with sanitary inspection.
74. Hotel inspection Jan. 1 to June 30, 1914.
75. Plumbing division, Aug. 28, 1913 to June 30, 1914.

PUBLIC HEALTH
IN
AMERICA

An Arno Press Collection

Ackerknecht, Erwin H[einz]. **Malaria In the Upper Mississippi Valley: 1760-1900.** 1945

Bowditch, Henry I[ngersoll]. **Consumption In New England Or, Locality One of Its Chief Causes** and **Is Consumption Contagious, Or Communicated By One Person to Another In Any Manner?** 1862/1864. Two Vols. in One.

Buck, Albert H[enry] (Editor). **A Treatise On Hygiene and Public Health.** 1879. Two Vols.

Boston Medical Commission. **The Sanitary Condition of Boston:** The Report of a Medical Commission. 1875

Budd, William. **Typhoid Fever:** Its Nature, Mode of Spreading, and Prevention. 1931

Chapin, Charles V[alue]. **A Report On State Public Health Work,** Based On a Survey of State Boards of Health: Made Under the Direction of the Council on Health and Public Instruction of the American Medical Association. [1915]

Davis, Michael M[arks], Jr. and Andrew R[obert] Warner. **Dispensaries:** Their Management and Development. 1918

Dublin, Louis I[srael] and Alfred J. Lotka. **The Money Value of a Man.** 1930

Dunglison, Robley. **Human Health.** 1844

Emerson, Haven. **Local Health Units for the Nation.** 1945

Emerson, Haven. **A Monograph On the Epidemic of Poliomyelitis (Infantile Paralysis) In New York City In 1916.** 1917

Fish, Hamilton. **Report of the Select Committee of the Senate of the United States On the Sickness and Mortality On Board Emigrant Ships.** 1854

Frost, Wade Hampton. **The Papers of Wade Hampton Frost, M.D.:** A Contribution to Epidemiological Method. 1941

Gardner, Mary Sewall. **Public Health Nursing.** 1916

Greenwood, Major. **Epidemics and Crowd Diseases:** An Introduction to the Study of Epidemiology. 1935

Greenwood, Major. **Medical Statistics From Graunt to Farr.** 1948

Hartley, Robert M. **An Historical, Scientific and Practical Essay On Milk, As an Article of Human Sustenance:** With a Consideration of the Effects Consequent Upon the Unnatural Methods of Producing It for the Supply of Large Cities. 1842

Hill, Hibbert Winslow. **The New Public Health.** 1916

Knopf, S. Adolphus. **Tuberculosis As a Disease of the Masses & How To Combat It.** 1908

MacNutt, J[oseph] Scott. **A Manual for Health Officers.** 1915

Richards, Ellen H. [Swallow]. **Euthenics:** The Science of Controllable Environment. 1910

Richardson, Joseph G[ibbons]. **Long Life and How To Reach It.** 1886

Rumsey, Henry Wyldbore. **Essays On State Medicine.** 1856

Shryock, Richard Harrison. **National Tuberculosis Association 1904-1954:** A Study of the Voluntary Health Movement In the United States. 1957

Simon, John. **Filth-Diseases and Their Prevention.** 1876

Sternberg, George M[iller]. **Sanitary Lessons of the War and Other Papers.** 1912

Straus, Lina Gutherz. **Disease In Milk:** The Remedy Pasteurization. The Life Work of Nathan Straus. 1917

Wanklyn, J[ames] Alfred and Ernest Theophron Chapman. **Water Analysis:** A Practical Treatise on the Examination of Potable Water. 1884

Whipple, George C. **State Sanitation:** A Review of the Work of the Massachusetts State Board of Health. 1917. Two Vols. in One.

Selections From Public Health Reports and Papers Presented at the Meetings of the American Public Health Association (1873-1883). 1977

Selections From Public Health Reports and Papers Presented at the Meetings of the American Public Health Association (1884-1907). 1977

Animalcular and Cryptogamic Theories On the Origins of
Fevers. 1977

The Carrier State. 1977

Clean Water and the Health of the Cities. 1977

The First American Medical Association Reports On Public
Hygiene In American Cities. 1977

Selections from the Health-Education Series. 1977

Health In the Southern United States. 1977

Health In the Twentieth Century. 1977

The Health of Women and Children. 1977

Minutes and Proceedings from the First, Second, Third and
Fourth National Quarantine and Sanitary Conventions. 1977.
Four Vols. in Two.

Selections from the Journal of the Massachusetts Association
of Boards of Health (1891-1904). 1977

Sewering the Cities. 1977

Smallpox In Colonial America. 1977

Yellow Fever Studies. 1977